NO MORE
SILOS

Metadata strategy for online publishers

Michael C Andrews

Cover image: Information, like seed corn, should move around so it can be productive, and not be stuck in a silo (corn pit) in hopes it might be used later.

Image by George B. Cornish, "A Car Load of Texas Corn", ca. 1910. Public domain image courtesy of The Metropolitan Museum of Art, which appeared in the exhibit "Faking It: Manipulated Photography Before Photoshop."

ISBN: 9781793097811

CONTENTS

CHAPTER 1:
INTRODUCTION

This book argues that organizations that have a significant online presence need a strategy for their metadata — how they describe their most important information so computers understand it. By having a metadata strategy, organizations can overcome internal silos that prevent them from providing information to customers effectively. A metadata strategy can make the information published on the web more useful and productive.

Lots of people have opinions about silos (they can be annoying) and about strategy (if done right it's much needed). But fewer people have strong views about metadata. Metadata may sound complicated and scary. This book aims to make metadata relevant to those who work with online content in some capacity.

The basic objective of a metadata strategy is actually quite simple. If someone outside your organization needs to use your information, you should use external metadata standards to describe the information. Doing so will make the information much more valuable for everyone — your customers, your partners, and yourself.

If metadata can be so useful and powerful, why doesn't it get more love? One reason is that the applications of metadata for online publishing still aren't widely appreciated.

The writer C. Northcote Parkinson, famous for his maxim that "work expands to fill the time available," developed another maxim that can help us understand why metadata is not discussed much within organizations. Parkinson's "Law of Triviality" states that people are prone to debate topics they are familiar with, and therefore have strong opinions on, while they remain silent and defer to experts on topics they don't understand. Writing over half a century ago, Parkinson imagined an organization debating plans for two projects: a new nuclear reactor, and an employee bike rack. The discussion of the reactor was quick, as most everyone was too embarrassed to speak up, afraid they would betray a lack of expertise. Meanwhile, the discussion of the bike rack went on for a long time, because everyone felt they were experts on bike racks, and everyone had an opinion. Parkinson's law highlights how the time spent debating an issue often has little relationship to the importance of the issue.

Metadata may not be as familiar and easy to understand as a bike rack. But it should not be seen as forbidding topic like nuclear reactors that only experts can understand. Unfortunately, metadata is too often viewed as esoteric and as someone else's problem to solve. When the organization discusses how to improve their publishing process, seemingly everyone will have opinions about drag-and-drop editing functionality in a new content management system (CMS), but few will voice any views about the metadata capabilities that the CMS supports. Despite the importance of metadata, it gets limited attention.

The good news is that metadata can benefit almost everyone involved with online publishing, and therefore everyone has a reason to become interested in it. They need to understand what metadata does, and how it can support different goals. When they have this understanding, they can help craft a strategy for metadata, so that metadata supports their needs and the needs of their colleagues.

Organization of the book

Part I looks at the value of metadata for online publishers. What is the nature of the current problem, and what is the opportunity? Why do publishers need a metadata strategy, and what does a metadata strategy cover? How does metadata relate to content strategy, and to business strategy? Part I provides the context for why metadata strategy is important and the business case for having a strategy.

Part II looks at opportunities to use metadata to support a range of internal and external goals. After reading Part II, the reader will have ideas about what specifically they would like to accomplish by having a metadata strategy.

Part III looks at how metadata is implemented, considering both the human and technical dimensions. This section discusses specific details relating to how to implement a strategy.

The chapters can be read in any order, depending on your current interests and knowledge. I encourage readers to use the book as a field guide to possibilities and practices. It is intended to spark ideas and suggest topics that are relevant to one's own situation as an online publisher. Readers should be led by their priorities and specific needs, and discover other topics they want to learn more about. They should feel free to skip sections or chapters that don't seem relevant to their responsibilities, especially in Part III dealing with implementation. Since only some readers will want to read the book from cover-to-cover, the book provides cross-references to other chapters when topics are also addressed elsewhere in the book.

Intended audience

The book is intended for people who are involved with creating, designing, developing, or promoting online content. It will appeal to content strategists, especially those interested in structured content and content engineering. It will also appeal to information architects and SEO professionals who are interested in learning more about how to display information in different contexts. Product managers who need to ensure the delivery of product-related information to customers across different platforms and channels will also benefit from learning how to tame informational silos using metadata standards. Developers and writers may also be interested in certain chapters.

The book focuses on strategy and does not explain technical concepts in any detail. Technical material such as code has been kept to a minimum. Readers with non-technical backgrounds should be able to understand the broader issues and opportunities associated with using metadata, even if they don't understand every detail.

Most of the concepts mentioned are introduced in my previous book, *Metadata Basics for Web Content* (Amazon, 2017), which provides some simple code examples for those interested. A growing body of online resources is also available that can explain technical concepts, though as yet there's no single resource that covers everything relating to metadata for online publishing.

Terminology

As I noted in my previous book, the terminology used to discuss metadata is — ironically — not standardized. Different experts, vendors and even standards organizations use different terminology. Some terms are more or less formal, while certain terms are favored by different communities interested in metadata. Rather than belabor sometimes minor differences in usage, this book will use many terms interchangeably that are close in meaning. Readers are not expected to know all this terminology: they will have the opportunity to become familiar with the range of terms as they read the book.

The concept of external metadata standards will also be referred to as vocabularies or external vocabularies; as structured data or structured metadata; and as semantic metadata or RDF or linked data. These terms are largely equivalent, and most readers interested in strategy won't need to worry about any differences in nuance.

What's most important is for readers to appreciate that many publishers are working toward similar goals, even if they sometimes refer to the approaches they use by different names. In fact, these differences in terminology when discussing metadata are a major reason why the concept of metadata strategy has lacked wider visibility so far.

While many terms can refer to the same general concept, in a couple of areas, similar-sounding terms need to be distinguished.

This book draws a critical distinction between proprietary and external metadata standards. Unfortunately, some terms associated with metadata can blur this distinction. Two topics that are confusable deserve mention. The first relates to metadata syntax. JSON and JSON-LD are similar in name and form, except that JSON tends to be used for proprietary metadata, while JSON-LD is used for metadata based on external standards. The second relates to data models for linking metadata, known as "graphs." Graphs are used in linked data or semantic metadata, but not all graphs use external standards. Since these distinctions can sometimes be overlooked, the book will discuss how similar-sounding terms can differ where that's important.

An appendix provides a glossary of terms used in the book.

PART I. WHY ONLINE METADATA IS SO IMPORTANT

Part I looks at the connections between external metadata standards and organizational goals, and how standards can fight one of the chief obstacles to realizing goals: silos.

The interaction between goals, standards, and silos can be hard to perceive, so different chapters in Part I will address the topic from different perspectives: organizational culture, technology, content, and business strategy. Although each perspective will be addressed only at a high level, later chapters in Parts II and III will provide more concrete examples how metadata can support publisher goals.

I once worked with the CTO at a large organization that has tens of thousands of employees and had over half a million web pages online. The organization had different divisions in different locations. When asked the proverbial question of what-keeps-you-up-at-night, the CTO replied silos. Each division was publishing content in its own way. It was hard to even unify information from the divisions on the homepage of the organization. The organization faced the problem of distributed publishing, which will be discussed in Chapter 17.

Another large organization I worked with faced a different silo problem. A Vice President at a well-known international financial institution asked for help with their intranet. He hoped that tweaking their intranet taxonomy would help colleagues in other countries and in other divisions find their information. Unfortunately, the Vice President could only manage his own division's intranet, which was not aligned with information available from other divisions and was not aligned with information on the public website. The intranet was hosted on

Microsoft SharePoint, which has historically been indifferent to metadata standards. The intranet had information that related to other published content, but it remained a disconnected silo because no common metadata standards connected different information sources within the organization.

Anecdotes don't of course prove anything but they can illustrate the kinds of silo problems that organizations face and role that metadata can play in their resolution.

CHAPTER 2: WHY ONLINE PUBLISHERS NEED A METADATA STRATEGY

Today, almost every organization is an online publisher. Corporations, government departments, and NGOs create and publish content that ends up on websites, in apps, emails, and other channels. Online publishers work hard to sculpt their content: the messages they are communicating to audiences. For the most part, publishers don't consider metadata an essential part of their messaging. They are shortchanging themselves by doing that.

Online publishers tend to follow a stovepiped process when planning how customers are informed and make decisions — often without realizing it. On one side are people who think thematically about narrative "content", such as written articles, video stories, or podcast interviews. On the other side are people who think minutely about "data": the specifications for products, the details about services, or the facts about people and locations. A yawning cultural gap separates these groups.

These groups share in common the need to track, manage, deliver, and repurpose customer-facing information. This information may live in databases and gets displayed within content. The secret ingredient that allows the information to move between the two worlds is metadata. Metadata enables information to be customer-centric because it can integrate different kinds of information that may be needed by the customer.

Modern web publishing could not exist without metadata. But despite their reliance on it, very few publishers do a good job managing metadata. Few have a strategy for their web content metadata. And as a result, their information can be tied up in a tangled jumble of pipes. Audiences want information at their fingertips, but too often the information they seek is trapped in isolated silos that are hard or impossible to access. The information is in the wrong place, because it can't get to where it is needed, when it is needed. The customer encounters a link redirecting them to another website, or worse, hits a dead end, and has to return to a search engine to find what they need.

Before we can explore how to connect information by using metadata, and the benefits such connections can deliver to an organization, we must first acknowledge the extent that information is disconnected currently. To do this requires us to peer into the grubby, grimy subterranean plumbing that manages the content and information that gets published. Online content by its nature is complex. But unfortunately, the internal processes and IT implementations in many organizations manage to make online content even more complex than it needs to be. Everyone involved with content, whether technical or not, should appreciate how patchwork systems cause problems.

Silos are a metaphor for a phenomenon that is all too real in many organizations. Silos can have a psychic quality to them, reflected in how different groups view each other. During a large conference call, many attendees may have trouble paying attention. They can't follow how specific issues discussed are immediately relevant to them. More tangibly, silos also are embodied in physical systems. Silos prevent an organization from accomplishing what it needs to do efficiently. And silos prevent customers from receiving what they want.

An absence of strategy creates stovepipe systems

A publisher tries to do many things with its content, but often does so in a piecemeal manner. Various IT team members consider what systems are needed to support different functionality. Unless there is a metadata strategy in place, each system is likely to operate according to its own rules:

- Content structuring relies on proprietary templates
- Content management relies on proprietary CMS data fields
- SEO relies on meta tags
- Recommendations rely on page views and tags
- Analytics rely on page titles and URLs
- Digital assets rely on proprietary tags
- Internal search uses keywords and not metadata

- Navigation uses a CMS-defined custom taxonomy or folder structure
- Screen interaction relies on custom JSON
- Backend data relies on a custom data model.

Many stakeholders won't understand exactly what each of these classification systems is. That confusion embodies the heart of the problem: there are many ways to classify content that don't follow a common set of terminology. They aren't intelligible to those who use a different classification system. The meaning has become wrapped up in the means of expressing the classification. Tags, fields, templates, and keywords can all describe the same stuff using different terminology and using different devices.

Sadly, such uncoordinated labeling of content is quite common. It's a sign that the publisher is lacking common standards for metadata.

Babel

What things are called, and how they are identified, has consequences. Terminology influences a publisher's ability to exchange and understand information.

Terminology differences between different groups and systems are the most visible manifestation of silos.

> "**Silo** (*noun*): 'A system, process, department, etc. that operates in isolation from others.' (*verb*): 'Isolate (one system, process, department, etc.) from others'."[1]

-- Oxford Dictionary

In large organizations, whether corporations, government agencies, or multilateral organizations, a Tower of Babel situation arises. Multinational organizations may not necessarily speak a single common language. But even if they do (using English, for example), different divisions and operating units rely on their own terminology to describe the things that matter to them. Product engineers may describe things differently than the customer service team — perhaps talking about product features instead of user options. The finance team tracks things their own way.

Organizations expect their staff to collaborate across boundaries. The amount of communication needed to support collaboration is increasing. But communication isn't always effective as it could be, because different participants have different reference points.

Outside the organization, the firm's customers are expected to serve themselves. Everything they need is supposed to be readily available from the screens of their smartphones, so they never need to talk to someone. But the seamless integration that was promised is often incomplete.

The companies that are most successful, most efficient and have the highest customer satisfaction, are the ones able to integrate information seamlessly. Metadata allows for information created by different persons and stored in different systems to be integrated together. To achieve that integration, metadata needs to follow agreed standards.

Silos (from the ancient Greek *siros*) literally mean corn pits. Metadata is like corn. It needs to be spread around, not just stored. It can seed new content, if allowed to disburse. But freely-circulating metadata doesn't happen automatically. It requires much planning, agreement, and enablement. It requires a strategy to make it happen (which will be discussed in more detail in Chapter 6).

Much of the web content infrastructure (CMSs, DAMs, APIs) is built around keywords, key-value stores and tag labels - the digital equivalent of post-it notes. These descriptors aren't semantic metadata: they involve a self-defined understanding, or a vernacular description that machines can't rely on. Tags and keywords aren't strategic. Publishers can't successfully scale operations relying on tags and keywords. The value of tags and keywords declines the more content one has. Metadata standards are an important tool for supporting content operations.

---

[1] https://en.oxforddictionaries.com/definition/silo

Strategy guides choices

Since metadata is poorly understood by publishers, it may be tempting to delegate all metadata decisions to a single person. Perhaps a metadata strategy isn't needed; what's needed is a metadata czar. Perhaps an all-knowing czar can make sure everything fits together correctly. But the root problem isn't simply a matter of missing expertise. Sometimes overconfidence can lead to problems.

Some organizations decide to treat their information consistently, but design their own "standards" that are proprietary. Even the most elegant solutions are of limited value if they are idiosyncratic and at odds with widely used standards for metadata. Because many organizations refer to internal data models as "standards," it is necessary to differentiate internal standards from external ones. Internal standards are proprietary, while external standards are publicly available. Internal standards support internal uses of the data — of interest primarily to internal systems and stakeholders. External standards support external uses of information — the kinds of information customers care about.

Figure 2.1. Publishers face a choice about how to manage their online information: Whether to use proprietary standards, or embrace external, publicly available standards.

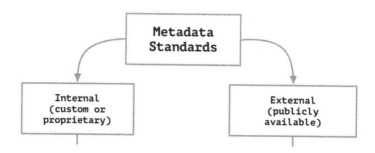

Internal standards tend to be closely tied to underlying IT systems (Figure 2.2). Often, the technology chosen ends up dictating the conventions that are implemented. The result is a mishmash of "data," rather than clearly defined information. With proprietary data, the meaning of the data is wrapped up in the system storing it. Information described with internal standards can be isolated from related information. It can be difficult to connect it to other information. The big risk is when information that customers need is stored as proprietary data. It makes it much more likely they won't be able to access it when they need it.

Figure 2.2. Proprietary metadata 'standards' lock information in silos.

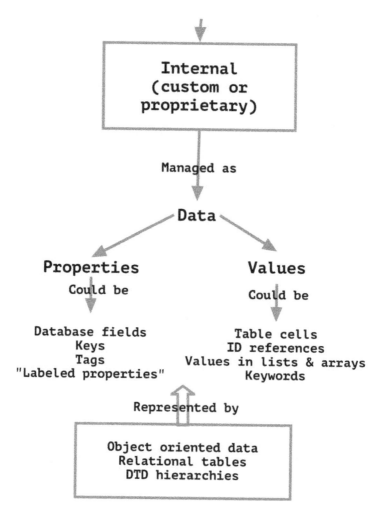

External standards connect information (Figure 2.3). They involve vocabularies to indicate entities and properties (known as property vocabularies) and values (known as value vocabularies). The information described with external standards does not depend on the IT system that it is stored in (discussed more in Chapter 5).

Figure 2.3. External standards classify information according to publicly available vocabularies.

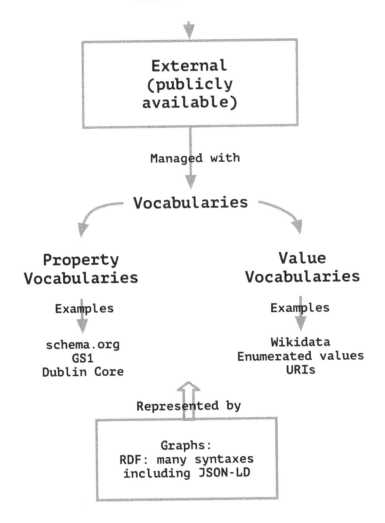

The history of the web demonstrates that common standards promote wider usage and new applications of information. But many publishers take a "late majority" approach to adopting external standards. They worry about standards only when it is clear that most of their competitors are already using them. They fail to consider standards as a strategic issue.

The path of embracing external standards requires persistence. Online publishers that lack a metadata strategy are prone to develop proprietary solutions, because such solutions often present themselves as the easiest or fastest way to complete a project, even when they create problems for others, both immediately, and later on.

Publishers need a strategy to develop metadata that is useful for all kinds of situations. Online information is only valuable if it can connect to where it is needed.

CHAPTER 3: WHY DO WE KEEP BUILDING SILOS OF INFORMATION?

I n a world where people and information are more connected, you might expect silos are disappearing.

Most people agree in principle that silos are bad. Nearly everyone has had the experience of encountering fragments of information that are difficult to piece together and make sense of. Surely no one would wish that on others.

Despite our collective dislike of them, silos persist. And more silos are being built every day. Owing to both internal and external influences, silos in content operations stubbornly continue instead of disappearing.

Silos inhibit the use of metadata standards. Metadata standards inhibit the persistence of silos. The choice is obvious. To counteract silos, publishers must first understand how they arise.

The human factor: routines and familiarity

Silos seem to happen, often unconsciously. Although a few people may intentionally build silos to hoard information, most silos occur without deliberate effort. Often, default behaviors make sitting on information the path of least resistance. Unless of the owner of the silo feels the pain of dealing with it, they may have limited awareness there is even a problem.

This disconnect raises the first characteristic of silos: the people most burdened by silos are the ones who are least able to change them. The people least burdened by silos are often the ones who can do something about them.

The second characteristic of silos is that is easier to complain about them than to fix them. Fixing silos requires a lot of up-front work, even though in the long term it reduces work for everyone.

Employees follow routines and habits that can make silos more likely to happen. Call it the inertia factor.

Most employees are focused on managing their own information — information they've created or are responsible for. They aren't necessarily aiming to share the information widely, especially with people they don't know. Not many people are concerned with how to maximize the number of connections of the information they've created. They are most interested in sharing information with other people who they know will use the information. Generally, those people are people they know already — their immediate colleagues or existing customers.

Silos feed off the inertia of routines. Employees share information based on known use-cases, such as routine procedures or existing customer tasks. They have little incentive to share information in the uncertain event someone else might need it. A fixed mindset about the value of information inhibits collaboration and innovation. This way of thinking influences how teams think about the design of information that's delivered online. They are focused on specific existing uses for the information only, and not on potential new uses of the information. They never ask: What are all the ways this information might be useful to someone, now or in the future?

Like other people, employees tend to rely on their personal experience to categorize and describe information. They belong to a group of colleagues, who use a set of shared terminology to discuss and interact with information. Shared understanding is often local, specific to a group that interacts with each other. The terminology used by a group will often show up in custom metadata. People narrowly define information according to its immediate relevance to them, a process referred to as "*extreme pigeon-holing*, [which] does not recognize how materials can easily be relevant to multiple topics."[2] What's convenient for an individual user can be restricting to a larger group of users.

It is easy to create information silos that can't connect to other information. Islands of information get formed, which are surrounded by water but not connected by bridges. Information may be in different formats, follow different instructions, and use different labeling. For example, many online publishers store digital assets (e.g., photos, videos, or PDFs of whitepapers) in separate systems that are not organized according to a common standard.

Employees tend to focus on the information they routinely use in their work. People are most comfortable communicating with people who are like them and who talk in similar ways — what sociologists refer to as homophily.[3] The filter bubbles we encounter online are an example of this behavior. While people in their personal lives may choose to self-select who they talk to, people in their professional lives have an obligation to make sure their information is available to everyone who needs it. It is easiest to share information with others who have a shared understanding of the information means. It takes a lot of effort to come up with a shared vocabulary to describe things in a way that is clear to everyone.

Familiarity can be the enemy of collective clarity. It's common for various teams to apply a simple standard for how to describe information: the it-makes-sense-to-me standard. They decide for themselves what feels clear or is easiest to do. But ideally, they should consider how others will use it.

Employees often see sharing as involving extra work. Even governments, which should be in the business of sharing information, need a nudge to share what they have.[4] Employees need more than a nudge to make the online information they create useful to others. Individuals and teams won't contribute to the pooling of information using common metadata standards unless they have the right support.

---

[2] http://bibblio.org/blog#trees-vs-networks

[3] https://en.wikipedia.org/wiki/Homophily

[4] Open data proponents have been known to shame governments for failing to fulfill their open data obligations. The US Government Accountability Office, an official watchdog agency, recently criticized the lack of metadata relating to federal spending: "The Secretary of the Treasury should fully comply with OMB's requirements by providing metadata in a single location that are easy to find on the USAspending.gov website." https://www.gao.gov/products/GAO-19-72?mobile_opt_out=1#summary_recommend

The institutional factor: pressures and incentives

A host of systematic factors contribute to the emergence of silos.

Just as individuals have difficulty thinking about the needs of distant colleagues, teams have a similar difficulty thinking about the needs of a distant time in the future. Organizations can have difficulty planning for long-term needs.

Long-term, cross-discipline goals are not any single person's responsibility. They are rarely allocated a budget. As one team of metadata experts noted: "The task of making those data available across disciplines and over time is, in general, an *unfunded mandate* — it requires a special kind of altruism to carefully code your data in ways beyond what you need for their immediate use."[15] One's colleagues aren't necessarily selfish. They just can't take on the burden of an unfunded mandate.

The neglect of long-term needs reflects the bias toward novel ideas and solutions. Online publishers, like teen social media users, are not immune to the "Fear of Missing Out" phenomenon. Such herd behavior has a long history, starting with the Dot-Com bubble and the proliferation of websites built with Flash and Shockwave. A few years ago, digital publishers rushed to build microsites and mobile apps. Most of these standalone products weren't used much by users and quickly became out-of-date as publishers abandoned them. Fear-driven decisions are often short-sighted ones that result in more silos.

Siloed thinking results in one-off products that are later abandoned. Many web publishers have built digital products such as mobile apps that prove difficult to maintain. The proliferation of channels is fragmenting the market. It is easy to create new silos if the publisher decides to chase each new opportunity without forethought to how these can be maintained or repurposed later.

Online publishers are being pulled into the rush to get on the next channel. Chatbots and voicebots are the latest examples. But it could easily be VR or AR, or some cloud-linked home appliance. A common assumption is that because a channel is new, it is necessary to create different proprietary implementations because the publisher doesn't know which company's proprietary platform is going to win the race and become the default. Teams can fall in the trap of designing content for Facebook or Amazon or some small company that could be bought out by them, instead of designing content that can work with different platforms. Platform vendors, both incumbents and startups, often encourage this thinking. In reality, no product can be an island. Any product that expects content to will be specially designed for it will not succeed in the long term.

Another tension arises from certain product development practices that focus on incrementalism, expecting that what's needed will organically be built if a team keeps fixing problems that arise. Projects frequently have a short-term focus and will downplay the development of long-term capabilities. In the "sprint and ship" focus of agile delivery, designing long-term capabilities can get sidelined. The new field of design operations ("DesignOps" or "Des Ops"), which looks at how design requirements need to be considered holistically, is providing a counter-narrative to the incrementalist approach.[5] Metadata can develop in stages over time, and often should be. But if there is no forethought to how different pieces of information will need to connect and interoperate, custom metadata generally results.

Second, publishers can become preoccupied with the frenzy around martech, AI and automation.[2] Content is always the trailing consideration in these discussions. Many of these tools boldly claim they can target people with the right content, even unstructured text (content with no metadata). Each of these solutions is a silo. They try to solve one problem but don't help overall. Vendors try to make their solutions ever more comprehensive, but all they do is lock the publisher into their proprietary approach. The reality is that no one solution can address all the challenges of content. And getting many proprietary solutions to work together in harmony is at best time consuming and frustrating.

IT vendors routinely ignore external metadata standards, resulting in vendor lock-in.[8] Vendors frequently claim their product has the flexibility to do anything. When that claim is investigated, it turns out the product requires custom metadata to work with custom code. Demo-friendly features overshadow long-term needs. "Newer" is positioned as being better, even if it doesn't comply with widely-adopted standards. For example, widely-used metadata standards depend on a concept known as graphs for data. Graphs have been evolving over the past decades, and have been steadily building interest. Graphs have attracted enough interest to entice vendors to develop proprietary graph databases (called labeled property graphs — you provide your own labels), which vendors tout as being better than the original.

Too many vendors seem happy to sell silo solutions: it keeps publishers locked into them — at least as long as they keep selling their product. The opposite outcome of vendor lock-in is vendor lock-out: when a vendor decides to stop supporting a product, such as when Adobe, one of the largest content management systems vendors, decided to exit the CMS field. Vendor dependency is a risk and a burden.

Vendors can promote a myth that custom tools are necessary to extract valuable information. Vendors spread the idea that custom metadata fields are better. Even consultants that rate vendors, such as Gartner, may repeat this false idea. A recent Gartner report contained the following evaluation criteria: "*Content metadata management*: Ability to assign **custom attributes** to content that extends beyond basic descriptors."[9] The assertion that custom metadata is better is at best misleading and in many situations is fundamentally counterproductive — customizing metadata can create a diversion that undermines overall success. The notion that metadata standards are "basic" and need to be supplemented with custom tags managed by a specific vendor's code betrays a lack of knowledge about the coverage available in external metadata standards. External metadata standards can be used to address common analytics or delivery scenarios most publishers will have. For most consumer-facing web publishers, custom metadata for externally published information is rarely required, if at all.

All organizations, even small ones, must work to resist the pull of silos. Publishers need discipline to mobilize a sustained program that forges a common purpose and develops a shared understanding within the enterprise. That's one reason why metadata strategy is important. The strategy identifies how publishers can unify fragmented systems and processes.

Large organizations struggle with how to manage complexity. Typically, they manage complexity through the separation of functions and responsibilities. By creating different units focused on well-defined tasks, large organizations hope that order will be maintained. But dividing organizations into smaller and smaller autonomous units makes the task of communicating across the organization more difficult. A razor-focused team can become a silo that is detached from the rest of the organization.

Gillian Tett, a business journalist with the *Financial Times* who has a background in anthropology, observes that organizations erect structures that make cooperation harder to realize. P&L responsibilities drive divisions — where each unit is run like a separate, accountable business with its own targets for sales and profits. Organizational boundaries are also justified as providing independence. Different professional roles can have subcultures. Tett quotes the former CEO of Sony, Howard Stringer, explaining what the silo means to a silo-ridden Sony Corporation: "The silo metaphor in business is really a description of the subcultures within an organization that have become islands and don't communicate horizontally or even vertically within their own organization."[10]

[5] F. Millerand and G. Bowker, "Metadata Standards" in M. Lampland and S.L. Star, *Standards and their Stories* (Cornell University Press 2009) p. 150

[6] "Even if design is also an agile process, it's very common that after the design phase, the designer loses control over the design." https://divante.co/blog/design-ops-design-systems-practice/

[7] The frenzy is famously represented by the "Marketing Technology Landscape Supergraphic" poster that shows 6000 vendor logos.

[8] "In economics, vendor lock-in, also known as proprietary lock-in or customer lock-in, makes a customer dependent on a vendor for products and services, unable to use another vendor without substantial switching costs." https://en.wikipedia.org/wiki/Vendor_lock-in

[9] Gartner, "Magic Quadrant for Content Marketing Platforms", March 2018

[10] quoted in Gillian Tett, *The Silo Effect* (Little Brown 2015), p. 71.

Redefining ownership and responsibilities

The problem with silos is not simply that people work separately, in isolation from each other. They also think separately. Staff working in different roles think about issues in different ways. They have different mental models about problems and goals. They use different reference points.

Due to the imperatives of the network economy, autonomous units can't work in isolation. Customers and services are becoming ever more connected and integrated. The enterprise needs to be more connected as well. The larger ecosystem in which employees and customers interact must be simpler to use and more integrated. Small groups can work collaboratively to transcend some of the silos that exist in large organizations. But small teams don't solve silos. Only better connections between groups can do that.

Content teams have an opportunity to bridge silos by implementing standards to describe information used in online content. They can encourage colleagues to use the same terminology, and follow agreed definitions for terms used within an enterprise. They can help develop a common mental model to describe information used in content.

The path to a shared model of information used in content starts with building awareness of metadata's value. Staff can learn about the numerous applications of metadata standards that mutually support each other. Organizations can help different roles discover the relevance of metadata to their work.

Metadata is pivotal to connecting information within organizations. Metadata standardization is important to facilitating enterprise communications.

Fortunately, metadata standards are available that can enable the communication of digital information across the organization, and to customers wherever they may be. But general awareness of these standards is limited. Even content teams may be unfamiliar with metadata standards and not understand their application. Publishers often think about metadata only when looking at their search engine optimization. A widely-held but inaccurate belief is that the most commonly used standard for web content, the schema.org metadata vocabulary, is useful for SEO only. Many individuals both within and outside of the SEO community equate schema.org with SEO. The challenge is resetting beliefs. As one software architect put it: "I believe that if people understand schema.org they will find a myriad of uses well beyond SEO."[11]

Improving the exchange of information is an urgent business issue. Metadata standards are an under-utilized tool to improve the exchange of information, and bridge silos across an organization. Staff must be made aware of the possibilities that metadata standards offer. They can then advocate that their organization develop metadata capabilities based on external standards.

---

[11] David Gibson, Southern Cross Health Society,
https://lists.w3.org/Archives/Public/public-
schemaorg/2018Feb/0008.html

CHAPTER 4: THE COSTS OF SILOS

Many employees have had the experience of feeling their organization is disconnected internally. They've had trouble communicating with a colleague in a different unit, or have been blindsided by some event in their organization that they were unaware of. They've encountered silos. Their annoyances are symptoms of more systemic problems. Many employees focus on the hassles that silos cause them personally. They may not focus on the overall financial costs that silos produce. Silos waste money.

Silos are a universal problem in larger organizations. Silos emerge when different groups of people work on related tasks or projects in an *ad hoc* or uncoordinated manner. Different activities are not visibly connected to each other in a way that everyone can easily see how they are related. Those who work with online content encounter silos as well. Consider a typical division of responsibilities. A creative team may work with an external agency to develop images or videos. Some of their assets are in a DAM. The development team is tweaking the navigation based on a new taxonomy to accommodate some new content requirements. Someone elsewhere in the company is working a data warehouse initiative, though no one on the web team seems to know what it is about. The SEO team is trying to keep up with the volume of work and with changes in SEO guidelines. Some writers are trying to figure out what content needs revision based on analytics data. Other writers are developing content for a new product release. Everyone is working to get their jobs done, meet deadlines, and clear the backlog. But it is difficult to connect the dots between these activities to see how they are related to each other. That's because there's no metadata strategy in place that can reveal how different activities are related.

The good news is that publishers *can* minimize silos, though it requires persistence. Adopting and implementing metadata standards within an organization can reverse the tendencies of silos. But like physical exercise, these benefits require a sustained effort before they are fully realized. To build momentum, online publishers should be mindful of the costs of *not* adopting external metadata standards. Nearly everyone agrees that silos are bad and unpleasant. But the more significant issue is that silos are a hidden expense. And the cost of silos far outstrips the cost of fixing them with external metadata standards. Fixing silos by adopting metadata standards will save money.

Publishers will want to understand the financial dimensions of their silo problem if they expect to fix it. They need to understand what kinds of investments will be effective. Some organizations believe they will solve their silo problem by spending heaps of money on data initiatives. They imagine that storing all their data in one big "lake" will allow them to understand what's going on in their organization. They get suckered into a false hope: believing massive technology spending will solve problems that have intrinsically human aspects to them. The data may be centrally located, but it remains disconnected from the stakeholders who need it. Their silo problem persists, except that it has become even more expensive.

Gillian Tett of the *Financial Times* cautions against magical thinking about data: "Data does not organize itself, or break down silos by itself."[12]

The cost of silos is diminished productivity. When web teams can't coordinate their activities on the basis of shared metadata standards, they will need to do more steps and will experience delays. These costs can be divided into two types: current costs (extra expenses), and opportunity costs (potential lost revenues).

Silos impede efficiency. Online publishers can learn from the manufacturing sector, which pioneered efficiency methods such as the Toyota Production System. Manufacturers developed the concept of "process waste" that is relevant to online publishers that create and manage information.

When content, information, or data is moved from one silo to another, it most often results in some form of process waste. These silo-to-silo handovers can be:

- People-to-system handovers (e.g., uploading files, manually updating fields)
- System-to-people handovers (e.g., downloading, manually monitoring)
- System-to-system shuffling.

Handover inefficiencies arise when getting information from one form to another, such as collecting information in a spreadsheet and getting it loaded into a system, or migrating from one system to another. Or they may arise from complicated APIs designed to get two different systems to communicate with one another. When different actors (staff or systems) use their own classifications to manage information, it results in process waste.

Data wrangling is problematic: The issue of technical debt

Developers take pride in their ability to wrangle a messy pile of data into something that works. But that data wrangling can be an unnecessarily painful process.

How did the data become messy to begin with? The problem often develops from the proliferation of custom metadata in response to various requests from different silos within the organization.

Data wrangling can resemble one of those "spot the difference" puzzles in a glossy magazine, where two nearly identical photos are side-by-side, and the reader has to spot minor differences between the images. A recent article provides an example of this sort of problem. A developer was using code developed by someone else. The developer confessed:

"After three days of importing (almost half of the XML was imported during this time), I realized that I'd made a mistake: the ParentID attribute should have been ParentId."

When a developer needs to use data that's described with non-standard attributes, there is plenty of scope for coding errors like this. Such errors arise because of *technical debt* — past practices that make things harder than expected later on.

Unfortunately, much web content is described with custom and proprietary metadata. Developers create their own attributes to describe the content. When this happens, it means other developers have difficulty using the content. And it means that other machines can't access the content easily either.

Customer-facing information is different: it is persistent, and it is used by many people, not just one or two systems. It needs to be handled with special care. Custom metadata is not sufficient: customer-facing information requires external metadata standards.

Developers spend much of their time developing custom code to do things. In the process, they can treat customer-facing information as a custom variable within their code. When focused on building an app for a specific project, they may not be thinking about other uses of the data or future changes that might be needed. Inefficiencies can arise when developers treat all data, whether it is customer-facing information or temporary variable in code, as being the same.

Consider the current fashion for using JSON in web content. Many developers rely on JSON to specify data. JSON syntax is simple, and it is easy to create a dictionary in JSON presenting attribute names and associated values. Developers can build front-end interactivity using JSON-defined web content, and build APIs around that JSON as well. JSON syntax is handy when writing programming scripts, but it isn't ideal for describing content. JSON creates technical debt. It is hard for the information to be used later for other purposes. JSON data is generally single-purpose data.

> *"Applications built with components that use JSON to serialize/deserialize data moving between them have a tendency over time to create **JSON property soup**. As requirements evolve, and developers are left to their own devices to modify features and adapt the codebase, properties are introduced into JSON on an ad-hoc basis. JSON entropy increases. What may have started out as a simple, clean JSON model, tends towards one of mess and complexity."*[13]

-- Paul Wilton

Metadata described using the JSON syntax generally lacks a published schema defining what the attributes represent (in contrast to metadata using the newer JSON-LD syntax).[14] Developers create "schema-less" databases using JSON.[15] The database is a bag of keys and values. Developers need to know what those keys were meant to represent in order to use them. Unfortunately, deciphering what the keys mean requires documentation. If a front-end developer wants to access an attribute, they need to see if there are comments in the code explaining what the attribute relates to. If someone outside the organization needs to access a value, they need to read through API documentation.

Developers who prefer HTML to JSON are also often guilty of creating technical debt. They try to describe content using "class" attributes meant for CSS styling. The result is often a motley hodgepodge of made-up names and IDs.

Whenever developers invent their own names to describe what's in the content, it creates a huge problem to deal with sooner or later. It may seem simple to define one's own attributes. The project may not need thousands of attributes, so why bother using a metadata standard such as schema.org to describe the content? Defining one's own attributes may seem faster. And what those attributes mean should be obvious to others, a developer might imagine.

Some developers prefer to create their own data model instead of relying on standards developed by others. They embrace a "not invented here" attitude toward data models that others have developed. Other developers opt for a "minimally viable" solution that creates a simple set of attributes that gets the job done in the short term, and defers other issues until later. No matter the motivation, self-defined metadata creates extra work later. Special documentation such as a data dictionary must be produced whenever one doesn't rely on standards — a task that is often neglected. For outside parties to use the data, a special API must be created (and documented). One developer quipped that technical debt should be referred to as "MacGyver debt" where developers have to "solve problems using his Swiss army knife, duct tape, and whatever else was on hand."[16]

But when content and information are described using standard metadata vocabularies, the content is ready for any contingency. If one developer leaves to work elsewhere, other developers can decipher the meaning of metadata by referring to the published standard.[17] If the company publishing the content merges or is bought out by another company, the other company can understand what the content means by consulting the standard. When using a metadata schema based on open standards such as schema.org, there is no longer a mystery what "EndDate" refers to.

Developers may lack a detailed knowledge of what attributes are covered by external standards for web metadata. Their focus is often on enabling transactional functionality, rather than on disseminating information. They may not have worked with schema.org, Wikidata IDs, or the United Nations CEFACT standards that indicate units of measure. That's one reason why a metadata strategy needs to be a team effort — developers already have many responsibilities and need support from other roles to decide what metadata standards to use. Fortunately, details of these standards are available online, and anyone can consult them. Learning about an unfamiliar standard requires effort, but that effort is shared by everyone. With standards, no one adopts the perspective that others need to learn their way of doing things. There is a common way that all must learn about.

---

[12] Gillian Tett, *The Silo Effect* (Little Brown 2015), p. 250.

[13] "Publishing JSON-LD for Developers"
https://datalanguage.com/news/publishing-json-ld-for-developers

[14] "The big picture is that JSON-LD allows applications that use it to share data and interoperate in a way that is not possible with regular JSON, and it's especially useful when used in conjunction with a Web service or a document-based database like MongoDB or CouchDB." Manu Sporny, "JSON-LD is the Bee's Knees" http://manu.sporny.org/2013/json-ld-is-the-bees-knees/

[15] A common complaint about traditional database schemas is that they are rigid and difficult to change at a later time. However, the schemas of modern metadata vocabularies based on the RDF data model are easy to modify or add to as needed.

[16] A reference to a popular TV action series in the United States called MacGyver, where the protagonist heroically but unrealistically fixes any problem with tape. https://engineering.riotgames.com/news/taxonomy-tech-debt

[17] Stories about trying to decipher the meaning of data designed by past employees are common: "These stories include eerie phrases like 'I'm not sure where that comes from', 'I think that broke a few years ago and I'm not sure if it was fixed', and the ever-ominous 'the guy who did that left'. https://caitlinhudon.com/2018/10/30/data-dictionaries/

Shared benefits

Adopting metadata standards means sharing responsibility. Everyone must think beyond their immediate needs to consider what others might need later on. Yet any extra effort is more than offset by the shared benefits realized. Creators of metadata benefit by using standards because the standards make it easier for them to use the metadata themselves. When following an agreed standard, the naming and capitalization of attributes are no longer left to chance or individual preferences, and the scope for programming errors is reduced. Because the metadata is predictable, the code is more predictable.

By investing in metadata standards, developers make follow-on tasks easier for both internal and external consumers of the metadata. By relying on external standards, less documentation is needed. The development effort is reduced when using metadata standards since there is less need to rely on custom-made APIs to exchange the information with other parties. The data is more portable and flexible as well. Libraries exist that allow standards-based metadata to be converted between different syntaxes if required.

One goal is to be able to reuse the information as much as possible (see Chapter 13 on reusing information). The key questions that authors and developers should ask themselves are:

- Do users care about this information, or does only the publisher care (in which case custom metadata is fine)?
- If users do care, how can this be expressed using standards?

Developers will find external standards will help make their work easier over the long term. And other members of the web team will be able to use the information more flexibly as well.

Identifying inefficiencies

Silos emerge from the fragmentation of information. Online publishers like find many examples of silos in their content and information. These might include:

- Redundant metadata, which will often be conflicting
- Different metadata implementations, which lack the required flexibility to meet reporting/analysis criteria
- Disconnected metadata, where metadata stored in various systems isn't linked
- Lax quality, due to no common standard.

The cost of metadata silos is captured by the Japanese concept of *muda*, or futility.

> *"Muda is a Japanese word meaning 'futility; uselessness; wastefulness', and is a key concept in lean process thinking, like the Toyota Production System (TPS) as one of the three types of deviation from optimal allocation of resources. Waste reduction is an effective way to increase profitability."*

-- Wikipedia

Taiichi Ohno, the developer of the Toyota Production System, identified seven kinds of waste. We can consider metadata silos in terms of the common types of process waste:

1. **Transport** — the unnecessary movement of stuff

Examples of unnecessary transport include server calls between systems, or extra steps involved.

2. **Motion** — the unnecessary work by people

Examples of unnecessary work are numerous: Manual downloading and uploading of information; Difficulty locating content assets due to poorly defined metadata; Developing special APIs to let systems talk to each other; Manual reconciliation of analytics; Extra discussions and meetings to clarify the meaning of information.

3. **Inventory** — work-in-process that has no added value

Unnecessary inventory could involve: The translation of properties or values into a different kind; Having redundant information stored in different locations.

The values for many metadata properties are constants: they shouldn't exist in multiple places, because they could get out of sync.

4. Waiting

Examples of waiting include system latency when exchanging information between systems using different metadata standards, project bottlenecks coordinating teams using different standards, and longer time-to-market when introducing new products and services.

5. **Over-production** — generating content more, sooner, or faster than is required.

Duplicate and redundant content are common problems. When content is produced in a stovepiped manner, some groups will work more quickly than others, resulting in imbalances. Writers have the copy ready, only to realize that the graphics aren't ready.

For example, when an individual knows that it can take time to get a request filled, they may be inclined to ask for things "just in case" it might be needed at some point when they can't wait for others. Metadata can help different parties coordinate their outputs, and understand the stock of content and information that's currently available to reuse and modify.

6. **Over-processing** — checking or manipulating information beyond what was required by the customer

Over-processing could entail the amount of review or QA required, because there are no common standards that allow for automation.

7. **Defects** — unusable or rejected by the customer

Avoidable defects could be formatting issues in the content, or updates not uniformly propagated.

Opportunity costs

Information silos don't just slow things down. They can obscure what is going on. This problem affects all stakeholders in the organization, not just developers.

> *"Fragmentation can create information bottlenecks and stifle innovation."*[18]

-- Gillian Tett

It's harder for different stakeholders to work toward common goals when they lack a common description of their online content. It's difficult for them to see relationships. Project teams can't cross-reference information from different systems. They can't re-organize information, because different proprietary metadata descriptions are not structured for flexibility. Teams lack a common basis to interpret information (discussed further in Chapter 16 on operational coordination).

Teams can miss out on chances to execute quick projects when they don't have a shared metadata resource capability. Frequently, each function participating on a web team has its own framework for thinking about the importance of priorities, often based on scheduling or staffing, instead of using a framework that is shared across all functions working on web content. Metadata can allow projects to be considered in terms of the information that is already available, the information that needs to be available, and the benefits expected by offering such information to customers.

By habit, individuals talk about online information according to the lingo of their tribe, which could be technical, based on lines of business, or centered around user experience. Individuals need a common language to talk to others outside their tribe. For example, a cross-functional team may want to understand what's happening when users click a button on a page that says "view details." Different roles will consider the button in different ways: as a clickable element, as a stylized graphic feature, or as a conversion path relating to a specific product. When considered through the common language of metadata, the button represents a *potential action* that is associated with presentation of specific information before and after the action is taken.

The problem of terminology is severe when dealing with different lines of business and different geographic regions that refer to similar things in different ways. One executive at a multinational firm that has 60 operating units complained to a team of McKinsey consultants about the human cost of silos: "'We were like the UN without translators,' one executive noted, 'with different language and terminology describing nearly every process'."[19]

Inertia can contribute to the rise of separate terminologies. But it is not an excuse. An individual may not have developed the custom classification system he or she is using, but they haven't challenged it either. Gillian Tett notes: "Most of us simply accept the classification systems we have inherited."[20]

It bears repeating: for teams to collaborate, they need to speak a common language. Nearly every management consultant advising on the now-hot topic of "digital transformation" will offer some variation of this advice: "Create cross-functional teams that break through silos and work close to the consumer."[21] Common terminology is essential for cross-functional teams to collaborate. Common terminology is the outcome of adopting external standards for metadata.

A common sign of silos are "atomized processes" where different groups are each doing their own thing, with limited coordination across groups or over time. Proprietary metadata contributes to the formation of atomized processes. Proprietary metadata can't be shared easily with other systems and is hard or impossible to migrate if the organization changes systems. Proprietary metadata is a sunk cost that's expensive to maintain instead of being an investment that will deliver value for years to come. Unlike metadata based on external standards, proprietary metadata is brittle — new requirements can mess up an existing integration configuration.

Using external vocabularies for metadata is a powerful, but often overlooked, way to stop the waste. Data stops being a maintenance cost and starts delivering value because it can be more widely used across different projects and can support more goals.

---

[18] Tett, *The Silo Effect*, p.14

[19] From McKinsey article "Making collaboration across functions a reality" Ruben Schaubroeck, Felicita Holsztejn Tarczewski, and Rob Theunissen, McKinsey Quarterly March 2016, https://www.mckinsey.com/business-

functions/organization/our-insights/making-collaboration-across-functions-a-reality

[20] Tett, p.249

[21] "The Digital Marketing Revolution Has Only Just Begun", https://www.bcg.com/publications/2017/sales-consumer-insights-digital-marketing-revolution-has-only-just-begun.aspx

CHAPTER 5: THE IMPORTANCE OF EXTERNAL METADATA STANDARDS

What words mean is a problem that has long bedeviled written content. The problem is no longer limited to lawyers arguing in a courtroom. The rise of professional specialization, globalization, and social subcultures means that even common words can mean many things. Different audience segments will interpret words and phrases in different ways.

When implemented correctly, metadata defines what the information in content means in a uniform, unambiguous way. It provides a basis for other parties to understand the meaning without needing an interpreter.

It's not just people who can understand meaning differently. Different machines can understand text values in different ways as well.

Consider an everyday example. How large is a large egg — or the chicken that may have laid it? Various countries have different ideas about how to grade eggs (or chickens) according to size — even countries that all speak the same language (English). Australia has a different idea about how to label big eggs compared to the United States. When Amazon was designing skills for its Alexa voice interactive device, it faced this issue (see Figure 5.1). Recipes call for extra-large eggs. But extra-large according to whose definition?

Figure 5.1. People refer to food items as large or medium. What that means depends on the item and even the local market. Voice interaction designers are

FoodCount.Size Enumeration &

Value	Description for selected food items
EXTRA_EXTRA_LARGE	In Australia, used for eggs that weigh 71.7 - 78.5 grams (same as King and Mega)
JUMBO	Eggs: In US/Canada, weight more than 2.5 oz or 70 grams
EXTRA_LARGE	Eggs: US/Canada, weight more than 2.25 oz or 63 grams Potato: US, diameter of 2 3/4 to 4 1/2 inches, same as "Chef" size
LARGE	Eggs: In US/Canada, weight more than 2 oz or 56 grams Whole Chicken: US/Canada, same as "Roaster" Potato: In US, diameter of 3 to 4 1/2 inches
MEDIUM	Eggs: In US/Canada, describes eggs that weigh more than 1.75 oz or 49 grams Whole Chicken: In US/Canada, same as "Broiler" Potato: In US, diameter between 2 1/4 and 3 1/4 inches
SMALL	Eggs: In US/Canada, describes eggs with weight more than 1.5 oz. or 42 grams Whole Chicken: In US/Canada, same as "Fryer" Potato: In US, diameter between 1 3/4 and 2 1/2 inches

encountering these issues. Source: Amazon Alexa.

Even numbers can mean different things to different people. Let's move from eggs to clothing. Every country has its own numeric system for clothes sizes. Some European countries use both national and EU systems. Is the clothing size for Australia (AU), Brazil (BR), China (CN), Germany (DE), the European Union (EU), France (FR), Italy (IT), Japan (JP), Mexico (MEX), the United Kingdom (UK), or the United States (US)?

Next, how do you encode that clothing size in metadata? What codes or abbreviations do you use? What property name do you use? Different online merchants follow different schemes. Should you follow the practices of Google Merchant Center, Amazon, or Alibaba?

Silo-busting with standards

Metadata standards break down content silos. Standards help to promote a mutually-understandable way to talk about content.

An absence of well-defined metadata standards hurts the customer experience when customers can't access information on different applications or devices. They may need to visit different websites, use different apps, or log-in to different systems. The multitude of apps on our phones, many of which seem similar or related (and are sometimes from the same publisher), is one symptom of the failure of online publishers to implement external metadata standards diligently.

> *"Today, metadata is mostly local, in the sense that often the meaning gets lost when moved from one system to another."*[22]

-- Nokia Research

Many businesses operate under the assumption that external metadata standards aren't relevant to them. They can build their own data models. If they need to share content, they can build an API to do that. They embrace a very enterprise-centric perspective. They expect the world will adapt to them, rather than seeing the need to adapt to the rest of the world.

Publishers of online information can be divided into two camps: those who need to seek out people who might be interested in their information, and those who expect people to come to them for information. Publishers that are focused on delivering content to a broad audience have been forced to consider how their customers find their information. Firms that are focused on technical information, which has a specialized, often captive audience, have been less concerned with considering audience needs. They're more focused on managing internal data.

A *Bloomberg* article describes the difference in attitude between publishers of broad ("horizontal" or cross-sector) online information and specialized ("vertical" or sector-specific) information:

"[Online consumer] publishing and geospatial [information] may be industries leading the way in [metadata] standardization, [but] some industries are not quite there

yet. Perhaps they have been exchanging data but are not necessarily required to distribute it cross-industry or cross-supplier."[23]

The broader the range of customers who need to access an organization's information, the more important using metadata standards become. But all providers of online information, whether serving broad or specialized audiences, should make it easy to exchange information and encourage its usage. Publishers can make sure other parties can easily understand the meaning of their information by using external metadata standards such as precise data formats and syntaxes, semantic schemas and ontologies, and enumerated values and web-accessible identifiers for values.

Internal standards, whether proprietary data models or bespoke rules for "tagging" content, are of limited value outside of one's own organization. External standards let publishers connect their information to outside parties. What criteria define what qualifies as an external standard?

The Open Data Institute (Figure 5.2) classifies internal and external standards along a continuum:

- **Closed** standards

  o   Internal access (only available to insiders)
  o   "Named" access (available only to those sign a contract)

- **Shared** standards

  o   Group-based access (authenticated: available to those who join as members of an association or group)
  o   Public access (licensed: available to all, but some conditions on use apply)
- **Open** standards (open license: no conditions on use).

Closed standards create problems. For example, the US Government relies on proprietary DUNS numbers from Dun & Bradstreet to track contracts. The US Government Accountability Office noted that "we found that Dun & Bradstreet had placed restrictions on DUNS numbers that limit the purposes for which the government can use the data, and hamper the ability to switch to a new numbering system."[24]

Shared and open standards typically come from international bodies such as the W3C, GS1, ISO, trade associations, and the Wikidata community. There are different levels of openness in both the standards-setting process and standards adoption. Some standards are open to all to use. Shared standards (such as public access standards offered by some trade associations) provide some of the benefits of open standards. They improve on closed, proprietary standards, but they may be subject to licensing conditions.

Figure 5.2. Openness exists along a spectrum. Source: Open Data Institute.

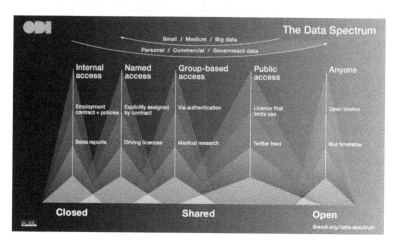

Open metadata standards support different roles:[25]

- Provide common, shared vocabularies
- Facilitate the exchange of data
- Provide guidance on how to manage information.

Open metadata vocabularies standardize how information is characterized, including:

- Concepts
- Words or terms
- Attributes or properties
- Relationships
- Standard codes and identifiers
- Units of measure

- Models of organization.

Open metadata standards support the *exchange of data* at all levels, from bits to bundles:

- Formats for content and information
- Data types
- Data transfer
- Rules
- Maps.

According to the Open Data Institute, open metadata standards offer four key benefits:[26]

1. Interoperability
2. The ability to compare information
3. The ability to aggregate information
4. Linkability.

Despite these benefits, open standards are often dismissed as entailing too much effort. Yet semantic metadata, an umbrella term for open metadata standards, is shedding its reputation from the aughts as an academic curiosity that is difficult to put to practical use. Although semantic metadata has its origin in the needs of academic and scientific research, it has been large, for-profit companies that have been the major drivers in promoting the development and popularizing the implementation of metadata vocabulary standards.

Best Buy was one of the first major corporations to implement new semantic metadata standards. An article from 2010 notes that Best Buy was using the then-new RDFa syntax and GoodRelations ecommerce vocabulary a few years before the emergence of the schema.org standard. Already, Best Buy was thinking about how to make the process easy for employees:

"Best Buy employees entered information into the blogs every day, using online forms that output RDFa. Myers told us that the use of RDFa makes 'human input from our store employees more visible on the Web.' Best Buy is using Good Relations, a Semantic Web vocabulary for e-commerce that describes product, price, and company data."[27]

Since Best Buy's pioneering efforts, the momentum for external metadata standards has been growing steadily. Search engines, through their stewardship and promotion of the schema.org vocabulary, have encouraged nearly all online publishers to adopt semantic metadata standards to some degree. But search engines are no longer the only rationale for using these standards. Internal use cases can be implemented more efficiently when using external metadata standards. It doesn't make sense to maintain two sets of standards covering the same information, where companies use external standards for publicly published content, but maintain proprietary standards to manage that information when it is communicated internally. Many firms are starting to realize they are duplicating their work by maintaining separate metadata for externally-facing and internally-facing use cases.

---

[22] Juha Lehikoinen, Antti Aaltonen, Pertti Huuskonen, *Personal Content Experience: Managing Digital Life in the Mobile Age* (Wiley 2007), p. 116.

[23] Adrienne Tannenbaum, "Finding Maturity in Your Metadata Strategy", *Bloomberg*, December 22, 2014, December 22, 2014, https://www.bloomberg.com/professional/blog/finding-maturity-in-your-metadata-strategy/

[24] https://www.gao.gov/assets/700/696023.pdf

[25] "Types of open standards for data", http://standards.theodi.org/introduction/types-of-open-standards-for-data/

[26] The Open Standards Institute, "When to Use Open Standards", http://standards.theodi.org/introduction/when-to-use-open-standards-for-data/

[27] "How Best Buy is Using The Semantic Web", Richard MacManus, June 30, 2010, *ReadWrite*, https://readwrite.com/2010/06/30/how_best_buy_is_using_the_semantic_web/

What does 'open' mean?

This book will generally refer to *external* standards, rather than *open* standards, to avoid confusion about what is technically open. The word *open* is widely used in different contexts, modifying different concepts. These terms are frequently confused because they can sound similar and often have overlapping focuses.

At its most fundamental level, *open metadata standards* provide a common way to describe content that is available for anyone to use. For example, a standards community might decide to always refer to the property for a state or province within a country as a "region." The description or vocabulary is *open* (non-proprietary) because it is standardized and the published standard is free to use. The W3C is an example of a community that creates open metadata standards. The value of open metadata standards is that they enable access to information, and support the correct understanding of the meaning of the information.

Open data concerns making information freely available for other parties to use without any copyright restrictions. Governments and international organizations such as the World Bank that have a public service mandate publish open (non-proprietary) data. For-profit enterprises are less interested in releasing open data, although there are some notable exceptions. Open data does not have to use open metadata standards, but often does.[28] Open data concerns reuse rights, while open metadata standards concerns access and exchange.

Using open metadata standards can facilitate third-party *access* to information, but does not force the data to be "open" — available for others to reuse without restriction. Online publishers can use metadata standards to assert copyright and indicate distribution licensing.

Open source is related to computer source code, not to metadata standards. Open source projects often utilize open metadata standards, so online publishers who follow open metadata standards can get access to many useful open source tools. But just because the software is open source, it doesn't mean it necessarily follows open metadata standards. WordPress, the most popular CMS, is open source but has poor support for open metadata standards.

Open linked data is a combination of open standards, open data, and machine accessibility. The term *linked* refers to the connecting or linking of information specified within metadata that has been published on different websites.[29] Linking makes it clear how information from different publishers is related, and whether or not such information refers to the same entity. When the data is open, different publishers can link their information so that it can be combined easily without licensing restrictions. It is possible to have linked data that uses open standards but that is not open data; it would not be *open* linked data if the publisher asserted a copyright to the information.[30] Open linked data can be a valuable resource. But it is not always the goal of commercial firms, who may want to control the use of some of their information.

Different forms of openness provide online publishers with freedom and options. One motivation to use open standards, according to one formulation, is "to liberate data from the tyranny of applications."[31] With open standards, information isn't locked into any vendor's proprietary system. Online publishers don't have to use open source systems to get the benefits of open metadata standards. Their content can work with any system, either open source or commercial, provided the system supports open metadata standards.

External metadata standards have become increasingly sophisticated in coverage. They can now address many dimensions of online information that previously could only be managed using proprietary relational databases. Some major developments in recent years include:

- The growth of entities and properties in the core of schema.org vocabulary, now covering:

  o 597 Entity Types
  o 862 Properties
  o 114 Enumeration values
- New extensions to schema.org covering in detail vertical sectors such as autos and healthcare
- The development of GS1 web standards for products, providing detailed properties for product information
- The release of tens of thousands of Wikidata unique identifiers, allowing specific multi-lingual identification of things and concepts
- A mechanism to validate values using the new SHACL standard
- The introduction of a web-friendly syntax (JSON-LD) that gives more options to developers.

Some online publishers may not be aware of all the progress that external standards have experienced. And that progress shows no signs of slowing down. But it must also be noted that not all sectors can benefit equally from external standards. Some sectors such as retail, finance, and healthcare have very deep coverage, while other sectors (for example, houseplants) lack detailed coverage. Some sectors have been early adopters of external standards and as a result benefit from more options. Other sectors have been passive and not engaged, and haven't proposed and developed more specific properties relating to their sector. Even if coverage relating to one's sector is currently limited, publishers have the opportunity to develop common metadata standards relating to their sector (discussed in Chapter 21 on defining scope).

---

[28] Information in a spreadsheet that is posted online can be open data, even though it doesn't follow open metadata standards.

[29] Or more formally, within different content repositories.

[30] Some enterprise Knowledge Graphs (discussed later) could be categorized as *closed* linked data, available only via internal or closed access.

[31] See Alexander Coley, "Silos are architectural heritage from the pre-data era: it is time to move on", https://www.epimorphics.com/silos-are-architectural-heritage/

The decline of vertical (single-purpose) portals

Much content is discovered through web searches. The needs of web search engines have been the big driver of web metadata standards. Organizations can no longer expect that audiences will first go to a specific portal to search a database. For example, libraries have used idiosyncratic metadata standards to describe books that could be searched on the portals of libraries. Increasingly, libraries are looking to adopt the same schema.org standards that are used by online book retailers and other consumer websites. Readers are looking for information about books. They don't want to first decide the source of the information.

The rise of standards is eroding the appeal of specialized websites that aggregate previously hard-to-aggregate information. Job websites would scrape information from different sites and pull them into a common database. Now, job postings are described with standardized metadata, meaning that posting on different websites can be discovered easily in search (discussed further in Chapter 11 on search discovery).

Publishers now need to get information to where customers are, instead of trying to get the customer to come to where the publisher holds the information.

Overcoming the legacy of silos

Despite significant progress, plenty of content silos are still around.

Metadata researcher Alex Stolz describes the continued problem of "heterogeneity" (variety) in online information. Instead of content following standards, content is "developed independently by different parties, and serving distinct purposes", he notes.[32]

> *"Among the prominent examples for a proprietary classification system on the Web is the Google product taxonomy."*

-- Alex Stolz *metadata researcher*

Even Google, a strong promoter of common metadata standards for web content, has also been guilty of creating silos on the web.[33] One presumes this is because Google is a big company with many active projects that were started at different times, and as a result, not every project is aligned with common standards.

Many organizations are proud of the taxonomies they've developed or data models they've designed for their specific needs.[34] Stolz notes the limitations of such go-it-alone approaches: "The problem with (custom) classifications is that they are often *designed for specific purposes* and thus apply to different contexts, and categories may be arranged in distinct structures and expressed using different terminology."[35]

Purpose-built solutions don't adapt easily to new contexts. Silos arise when companies define enterprise metadata standards that are inwardly focused, and which fail to consider how enterprise web content connects the organization's processes to the customer's decisions. Companies may have a master data model developed for business intelligence and data mining, using definitions that are unrelated to how customer interactions are described in web content. Master data models may use proprietary properties or sector-specific industry definitions instead of building upon external metadata standards. Master data models can be cryptic, where only a handful of people even understand what they describe.

External, community-backed standards can evolve to address new contexts. They are powered by the resources of a community of participants facing similar requirements. They are far more resilient than proprietary approaches, because a diverse pool of contributors participates is expanding and updating these vocabularies.

External metadata standards are increasingly important because all kinds of services are conducted online — and not just B2C (business to consumer) marketing. Standards promote the exchange information that supports a range of interactions:

- B2B (business-to-business)
- G2C (government-to-citizen)
- C2B (consumer-to-business)
- C2G (citizen-to-government).

External standards should be the default for customer-facing information, with custom properties the exception in cases where external standards aren't available.

---

[32] Alex Stolz, "Deep Product Comparison on the Semantic Web", https://d-nb.info/1128618265/34

[33] Custom product taxonomies are a widespread problem and inhibit comparison of products from different vendors. Online publishers should be using external standards such as GS1's product value vocabulary to classify products.

[34] Custom taxonomies are sometimes needed to indicate distinctions of particular interest to the publisher. Publishers should always question whether these requirements are truly unique, or whether external controlled vocabularies can be used. Taxonomy values should use standard property vocabularies to indicate that the terms mean. Too many CMSs use custom taxonomies as a way to avoid support for metadata standards.

[35] *Ibid.*, emphasis added.

Key point 1: Save yourself (and others) some work

Don't reinvent the wheel --

Many organizations develop their own "data model" to describe information in their content. But rarely are these data models relating to web information that unique — they are just different enough to be difficult to use. Data models are valuable for enterprise data that is used internally, but for externally-facing information delivered online external metadata standards can provide a ready-to-use model to describe the information.

> *"The structure of schema.org, as a massively peer-reviewed, Internet-ready, semantic 'model' saved so much specification time."*

-- David Gibson *Southern Cross Health Society*

Don't write unnecessary documentation: leverage other people's --

Custom documentation can be a bottleneck. Instead of drafting extensive explanations, publishers can link to the most up-to-date version of the standard.

Don't make people read your documentation: use familiar terms --

Users and developers will avoid reading documentation if they feel they can get away without reading it. Any documentation publishers do produce should be so familiar that developers don't have to look at it closely. The more publishers use standards that are being used elsewhere, the more familiar their metadata will seem. For example, nearly all standards use the ISO date format (year first, followed by month then day). Few developers need to check the formatting of dates — it is second nature.

Give people a common way of thinking about entities and properties. Help everyone chunk and cluster information in their minds easily by using a common framework that is used over and over, and becomes second nature. External vocabularies can promote clarity about the information teams are managing.

Key point 2: Make your contributions interoperable

Online publishers should let others use their information without forcing others to reinterpret the information in some way. And they shouldn't require others to change their current IT setup to consume their information. Their information should be plug-and-play ready.

External metadata standards promote interoperability — the ability of different parties to exchange information easily. Interoperability allows everyone who uses the information to do some on their own terms. Metadata standards define common concepts — units of information — that can be expressed differently in various human and computer syntaxes.

Standardized metadata for online content supports three kinds of interoperability:

1. The ability of different audience segments to understand common information
2. The ability of different processes to use common information
3. The ability of different IT systems to use common information.

Interoperability applies to people as well as to systems. People at times need different labels to describe concepts such an administrative region where one lives. But also need information to be reliable, so that different administrative regions can be compared. Metadata standards can support both those needs.

Customers want a common definition of what a concept means — for example, what "no added sugar" means. They want to reliably understand the meaning of the concept. If an online publisher defines a concept differently than the standard used by other publishers, it will be at a disadvantage. It is important for publishers to follow standardized, common definitions of concepts. But how a concept is labeled and presented to different audiences won't always be the same. Linguistic and national differences can necessitate the use of different labels.[16] Even when using English, different countries may refer to the same concept using different terminology (e.g., trucks versus lorries). Metadata standards can support variations in labels and values such as prices that are presented to different audiences. Even though different segments may see different labels, the meaning is consistent (see Figure 5.3).

Figure 5.3. How to describe a self-driving car will vary. Metadata standards support interoperability in terminology.

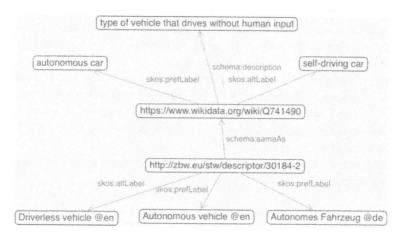

While web-facing content expresses the priorities of customers, the enterprise manages internal processes to support these customers. At times these internal processes will describe information differently from how it is presented to customers. For example, an ecommerce vendor may make an internal distinction between whether an item is out-of-stock or whether it is back-ordered. Consumers may not be interested in that distinction: they want to know whether or not the item is immediately available to purchase.

Different enterprise functions may be interested in more or less granular information than is presented to customers. The metadata standard can facilitate interoperability between web-facing information and enterprise process indicators. It can indicate the equivalence between properties and values used in web content and those tracked within enterprise processes.

Different IT systems also need to be able to use the same information. Metadata standards support the exchange of information between systems by defining the schema and syntax for the data.

John Passey and Urs Gasser at Harvard University note the risks of pursuing a proprietary, non-interoperable approach:

"Designers of noninteroperable online services and devices run a high risk in ignoring general consumer preferences and limiting consumer autonomy."[37]

Interoperability does not imply integration — having a single technology platform — though interoperability provides a foundation for integration. Palfrey and Gasser draw a "distinction between *complete standardization* (in which the same technologies are adopted across the board) and *interoperability* (in which technologies merely need to work together in certain ways.)"[18] Content can use metadata to become interoperable. The more that the metadata follows external standards, the more easily the content can work across different systems without modification. How metadata standards can support operations will be discussed more in Chapter 16.

Companies should avoid the mistake of assuming they can set their own standards and expect others to adopt these standards. This thinking is most common in fast-growing companies that hope to become the dominant "platform" for their sector or service. While proprietary engineering standards can sometimes force customers to use hardware or software products, online content is different. Consumers have countless choices about what content they give their attention to. Content lock-in isn't viable. Publishers that have closed platforms will face a losing battle for attention.

John Palfrey and Urs Gasser argue that the traditional "strategy of exclusion" has become dated, and openness is now favored.[19] They maintain that interoperability is the key to long-term viability.

> *"More and more firms, especially in the information business, are shedding their proprietary approaches in favor of interoperability at multiple levels. The goal is not to be charitable to competitors or customers, of course, but to maximize returns over time by building an ecosystem with others that holds greater promise than the go-it-alone approach."*

-- John Palfrey and Urs Gasser *Harvard University*

Information doesn't thrive in a walled garden. In a few high profile cases, where no common standard was yet established, companies have tried to make their standard the dominant one. Microsoft did this with the Word document format, and Adobe did this with the PDF document format. In both cases, customers didn't want their content locked into a proprietary format, so both Microsoft and Adobe were forced to open their standard for everyone.[40] The benefits of using open standards are too great.

---

[36] Localization can encompass language, cultural norms, legal and regulatory requirements, and payment options.

[37] John Passey and Urs Gasser, *Interop*, p. 62

[38] ibid, p.91

[39] John Palfrey and Urs Gasser, *Interop*, p. 149

[40] Google's AMP standard is the most recent example of a proprietary standard announcing that it is now "open," though it remains to be seen how much publishers and Google competitors can change the existing standard.

Connecting information with RDF

Content and information are most valuable when connected to other content. Online information needs to be available on different platforms. Even closed ecosystems such as Facebook promote standards that are "open" (Open Graph) and compatible with W3C standards in order to ingest content easily. No organization can afford to be a walled garden with respect to content.

Numerous metadata standards are available, addressing a range of needs, both general and specific. Most of these standards, such as the popular schema.org vocabulary, are based on the RDF data model,[41] or can be readily converted into RDF.

One major virtue of RDF is that it is simple: "the RDF data model is very simple and can be understood by almost any person in less than an hour."[42] The simplicity enables flexibility: "The simplicity and generality of the RDF data model enables its use to model any kind of data that can be easily integrated with other data."

RDF is a valuable tool for bridging silos of information:

"RDF as an integration language. RDF is compositional in the sense that two RDF graphs obtained from independent sources can automatically be merged to obtain a larger graph. This property facilitates the integration of data from heterogeneous sources. One of the biggest challenges of the current era related with computer science is how to solve the interoperability problem between different applications that manipulate data that comes from heterogeneous sources. RDF is a step forward to partially solve this problem as RDF data can automatically be integrated even if it has been produced by different parties."[43]

RDF abstracts away the hassle of connecting information. Developers can use RDF without needing to understand the details of how it works. Not all developers will care about the inner details of RDF. But those who need to integrate information from different sources will appreciate its flexibility.

The big benefit of working with standard vocabularies is that online publishers can draw on multiple vocabularies to describe and connect their information more richly. Because all vocabularies use a common RDF data model, the vocabularies can be combined.

Major metadata vocabularies have properties that can be used to describe relationships between things — such as whether an item is used with another item, or has been replaced by another. Nearly everyone who has bought things online has experienced the confusion that can arise when trying to figure out which product is newest, or if a new part can be used in a non-discontinued product. Combining properties from different vocabularies is a powerful way to connect information to address highly specific use cases.

Within schema.org, important connecting properties include:

- schema:isRelatedTo
- schema:isSimilarTo
- schema:isConsumableFor
- schema:isAccessoryOrSparePartFor.

Within the GS1 Web vocabulary, properties are available to show how different products may be related:

- gs1:dependentProprietaryProduct
- gs1:equivalentProduct
- gs1:primaryAlternateProduct
- gs1:replacedProduct
- gs1:replacedByProduct.

Dublin Core has generic properties defining the parts of things:

- dcterms:isPartOf
- dcterms:hasPart.

Different external standards aren't competitive with each other; they complement each other. And if available standards don't support a publisher's requirements, publishers can extend existing standards or propose new ones that are open for others to use. They can encourage other parties in the publisher's ecosystem, business suppliers, IT vendors, and host platforms to adopt them and support their requirements.

---

[41] RDF is the Resource Description Framework, a W3C standard for modelling data as triple statements

[42] Jose E. Labra Gayo, Eric Prudhommeaux, Iovka Boneva, Dimitris Kontokostas (2018) Validating RDF Data, Synthesis Lectures on the Semantic Web: Theory and Technology, Vol. 7, No. 1, 1-328, DOI:

10.2200/S00786ED1V01Y201707WBE016, Morgan & Claypool,
`http://book.validatingrdf.com/bookHtml007.html`

[43] *Ibid.*

CHAPTER 6: WHAT'S INCLUDED IN A METADATA STRATEGY?

L arge organizations need to be able to deliver customer-relevant digital communications at scale. That is challenging to do. It is hard to package the right information into the content that audiences consume online. Audiences might get too much information, or too little, or have to cope with information not immediately relevant to their current needs.

Global enterprises are big and need to speak to many customers at once. But their customer is an individual, an audience of one. The enterprise has a lot to say. But the customer needs something specific and doesn't want extraneous information.

A metadata strategy provides a foundation for addressing the problem of scope and scale.

> *"Metadata strategy identifies the type and structure of metadata, also known as 'data about data' (or content). Smart, well-structured metadata helps publishers identify, organize, use, and reuse content in ways that are meaningful to key audiences."*[44]

-- Kristina Halvorson and Melissa Rach

A strategy is an antidote to the *ad hoc* manner that many organizations currently create metadata. The strategy guides the direction so that each decision supports the other. "The trap is to focus on individual decisions, rather than the sum, to pursue best practices rather than strategy," notes Bharat Anand of Harvard Business School.[45]

A web metadata strategy defines how organizations use metadata to:

- Connect content to business goals
- Connect content to audiences
- Connect content with enterprise functions.

A strategy will define goals for metadata. Online publishers should aim for metadata to support several business goals that represent different parts of the business: marketing, customer support, UX, business intelligence. Publishers may roll these goals up into a broader vision, which should appeal to a range of stakeholders within the organization.

A metadata strategy in action: the example of eBay

Before we explore the many dimensions that can be relevant in a metadata strategy, let's look at how a well-known company has approached metadata strategy.

EBay is familiar to many web users, though its scale is not all always appreciated. EBay is the largest exporter of Chinese goods around the world, according to its CEO Devin Wenig. EBay has partnerships with physical retailers: in the US with Best Buy and Target, and in the UK with Argos.

Several years ago, eBay recognized the status quo was not working. They needed a metadata strategy. Not having metadata standards was hurting growth. Wall Street was keenly interested in how eBay could change.

An investor website noted: "eBay and other marketplace sites have struggled with having identical or related products given very different names and descriptions by different sellers."[46]

An Oxford University professor noted: "Buyers on eBay often had to search for words in product titles and descriptions then scroll through page after page of results. This is a legacy of eBay starting as a marketplace where anyone can sell anything."[47]

Hal Lawton, North American head at eBay acknowledged: "Our marketplace was born 20 years ago when online selling was in its infancy. Sellers could write whatever they wanted as a description."[48]

A retail industry website described the scale of eBay's problem: "One of eBay's main bragging points — that it has 1.1 billion listings — has also become a source of weakness for the company. Organizing that many items is a herculean task, particularly when the bones of the site are now decades old."[49]

EBay had a metadata problem: "The lack of an ontology [standardized metadata properties] in the market reduces [the] number of transactions that can take place, because people have trouble finding a match even when one exists."[50]

EBay decided that the proprietary metadata they used in their content wasn't working, as it was preventing them from leveraging metadata to deliver better experiences for their customers. They embarked on a major program called the "Structured Data Initiative", migrating their content to metadata based on the W3C web standard, schema.org.

The goals for eBay's strategy are both concrete and aspirational:

"The massive data project underway at eBay aims to improve cataloging for products on offer, increasing the rate of discoverability from 42 to about 90 percent."[51]

Wall Street analysts have followed eBay's metadata strategy closely (Figure 6.1). Their adoption of metadata standards has enabled a "more personal and discovery-based buying experience with highly tailored choices and unique selection", according to eBay. EBay is using the metadata to work with new AI technologies to deliver a personalized homepage to each of its customers. It also used its metadata in its conversational commerce product, the eBay ShopBot, which connects with Facebook Messenger. EBay's experience shows the value of having a metadata strategy before adopting AI.

Figure 6.1. Ebay Form 8K for investors filed with the SEC mentioning their metadata strategy plans. Source: eBay.

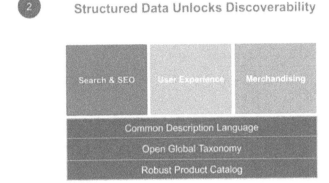

EBay saw the potential of metadata to serve multiple purposes. Metadata can support different goals: those of buyers, sellers, and the corporation and its shareholders. Metadata standards bridge different activities, such as online search (SEO) and the customer experience within the eBay shopping portal.

EBay's metadata strategy adopts the schema.org vocabulary, a W3C standard, for their internal content management, in addition to using it for search engine consumers such as Google and Bing. Plenty of publishers use the schema.org vocabulary for search engine purposes, but few have taken the next step like eBay to use it as the basis of their content operations. By following external standards, eBay is now well-positioned to take advantage of any new third-party services that can consume their metadata.

Figure 6.2. Diagram depicting eBay's metadata strategy. It illustrates the different stakeholders involved (customers, platforms, sellers) and articulates the key content for which metadata is needed. Source: eBay.

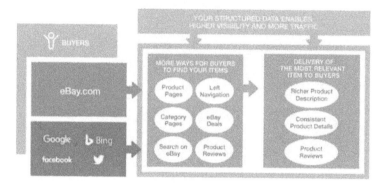

Figure 6.2 presents a diagram of eBay's metadata strategy, which reveals a critical issue. There are different paths to eBay's information about products for sale. Customers can reach eBay via search engines such as Google or Bing, social media such as Facebook, or from the home page or another landing page on eBay's website. Regardless of how customers start their journey, they are seeking something specific, and want to get to information about that product as easily as possible. All channels need to support the user's journey.

Often, web users will comment that it is easier to find content via a Google search than it is to locate it on a company's website. EBay recognized that their search and browse experience needed to match or exceed Google's search capabilities. If people couldn't find what they needed within eBay's website and had to rely on Google to find it, eBay faced the risk that those customers would consider other vendors who appear in the search results.

---

[44] Kristina Halvorson and Melissa Rach, *Content Strategy for the Web* (2nd Edition)

[45] Bharat Anand, *The Content Trap*, p. 249

[46]   https://seekingalpha.com/article/3998840-ebays-artificial-intelligence-says-challenges-marketplace-big-data

[47] Viktor-Mayer Schonberger with Thomas Range, *Reinventing Capitalism in the Age of Big Data* (John Murray 2018) p. 69

[48]   https://www.ebayinc.com/stories/news/leaning-into-the-future-of-e-commerce/

[49]   https://www.racked.com/2017/10/16/16473414/ebay-online-shopping-resale

[50] Viktor-Mayer Schonberger with Thomas Range, *Reinventing Capitalism in the Age of Big Data* (John Murray 2018) p. 69

[51] Viktor-Mayer Schonberger with Thomas Range, *Reinventing Capitalism in the Age of Big Data* (John Murray 2018) p. 70

Defining the context of metadata strategy

Metadata operates within a much larger business context.

When developing a strategy for metadata, organizations will want to identify how metadata is connected to their operations. Some foundational questions include:

- Who benefits from metadata?
- What stakeholders does the strategy need to consider?
- How might operations be different if metadata is adopted?

A web metadata strategy will address *what* is needed, and *how* to do it. It will provide:

1. A unified, enterprise-wide set of requirements for metadata for digital content
2. A plan to strengthen, assess, and govern the use of metadata for online content.

A strategy will express goals and requirements. It will be backed by a program that delineates activities needed to support the strategy.

A metadata strategy aligns all stakeholders around key considerations:

- The opportunity cost of *not* having standards (*What's the nature of our problem?*)

- Goals for adopting standards (*What can be done if we solve our problem?*)

- A plan of action for adopting standards (*How are we going to get there?*)

A metadata strategy and implementing program includes a range of activities:

- **Benchmarking** the current use of metadata
- Developing **metadata requirements**: standards and goals for one's web metadata
- **Training**: understanding of how metadata works

- Establishing **criteria for tool adoption**, including tool usability, deployment practicality, implementation readiness, and future-readiness
- **Governance** for metadata framework development, covering terminology, taxonomies, and APIs
- **Analytics** developed to leverage metadata to deliver more useful and actionable analysis.

In subsequent chapters, the book will provide details about specific focus areas that can be part of a metadata strategy. These include potential benefits of metadata, which suggest goals that can be included in the strategy. Subsequent chapters will also look at specific requirements publishers should address when crafting and implementing a strategy.

Before deciding on the details, publishers should first define their context: the scope of people and systems that will be affected by metadata. This scope will define some high-level requirements that will be used to develop the strategy.

Gap analysis and enabling change

The development of a strategy customarily begins with a discovery phase. Organizations need to understand where they are currently with respect to using metadata and start to identify areas where they'd like to improve. This is the gap analysis: assessing the organization's current situation and comparing it to where it would like to be in the future.

The metadata strategy that's created will reflect the priorities of the publishing organization. A metadata strategy for a consumer electronics firm will look different from one for a non-profit organization. These organizations have different specific requirements, but both share a common need: to use metadata to improve how they communicate information to their customers.

A strategy should review how the organization's potential to grow or accomplish key goals could be hindered if metadata capabilities aren't adequate. Metadata works in tandem with other content and business-related activities, such as process streamlining, automation, and editorial planning. Transformation initiatives will be only partly effective in the absence of quality metadata.

The strategy should address both the results that are desired and the means to achieve those results. Metadata can improve online publishing two ways, by boosting:

1. The **efficiency** of content operations (the capacity to address goals)
2. The **effectiveness** of published content (the results achieved).

As part of the discovery process, publishers will want to identify their resource gaps: the difference between what the organization expects to do, and their ability to deliver it.

The strategy should account for both current and future needs. It should look beyond current content goals and consider how goals might evolve in the foreseeable future. Metadata is a capability that needs to develop over time. To respond to future change, organizations will need capabilities that can support their response.

Thinking about future needs can be difficult if current projects or issues are pressing. Scenario planning can help organizations focus on the future. What might the publisher want to do with metadata in the future, or be forced to do, given business, consumer, and technology trends?

When considering the many factors that may be relevant, consider each in turn, and decide whether something is:

❏ Currently relevant
❏ Potential future opportunity
❏ Possible disruptive threat
❏ Will never be relevant.

Value chain analysis

The value chain helps define the scope of metadata to include in a strategy. The value chain consists of four dimensions of information:

1. Creation
2. Aggregation
3. Distribution
4. Consumption.

The value chain influences the publisher's capacity to deliver the right information to users at the time and in the form that they want it. Metadata is important across the entire the entire value chain. A value chain analysis can suggest properties that may be needed to support different scenarios of use.

By understanding the value chain, the publisher will be able to answer:

- Who supplies information?
- How is it packaged?
- How much is made available?
- Where is the information accessed?

By considering the journey of information from conception to use, publishers can form a picture of how their information flows and connects. Some publishers create a "data ecosystem map" to illustrate information flows.[52]

Creation — The parties that contribute content that an online publisher may need to work with, which may include:

- Brand publishers (product-centric marketing or customer service content creators)
- News and entertainment publishers (syndicated subscription or ad-supported content)
- White-label content producers (multi-client content, commissioned sponsored content, content studios and agencies)
- Authoritative content publishers of record (information from government sources, statistical agencies, medical and professional societies)
- Customer-contributed content (reviews, comments, fan material, parodies)
- Customer status information systems (orders, tickets, delivery services)

- Public information sources (weather, traffic, flight delays).

Note that only some of the information an organization publishes is actually created by them. The organization may be sourcing content and information from other parties.

Conversely, not all information and content an organization creates will be published by them exclusively. A publisher may be sharing content and information with other parties for others to re-publish.

When different parties use different metadata in their content or use no metadata at all, the task of integrating content is much more difficult, which limits how the content can be used.

Issues relating to creation: What metadata needs to be available to enable web content to integrate content from diverse sources? What metadata does the publisher expect from others, and what do other publishers expect from the source?

Aggregation — The parties that acquire content from many parties, and make it available to many parties, which may include:

- Search engines
- Social network platforms
- Podcast platforms
- Curation sites
- Aggregation platforms (e.g., product comparisons, pricing comparisons, rating sites)
- App stores
- Digital payment platforms
- Shopping portals
- Publications accepting sponsored content.

If content doesn't adhere to well-established metadata standards or uses metadata sparsely, it can limit visibility on many aggregation platforms. Publishers may not be successful reaching the audience reach they need to reach.

Issues relating to aggregation: What metadata needs to be available to enable web content to adapt to different aggregation platforms?

Distribution — The physical means of disseminating digital content, which may include:

- Broadband WiFi
- IPTV networks
- 2.5G/3G/4G/5G mobile networks

- NFC
- ZigBee
- Bluetooth
- WiMax
- RFID.

Issues relating to distribution: Metadata needs to allow web content to adapt to different network requirements. These networks support different delivery speeds and levels of interactivity, from simple feeds to context-aware alerts or rich media interactivity. For example, some new distribution networks have a short range and involve low power consumption. Evaluating distribution requirements can help to separate simple information that might be needed in many contexts, from more complex information that will be only delivered where connectivity is fast.

Online publishers that are not in the tech sector may not be focused on these issues. But consider how important speed has become for accessing information on smartphones. Developers have spent considerable effort to make their content less "heavy". Online publishers were caught flatfooted by Google's AMP. Now suppose a new wave of devices promises to deliver information wirelessly, but only if it is available in certain formats? Will publishers be ready?

New wireless technologies offer short bursts of information to people nearby. They are increasingly important for content for the retail sector, hospitality, and entertainment. Contactless payments provide one example of how communication can occur between devices outside of a formal network.

An emerging application of non-broadband distribution is the delivery of supplemental information about a product that is consumed on a nearby device. The product may lack a screen or speaker, but it could broadcast a signal that another device such as a smartphone could display. Think of it as a step beyond QR codes.

Consumption — The devices consumers use to access content, which may include:

- Smartphones
- Tablets
- Smart speakers and earphones
- In-car entertainment
- Wearables (smart watches/glasses)
- Gaming consoles
- Intelligent cameras
- Machine-to-machine appliances
- Public digital displays.

Issues relating to consumption: What metadata needs to be available to enable web content to adapt to different device requirements?

Devices have different "affordances": how information is conveyed to users, which depends on factors such as the size of screens or the properties of auditory "displays." Most online publishers don't make consumer electronics, so it may not seem obvious to them that all these devices will be relevant. But people expect to access information on devices they are using when it is convenient and relevant to do so. What's convenience has a lot to do with context, such as what else they are doing, or who else they are with.

Online publishers may be tempted to skip the task of looking at their value chain. They may just want to create content and attach some metadata to it. But digital information doesn't live in a fixed container. It can be used in many scenarios, which is why value chain analysis is helpful. Online information is no longer defined as a web page. Each level of the value chain shapes information. Even distribution can define information requirements; for example, notifications could be a short burst of text such as an SMS. A thorough strategy will discover potential silos before they emerge. The strategy will consider how information needs to be available in different contexts.

---

[52] This is similar to "content ecosystem mapping", except focused on information in metadata rather than on content items. See "Mapping Data Ecosystems", Open Data Institute, https://theodi.org/article/mapping-data-ecosystems/

Stakeholder analysis

Defining the scope of metadata requirements will depend on who will use the information: the various stakeholders the publisher must consider. Stakeholders include both audiences who directly read the information as well as third parties that use the information to perform tasks that are in some way related to the information.

Web content serves many different kinds of audiences. Organizations differ in how public they are. Government organizations need to be transparent, as they have many different stakeholders. Educational institutions, non-profits and other service organizations also aim for transparency and have many constituents. Although public companies may be less transparent, they rely on making their information discoverable and deliverable to different groups. Closely held companies are perhaps least transparent kind of organization. But even they require information to be portable.

Because different stakeholders have different needs, the metadata strategy needs to prioritize those needs and identify how best to support them.

Stakeholders related to a corporate publisher

Prospective and current customers

Whether a company serves individuals or other businesses, they need to reduce the friction customers experience when interacting with their organization. Customers want to access information they need without having to know what department or division of the company is responsible for it. But organizations still deliver information in a siloed way. Marketing information is frequently developed and managed separately from customer service information.

Despite growing awareness that marketing and customer service are less distinct than the organizational chart implies, most organizations have made modest progress integrating their information across different functions, where it is centered around customer needs, instead of around organizational responsibilities. Customer information should be available in whatever context it is needed.

In addition to supporting interactions with customers, metadata can also help to support customers communicating and sharing information with each other. A growing range of products and services, providing information relating to traffic, weather, fitness, games and outdoor recreation, let users post information to share with other users. For example, a recent project has explored the sharing of physical activity data.[53]

Employees and job applicants

Recruitment and retention are major concerns for any skills-intensive employer. Metadata is useful for describing job openings and highlighting topics in blog posts mentioning projects that staff are working on. Publishers need to link together different themes: specific vacancies that are open, product training the company may offer, general recruiting needs (kinds of roles or skills that are frequently needed) while showcasing cool projects, thought leadership, and speaking engagements at conferences. To cross-promote these themes, metadata can be used to identify connections between different content.

The metadata standards community is working on new standards relating to educational and career credentials. These will likely also be useful for hiring priorities.

Suppliers and vendors

Enterprises need to share information with suppliers and vendors. If an enterprise gets product specifications from partners or supplies information to them, they don't want to have to redo this information to use it within their content. That work can be avoided if the B2B suppliers follow the same metadata standards that B2B buyers follow. The buyer can integrate their information with its information. B2B buyers will want to get their suppliers onboard with metadata standards they are adopting.

Another example where common information must be shared is when a third party provides the warranty fulfillment for another vendor's product.

Business or strategic partners

The situation with business partners is similar to B2B suppliers, expect that the organization will be exchanging or co-developing shared information, instead of simply receiving information to integrate. Using external standards for metadata in joint projects will facilitate collaboration. Examples range from joint product development to co-branded marketing.

Shareholders, investors, and funders

Those who fund organizations, such as shareholders of public companies, equity investors for non public companies, and benefactors and donors for NGOs and non-profits, will want to know how the organization is doing, and what it has accomplished.

They may want curated content provided in an email newsletter or a targeted report. Because information needs to be up-to-date and accurate, there is growing attention to standards to describe financial information such as earnings, corporate officers, and filings.

Outside stakeholders

Because outside parties don't have a direct relationship with the publisher, the publisher is less likely to consider their potential needs. Even though outside parties do not contribute to revenues, they can influence how a publisher is perceived: how visible information is, and whether the information is considered reliable. The metadata strategy should make it easy for outside parties to use the publisher's information for their own purposes. Publishers should consider not only how it wants others to use their information, but also how others may want to use the information to support their own goals that are not directly related to the publisher's goals.

Media

Media outlets may be interested in events the publisher is sponsoring or is participating in. Metadata standards for information relating to events can help to publicize an event you are doing.

Government

Governments require organizations to be accurate and transparent with information relating to pricing, corporate activities, claims about products, and range of other issues. These requirements are especially important in heavily regulated sectors such as pharmaceuticals. Some tech companies anticipate more direct exchange of information between customers and government agencies such as the US FDA and EPA in the near future, where consumer devices can trigger the delivery of information to consumers.

Metadata helps ensure that information is consistent and available. Metadata can also support the exchange of information with government parties. Organizations may need to submit information to government regulators. External metadata standards are starting to play a role in the submission of such information. Conversely, some publishers will need to access information from government sources. Publishers should investigate the role metadata could play in the acquisition of government sourced information.

Competitors

Online publishers should know how their competitors are using metadata standards. They may choose to do a competitive audit to determine the strengths and weaknesses of competitors' use of metadata. Such an audit may point to competitive opportunities.

Metadata standards become especially critical when competing firms decide to merge, or when one firm acquires another firm or the business operations of another firm. This scenario is common and can pose significant integration costs that stymie the "economies of scale" that were expected to result from the merging. When one or both parties follow standard metadata vocabularies, the challenges of integration are reduced significantly.

Consumer groups and charities

As product information becomes more detailed, some consumer groups are paying attention to certain factors such as energy ratings.

Metadata standards can even provide some environmental information about products. For example, the GS1 web vocabulary provides a property to indicate "the process the packaging could undertake for recyclable & sustainability programs." Online publishers can indicate whether their packaging is reusable, compositable, or energy recoverable.

Charities are another kind of third party that can sometimes be involved with exchanging information with online publishers.

Trade associations

Trade associations have long been active in developing and promoting metadata standards. In recent years, they have recognized the value of participating in standards communities outside of their industry sector, so that their sector-specific needs are harmonized and integrated with more common, generic metadata standards. For example, the FIBO Financial Industry Business Ontology is standard developed by the EDM Council to meet the needs of the banking sector, but which has been integrated into the schema.org vocabulary as an extension.

Platforms

Platforms of different kinds need to be able to host content and information. Platforms actively shape the development of new metadata standards. Online publishers will want to monitor what proposed new standards will affect their business.

---

[53] "Prototyping with open sports data (report)", ODI, https://theodi.org/article/prototyping-with-open-sports-data-report/#1523281746233-4ba4564c-c656

Deciding on coverage: entities and properties

One of the most important aspects of a metadata strategy is deciding what information in and about content to describe, and which metadata standards to use. Coverage decisions will be prioritized according to the business importance of the information, the opportunities to use the information in multiple contexts, and the effort expected to develop the metadata. Publishers will need to identify:

- Information to track using external metadata vocabularies
- Information to track relying on custom metadata only
- Information not necessary to track with metadata.

The right coverage will depend on goals and resources. A small publisher may decide that extensive detail would be overkill, while a large publisher may decide that such an investment is needed.

Some information will only ever be needed internally. For example, the name of a staff photographer for a photo might be recorded within a DAM but is not needed by other users of an ecommerce website. Yet for a news website, the photographer would be important metadata to record with an external metadata standard such as IPTC.

While external standards offer many benefits, online publishers have discretion about how to adopt them. Not every item of metadata needs to follow an external standard, especially if the information has only one very specific use. But information that needs to be exchanged widely within the enterprise and shared outside the enterprise should strive to use external standards. Where possible, publishers should opt for an external standard, so that the metadata can support more roles in the future.

CHAPTER 7: THE ROLE OF METADATA IN CONTENT STRATEGY

A decade ago, Kristina Halvorson, the influential content strategy consultant, named metadata strategy as one of "a number of content-related disciplines that deserve their own definition" in her seminal *A List Apart* article, "The Discipline of Content Strategy".[54] Although awareness of metadata has increased over the past decade, the discipline of content strategy still hasn't given metadata strategy the attention it deserves.

Chances are, very few people in your organization are clamoring for better metadata for web content. Writers don't seem too worried about it. Developers believe the current situation is working good enough. And curiously, very few vendors are knocking on your door saying you have a metadata problem that their product will solve for you. Why should web publishers care about metadata standards?

If metadata standards haven't been on your company's radar, you are not alone. Few web publishers think about the topic in detail. And even fewer think about metadata as a strategic issue.

Fortunately, a handful of successful online publishers such as the BBC, eBay, and Electronic Arts, have been working on metadata as a strategic organizational priority. Their experiences suggest that the rest of us need to start thinking more about how we can use web metadata to support the online content in our businesses.

For anyone who values content as a shiny object, metadata will seem like a dull topic.[55] Metadata won't make content "compelling." It won't make writing poetic. Metadata won't grab customers' attention with glitzy visuals.

What metadata can do is maximize customer attention — so they don't tune out and switch off. Metadata makes content, and the products and services addressed by the content, easier for customers. Content strategists should care about metadata because metadata makes customers' lives easier.

Metadata can improve communications in two ways. First, it makes sure that the customer's time is not wasted. People get what they are looking for, rather than seeing stuff they aren't looking for and don't want. Second, it makes the content more convenient. Customers can get content where and when they have attention to give to it. They may not be able to give their attention while at their desk at work or on the sofa at home. But they may have attention to offer when exercising, cooking dinner, or driving in the car. Metadata makes it easier for content to be delivered through different channels.

| *"Unstructured text is unorganized."*

-- Steve Macbeth *Microsoft*

Some content strategists make the mistake of considering metadata as an IT issue, like installing a CMS. Metadata is not a product you buy and install. Metadata doesn't come pre-loaded with features. There is no vendor demo to watch.

Metadata can do lots of little things to support content, rather doing than one big thing. All those things it can do for content will make the lives of both customers and publishers easier. Content strategists have a self-interested reason to understand the use of metadata. Metadata can make their own work easier to do.

Metadata supports content strategy by bringing more precision to discussions about content. With metadata, content stops being a one-off item that is referred to by a title. Metadata reveals different features of the content, such as who created it, when it was created, its length, what it is linked to, what media assets are embedded in it, and importantly, what specific information the content addresses. With that precision, content teams can talk about managing many items of content. They can think about what features they want their content to have, based on what features have performed well already.

A content strategy, to have a sustained impact, needs a metadata strategy to back it up. A metadata strategy provides a plan for how a publisher can leverage metadata to accomplish specific content goals. It articulates what metadata publishers need for their content, how they will create that metadata, and most importantly, how both the publisher and audiences can utilize the metadata.

When metadata is an afterthought, publishers can end up with content strategies that can't be implemented, or are implemented poorly. Without a metadata strategy, a content strategy can get stuck in a firefighting mode. Many organizations struggle to improve their content output because they ask overwhelmed staff to track too many variables. Metadata can liberate staff from checklists, by allowing IT systems to handle low-level details that are important but exhausting to deal with. Metadata can keep the larger strategy on track. Metadata can deliver consistency to content operations and can enhance how content is delivered to audiences.

Content strategy comprises different dimensions:[56]

- **Editorial** (creating content)
- **Content experience** (designing content for audiences)
- **Content process** (workflow and review)
- **Content structuring** or content engineering.

Metadata is most closely associated with content structure, but it would be a mistake to view it as being a narrowly specialized function. Metadata can support editorial tasks, the design of content, and workflow as well. Metadata can support all aspects of content operations.

Enhancing content production and delivery capabilities

Many content teams feel overwhelmed by the demands placed on them. They may not be happy with the quality of content being churned out. Because they have difficulty managing what's been published, they push back and advocate producing less content. They are unable to handle the workload.

The absence of quality metadata limits content capabilities. Robust metadata can enhance content processes within organizations, improve the content experience for audiences, and help content creators find the right assets to use. The most respected online publishers, including the BBC, *Nature* magazine, and the *New York Times*, all have significant metadata capabilities they've built up over years.[52]

Vexing content problems generally have more than one cause, and their resolution requires a mix of different interventions. Metadata can support a range of these interventions. It works in conjunction with other approaches used in content strategy, such as those relating to process design and streamlining, training, or analytics.

Online publishers often face complaints such as these:

- Customers have a hard time finding our content
- Much of our content isn't viewed
- Our content is boring
- We are overwhelmed, unable to keep up with how much content we are expected to produce
- We can't deliver our content to "X" platform
- Content is not up-to-date
- Content is inconsistent
- We don't have a good sense of what content is most valuable
- We have trouble localizing our content
- We keep recreating the same sort of content
- Our content isn't getting in front of the right people.

Metadata can, to varying degrees, improve all these issues. It won't by itself fix them, because such issues generally have more than one cause. What metadata offers is more precision to manage, analyze, and deliver content. It does that by providing a common vocabulary, based on recognized standards, to describe different dimensions of the content in detail.

Online publishers are missing out on their potential by ignoring metadata. Any solution you try will be only partly effective in the absence of quality metadata. Publishing excellence depends on metadata excellence: there's no way around it.

---

[54] Kristina Halvorson, "The Discipline of Content Strategy", *A List Apart*, Dec 16, 2008, https://alistapart.com/article/thedisciplineofcontentstrategy

[55] The problem of viewing content as a "shiny object" was the subject of a Reuters Institute study at Oxford University. "Examples of the manifestation of 'Shiny Things Syndrome' cited by the participants included fixation with artificial

intelligence (AI), virtual reality (VR), automated reporting (AR), and over-reliance on social platforms for distribution (leading to panic about algorithm tweaks)." http://www.niemanlab.org/2018/11/journalism-has-a-focus-problem-how-to-combat-shiny-things-syndrome/

[56] following Kristina Halvorson's "quad" formulation of focal areas of content strategy.

[57] The examples of *Nature* and the BBC will be discussed in later chapters. For a discussion of the New York Times' experience building metadata capabilities, see "Build Your Own NYT Linked Data Application", *Medium*, March 30, 2010, https://open.nytimes.com/build-your-own-nyt-linked-data-application-8b91fb71fd23

Prioritizing content

Let's start with a basic editorial task: prioritizing content. The simplest form of prioritizing content is to weed out content no one is viewing. That may involve a content inventory that includes page titles and perhaps keywords. It can be labor-intensive and imprecise. Fortunately, metadata can help make the prioritization process more insightful.

Content is created to support business goals. Business goals will inform a publisher's content strategy. A major focus of content strategy is deciding what content to keep and create: how well existing content supports current business goals. The decisions may be to:

1. **Keep**: Existing content that is considered essential and non-negotiable.
2. **Chuck**: Existing content that is considered non-essential or detrimental.
3. **Debate**: New content that's considered negotiable.

Metadata can help with these decisions. It provides information that allows content strategists to understand the past or expected performance of content.

Metadata can offer more insightful analytics, which can be used to improve the maintenance and optimization of *existing* content, and with the pruning of old content (Optimization is discussed further in the chapter on reducing risks).

When publishers are debating the creation of new content considered *negotiable*, metadata can help them make decisions based on available facts. Since the content is new, publishers must rely on analytics data about how well similar content has performed. Metadata can reveal how similar the proposed content is to other content already published. Metadata can indicate the similarity in terms of topics, format, content type, and other properties.

Another issue that content strategist must deal with is how to create content with available resources. Resources gaps are a common problem. They are the difference between what an organization expects to do, and their ability to deliver. Metadata can help with the scaling of content to close gaps in existing resources.

Scaling content

One category of high-priority content is content that does not exist yet but which is considered essential. The discussion within the organization shifts from debating what content to create, to debating how to get the work done. In this situation, metadata can play a strategic role.

More and more organizations are concerned with scaling: the ability to take on a larger workload without diminishing performance. Even if the organization itself is not growing rapidly, they may need to complete a new large project quickly in order to respond to new circumstances.

Content sometimes needs to do heavy-lifting: for example, when content introduces a new brand to a market. The execution of a business strategy can depend on a big push where the organization needs a lot of new content quickly.

When executives indicate they need more content, they are affirming how central content has become to how businesses operate online. Online information is critical to support more self-service, interaction in new channels, new products, new features, and new training. Even if the business is not making headlines announcing new plans to the public, it may be undergoing a "digital transformation" that involves offering more digital content to support their operations.

The heart of modern businesses is online service, with content central to that. Business strategy can result in new partnerships, new initiatives, and new lines of business. In these situations, the staff tasked with creating new content aren't in a position to negotiate whether new content is necessary. The issue to solve is not about content priorities, but content necessities. Content teams have to make content materialize quickly and accurately to ensure these projects are delivered successfully. Metadata can help content teams extend existing content to meet new purposes.

Metadata helps content scale. Metadata helps content to be available in many channels and platforms.

Being ready for the next 'disruptive' thing

Online publishers are already familiar with disruption. The first major disruption was the smartphone, which upended webpage design, and forced publishers to think about how customers got their content on mobile devices. Now, publishers wonder about emerging paradigms, such as voice interaction, AI, and virtual reality.

Metadata standards are the only proven approach that allows content to adapt to new paradigms. When content is widely described with metadata standards, any new paradigm will have to adapt to the vast universe of content already available. The experience of content for tablets illustrates this phenomenon. When tablets such as the iPad where first available, publishers rushed to adapt their content for special apps. Most of these apps didn't survive long, because the effort to create special content for a narrow channel proved unsustainable. Online publishers realized that devices and apps needed to adapt to the content. It wasn't realistic to design special content for these new platforms. The needs of content trump the needs of platforms.

Many content specialists mistakenly think of metadata as a technical issue that's of interest only to engineers. It is easy to see why: metadata involves code and seems complex. But unlike AI and other digital technologies, metadata isn't executable software code. It is more like HTML: it describes content, rather than manipulates content. Metadata depends on other software to do things. Metadata provides a vocabulary to indicate to machines and to people important information associated with content.

If they allow themselves to become blinded by the technical details of metadata, content strategists may be inclined to dismiss the relevance of metadata to their work. They should appreciate that while metadata does have a technical dimension, it's fundamentally about content, not about technology.

Metadata *isn't* a new kind of technology (it's a set of standards that have been evolving over time). Metadata *isn't* a feature. Metadata *isn't* software.

Metadata *isn't* a detail that is irrelevant to strategy. Quite the opposite. Metadata *is* a strategic tool.

Metadata can be an ally to content strategists who are concerned that technology deliberations can sometimes hijack the focus away from content objectives. External metadata standards help content be technology-agnostic.

Standard metadata vocabularies enable technical flexibility. By providing a common vocabulary for information, metadata standards can be used with a broad range of software. External standards let online publishers get the most out of whatever systems they have already.

External standards can support basic goals or highly sophisticated ones. They can work in concert with the most advanced technical approaches for managing online information. But they also work with simple approaches, such as Javascript code that every website developer uses on a daily basis. No matter what a publisher's capabilities currently, they can be improved by adopting external metadata standards.

The information described by external metadata vocabularies can be converted and transformed so that it can work with most any technical approach. When using standardized metadata in their content, online publishers aren't locked into systems that they've decided aren't serving their needs well. Metadata unshackles information from the programming ecosystem.

External metadata standards *aren't* a disruptive new technology that promises miracles. Metadata is not an alternative to artificial intelligence. Metadata can complement AI but is very different.

Right now there is a lot of buzz around artificial intelligence, especially machine learning. Online publishers might wonder: Why bother structuring online information with metadata when many software products claim to evaluate unstructured content and deliver a fantastic result? Some of these technologies are significant and impressive. But they are not magic. AI has made progress by focusing on narrow problems. It has faltered when it has tried to solve general problems. Metadata standards, by contrast, are meant to be general purpose in their application.

There are as many marketing and content management solutions for sale as there are problems. But purpose-built solutions tend not to be flexible, able to address a range of problems. Few organizations want to keep adding new systems they have to learn and maintain.

The difference between metadata and AI is the difference between strategy and features. Features solve narrow problems, such as sorting items. Strategies realize larger goals. Metadata can help organizations realize high-level goals, such as building audience interest, and satisfying customer needs.

Audience insight through metadata

One of the most important dimensions of content strategy is understanding customers and their needs. Content strategists may develop personas to represent different customer segments. They conduct various kinds of user research such as interviews and surveys to understand customer needs.

Metadata hasn't so far played a large role in understanding customer interests and needs. That is poised to change. Online publishers have an opportunity to use metadata to understand their customers and motivations more fully. Better customer insights can help them develop better content, and realize better engagement.

How people use and interact with content provides valuable insights into customer motivations and needs. Metadata helps publishers understand what topics these interactions relate to.

Customer engagement with content reveals interests. It may be what they searching for, liking, viewing, discussing, sharing or highlighting. Content discusses entities (people, products, places, etc.), and the entities discussed in content items are a major indicator of how content items are different from each other.

Personas often focus on offline characteristics of the customer, such as information about the customer's life situation and their past history with the product or organization.

Content strategists can develop rich customers insights from their use of online content. Customer online content engagement is a valuable complement to user research about customers' offline lives. Online publishers can examine the relationship between content attributes (metadata properties such as topics and formats), and customer engagement (their interactions with the content).

How content engagement reveals customer insights

Online publishers generally haven't used metadata extensively to examine content engagement, and haven't developed customer insights from such data. They may wonder how it can be done.

Online publishers can learn more about their customers by adapting certain practices first used by social media platforms. Social media companies, Facebook especially, have developed deep customer insights by looking at how users react to content. Social media platforms have pioneered an approach known as *semantic analytics* that is started to be adopted by online publishers.

Social platforms track and analyze a user's interaction with entities, which are either mentioned within the content (e.g., liking a post about a concert performance), or are offline interactions in the real world (e.g., liking a restaurant). This data is used to develop a profile of users based on their expressed interests.[58]

All engagement with content is in some sense social, even if it involves only a single user and that user is anonymous. The aggregation of analytics data makes possible the comparison of similar users (known as lookalikes). For example, aggregated data may show that people who watched a video about entity "X", also tended to view content about entity "Y". The relationship may not be an obvious one. Hypothetically, someone who watches videos about Japanese food may be more likely to be interested in the topic of skiing. The power of *graphs* is that they reveal associations between entities.

Although few online publishers have the reach or the scale of social media giants like Facebook, they enjoy advantages that Facebook doesn't have. As first-party publishers, they have a deep knowledge about the topics they are writing about. Social media platforms use Open Graph metadata, which does not provide much descriptive detail. Unlike online publishers, social media platforms have to create metadata about content created by others. They have to identify what entities are being discussed in user postings and random published content that is shared by users. This text involves strings of characters, rather than things precisely described by a metadata vocabulary. Facebook needs to add metadata to content it didn't create, which is technically challenging. First-party publishers, in contrast, know the entities in their content and can easily identify them with metadata. They can use their own metadata to develop a deeper insight into the specific topics and media formats people most want to engage with.

Facebook doesn't reveal much about how it uses its data. But Facebook has provided clues in the past that show how content interaction yields customer insights. When Facebook initially introduced the tracking of entities in Facebook postings, users had the ability to explore relationships between entities themselves. For example, they could search for:

- Ski resorts my friends have been to
- Restaurants nearby that my friends like
- Photos of my friends from my high school
- Movies liked by people who like my favorite movies
- Music liked by people who like music I like.

To support these capabilities, Facebook identifies entities in user posts and connects them according to the relationships of these entities. They apply metadata behind the scenes to understand their user's interests.[59] Facebook puts people at the center of its graph that links together things (entities). Postings may discuss various things (restaurants, movies), but the emphasis is on what people like or have done relating to those things.

Facebook manages all these entities through its **Open Graph**, which Mark Zuckerberg announced in 2010.[60] Zuckerberg explained:

"The Open Graph puts people at the center of the web. It means the web can become a set of personally and semantically meaningful connections between people and things. I am FRIENDS with you. I am ATTENDING this event. I LIKE this band. These connections aren't just happening on Facebook, they're happening all over the web, and today, with the Open Graph, we're going to bring all of these together."[61]

Zuckerberg noted that other social platforms are using a similar approach to link users with graphs of entities:

"Yelp is mapping out the part of the graph that relates to small businesses. Pandora is mapping out the part of the graph that relates to music. And a lot of news sites are mapping out the part of the graph that relates to current events and news content. If we can take these separate maps of the graph and pull them all together, then we can create a web that is more social, personalized, smarter, and semantically aware."

As Zuckerberg explains, a user's interaction with content reveals a lot about their priorities. Online publishers can adopt this approach as well to understand their audiences more completely.

Another social media platform that uses metadata to develop customer insights is Pinterest.

On Pinterest, users "pin" articles they find interesting, which are shared with other Pinterest members. Pinterest uses two metadata vocabularies: Open Graph (like Facebook), as well as the more detailed schema.org vocabulary.

Pinterest has developed customer insights about topics of interest through a product they call the **Taste Graph**. Pinterest collects data on content usage to build a profile of preferences and needs.

Brian Johnson, head of knowledge engineering at Pinterest, likens the taste graph to a common vocabulary:

"The Taste Graph is a collection of technologies and data that define a common vocabulary for understanding our content, users, and partners. It helps us understand how a person's interests and preferences evolve over time across categories like food, fashion, home decor and more."[62]

There are two distinct relationships between content data and user data:

1. User data about past content usage predicts content preferences
2. Content usage data predicts user preferences for things beyond content.

Pinterest uses the Taste Graph to make "organic pin" recommendations. Originally the Taste Graph consisted of "roughly 400 interest-based targeting options that were segmented across 29 top-level interest categories."

Pinterest has now expanded the Taste Graph to cover more than 5,000 interests. According to a report: "Pinterest has worked to make Taste Graph better able to understand how people's interests change over time. For example, if someone uses Pinterest to research kitchen remodeling ideas, that user may not want to continue seeing organic and paid pins related to home decor long after the remodel is completed."[63]

Pinterest develops insights by aggregating engagement data. Johnson notes its value: "We can serve more personalized recommendations and other results based on not just what someone is interested in, but what their taste is." Because their service relies on a use log-in, they can track changes in user interests over time.

Facebook and Pinterest offer content strategists with ideas on how to understand their audiences better. Facebook and Pinterest have developed sophisticated (and proprietary) data about audience interests by looking closely at user interactions with content. Metadata has been key to revealing these insights.

Currently, most online publishers have outsourced the understanding of their audience to social media platforms like Facebook. But the emergence of semantic analytics capabilities is allowing first-party publishers to understand audience interaction with their content based on the entities involved, much like Facebook. Online publishers don't need to replicate the depth and sophistication of Facebook or Pinterest to benefit. But they should seek to think more like these companies to understand their audiences in deeper detail.

How publishers can use semantic analytics will be discussed in more detail in Chapter 19.

---

[58] Social media firms such as Facebook build profiles by also collecting demographic and other kinds of *personal* information to build marketing analytics. Semantic analytics, in contrast, is only concerned with how users interact with published content, not in personal information that is unrelated to their content use.

[59] Facebook needs to understand what entities were being discussed in user postings. They've used a combination of approaches, including named entity recognition which linked to entities in Wikipedia, and encouraging users to create entities by creating pages for these entities. As a Facebook engineer explains: "Facebook users are always creating new Pages for new concepts, interests, and places. Similarly, our imported data sources like Wikipedia grow by tens of thousands of pages every day." Eric Sun, "Under the Hood: The Entities Graph", https://www.facebook.com/notes/facebookengineering/under-the-hood-the-entities-graph/10151490531588920/

[60] The semantic web expert Ruben Verborgh explains: "Open Graph is similar to Schema.org, and is mainly used for Facebook integration. Facebook allows you to like and comment on items outside of the facebook.com domain. Facebook recommends the RDFa standard in its webpage mark-up instructions. You can even access Facebook data as RDF — if you have an API key." http://rubenverborgh.github.io/WebFundamentals/semantic-web/#open-graph .

[61] Mark Zuckerberg, https://www.youtube.com/watch?v=8uatF4eTlQo

[62] Brian Johnson, Pinterest Head of Knowledge Engineering, "Taste Graph part 1: Assigning interests to Pins" https://medium.com/@Pinterest_Engineering/taste-graph-part-1-assigning-interests-to-pins-9158b4c25906

[63] https://marketingland.com/pinterests-interest-based-ad-targeting-options-swell-5000-224580

CHAPTER 8: THE ROLE OF METADATA IN BUSINESS STRATEGY

How can a metadata strategy for online content support business goals? How can effective online metadata contribute to the most important initiatives of an organization?

Metadata is rarely the first topic firms think about when reviewing their business strategy. Business strategy concerns big goals and directions. Metadata, in contrast, seems narrowly concerned with details. What leverage can metadata provide business strategy?

Execution is where metadata meets business strategy. Business strategy will be effective only if it can be executed easily. Metadata shapes what's possible for businesses to achieve.

Business executives will want to know:

- What metadata capabilities are needed or useful to support business objectives?
- What investment is needed to build these capabilities?
- What is the ROI of investments to build metadata capabilities?

These wide-ranging and important questions defy short simple answers. The contribution of metadata is far-reaching, but will depend on specific circumstances of a business. But whatever the circumstances, the business case for metadata is compelling. This chapter will explore how to approach the many dimensions of business that metadata can support.

Metadata helps firms realize their business goals when two streams of activity work together. A metadata strategy builds metadata capabilities that can be used in different scenarios. A business strategy builds marketing and operational capabilities in pursuit of key business objectives. Both streams should be coordinated to achieve the greatest impact. This coordination involves the mapping of long-term business goals with the long-term goals for metadata — the capabilities necessary to realize different business goals.

How metadata capabilities support business strategy

Organizations need metadata capabilities to execute and sustain their business strategy. Many organizations learn this truth the hard way. They decide to launch a bold new business initiative, and find that their metadata capabilities aren't sufficient to support that initiative. Metadata is infrastructure. It can't be built on demand like a product feature. It requires sustained investment to build these capabilities.

Content teams involved with metadata requirements and implementation should understand the strategic context facing their organization. Unfortunately, it is rare for content teams to focus on that perspective. Staff may feel that worrying about these big issues is above their pay grade. They have immediate tasks to get done. They may feel that executives in the "C-suite" are the ones paid to worry about the big issues.

But reactively waiting for orders from above can be counterproductive. Staff are caught flat-footed when asked to deliver a big business initiative involving online information that they aren't adequately prepared for. A metadata program requires a sustained multi-year effort to build. It takes resources that need to be earmarked as an ongoing expense, rather than an optional one that must be re-justified year fiscal quarter.

When content teams are disconnected from the financial considerations of the business, the end result is more silos. Organizations find they lack metadata capabilities because no one championed building such capabilities. If metadata development and maintenance are detached from the business context, these activities are unlikely to get adequate executive support. Staff won't feel valued by C-level executives because executives don't understand what they are working on.

In order for a metadata program to be embraced and championed by executives, it needs to speak to larger business priorities. It must show where it supports these priorities, and demonstrate that metadata is not a maintenance issue that can be outsourced or deferred.

Every organization will pursue a business strategy that is tailored to its specific situation. But for any business strategy, online content is likely to contribute significantly to success or failure. Metadata allows content to pivot to address new requirements quickly.

Successful strategies depend on all parties sharing a common vision and common goals. When different parties use terms in different ways or use different terms altogether, the chances of synchronizing their efforts are vastly diminished.

Metadata standards offer a common vocabulary for information used by different functions. A common vocabulary helps to connect different activities within an enterprise. Without a common vocabulary, different functions in an organization can have difficulty knowing how their work relates to other functions. Cross-functional collaboration is hindered.

When different functions use different terminology, there is no 360-degree view of the business. Terminology differences indicate the enterprise is not aligned around objectives. Specifically, they arise from:

- Naming conflicts (*inconsistency in the labels different parties use*)
- Data representation conflicts (*the format information is stored in*)
- Scaling conflicts (*how different parties measure things.*)

Any or all can contribute to aggregation conflicts — the inability to summarize what is happening at a high level. That impedes the enterprise's ability to measure their success in meeting their business objectives.

SWOT and metadata

The SWOT framework of strengths, weaknesses, opportunities, and threats is a simple tool that can be used to think about how metadata could contribute to high-level goals of an enterprise.

The SWOT framework is a common starting point for considering where an organization needs to go. Online content and information often play an important role in changes that are needed. Metadata helps with the execution of content and information.

Enhancing existing strengths

An enterprise may decide that it has certain competitive strengths that could become even stronger. These strengths could be customer loyalty or efficient procedures.

Here the strategy is to double down on what is working well. To do that requires a more granular understanding of how current services are performing. Metadata can support semantic analytics to reveal how content is being used by customers in different scenarios (see Chapter 19).

Addressing current weaknesses

Some weaknesses that are holding back the organization may relate to content. For example, the organization may not be fully compliant with legislation or regulations, which requires disclosure of certain information in a prescribed way. Metadata can mitigate the risks of faulty information (see Chapter 20).

Capitalizing on opportunities

New technologies can offer opportunities. Online publishers have to cope with providing content on new platforms and new channels. Metadata can accelerate how content is ready for new platforms. Metadata enables channel flexibility (see Chapter 12).

New markets are another common opportunity. Metadata can help with localization, and with supporting content to address and integrate with the expanding range of products.

Countering threats

A common threat is having insufficient resources. Nearly all publishers face the challenge of having a yawning gap between what an organization is capable of producing, and what is needed.

Skills shortages are another threat. AI and automation are gaining popularity in content production in part because highly skilled professionals can't keep up with all the content being published. Subject Matter Experts have limited time to contribute and review growing amounts of content. Online publishers need to leverage content automation tools that utilize metadata to reduce burdens on skilled staff (see Chapter 18).

A SWOT analysis can reveal how metadata fits into the larger strategic context. Metadata by itself won't fix a strategic challenge facing an organization. But metadata can actively contribute to transforming a challenge. Metadata is part of the strategic arsenal of transformative capabilities, which include brand repositioning, product development, customer service platforms, and business intelligence systems. Any digital transformation project that doesn't include metadata strategy is unlikely to realize its full potential.

How metadata can support business growth

Corporate executives consider growth a top priority. A basic strategic decision they face is how to pursue growth. Should an enterprise try to improve what it is doing currently, or should it pursue something new? Should it seek to reach different customer segments or audiences? Or should it try to appeal to existing customer segments with new products? These decisions are encapsulated in a tool known as the Ansoff matrix, which represents four distinct business strategies.

	Existing markets	**New markets**
Existing products	Market penetration	Market expansion
New products	Product expansion	Diversification

Metadata can support the execution of all these strategies, even though each has a different emphasis. Metadata makes the information presented to customers more flexible. That flexibility helps business pursue different strategies.

Metadata allows different pieces of information to be used in a range of contexts. It defines the core information that a business presents to customers in its content. It can address new business requirements as they arise.

When businesses develop new requirements for the information they must present to customers, their metadata specifications will provide the basis for knowing what changes are needed. Metadata specifications can indicate properties of an entity that are new, and properties values that need changing. For example, a product may be sold under a slightly different name in a new market and have different pricing. Rather than recreate all the information for the new market, the business can build on existing metadata to make the information available in the content.

Existing products, existing markets: market penetration

Metadata supports content optimization — tweaking the exact presentation of information that is presented to audiences. Metadata, working with analytics and testing, can isolate information that needs improving. When content is optimized, it can result in more sales.

Existing products, new markets: market expansion

Web content metadata makes adapting existing content to new markets easier. Taking existing products to new markets involves localization. Metadata can help define parts of content that need different versions for different markets, elements such as trade names or legal terms and disclaimers. Metadata properties can capture other required information, such as customer ratings and reviews, that are needed for new markets (see Chapter 13 on reusing information).

New products, existing markets: product expansion

Metadata also supports information related to a product extension, such as introducing a premium version of a product, or accessories.

When introducing new products that to markets where a firm operates already, the firm must explain what the product is about, and how it relates to existing products. The firm may be introducing a new product that complements or interacts with an existing product. Metadata can be used to explain how different features of products are related to one another. It can accelerate the development of content about new products, by indicating what information can be reused from existing products, such as warranty information.

New products, new markets: diversification

When diversifying into new markets with new products, firms need a foundation of information to prepare for a range of needs that will arise. Metadata supports diversification strategies by allowing information to be used in flexible ways.

Executives may not be interested in the specifics of how metadata does these things (which will be discussed in later chapters). Executives will be most interested in knowing that metadata capabilities can make existing information more flexible, so it supports new products and markets.

How to think about the ROI of metadata

For some executives, it is not enough to know metadata will make their goals easier to accomplish. The CFO may want to know how metadata will influence the bottom line.

Appreciating the financial value of metadata can be important. Metadata is often not well understood, especially as it exists below the surface of executive visibility. Executives will ask what is the payoff of devoting resources to building metadata capabilities for online content.

Metadata offers many benefits, depending on how extensively it is used, and how it is applied. The very flexibility of metadata means that it is difficult to generalize about its benefits.

The ROI for digital investments can be very specific to a company, industry, and customer segment.[84] It can be reckless to generalize from specific examples. A common weakness with ROI formulas is that they reflect siloed thinking. They treat metadata as a discrete input that can be associated with a discrete output. In practice, metadata is an array of inputs that are associated with an array of outputs. Metadata capabilities are common infrastructure that support strategic initiatives. Strategic initiatives represent a bold move to implement new practices. It can be difficult to predict a precise ROI for such initiatives.

The disappointing news is that there are no simple rules of thumb about the financial payoff of metadata spending. No generic formula exists to calculate metadata's ROI because:

- Metadata doesn't always cost the same; it is a variable expense. Some metadata is cheap to add, other metadata requires human attention and costs more.
- Metadata can deliver variable results; it supports different goals, and even when supporting the same goals, different kinds of enterprises will achieve different financial payoffs.

Instead of trying to "prove" ROI with a misleading or simplistic formula, it is more productive to craft a unified *business case* for metadata. Metadata does deliver financial benefits. But these benefits will not accrue to only one division of a company or organization.

Metadata should be considered a shared *resource*, whether or not it treated as a shared *cost*. Metadata integrates different activities within an organization, and as a result, it belongs to everyone. It can't be associated with a single purpose and doesn't necessarily belong to a specific operating division or function in an organization.

When considering metadata as a resource, organizations will want to assess the *productivity* of the resource. How productive is online information currently, and how productive could it become?

A simple way to measure metadata productivity is to track how frequently information described within metadata is utilized. If specific information is used only once in content at any time, it has 1x productivity.[65] If two content items both used the same information, the productivity of that information is 2x. Some kinds of information might be widely used across content, and have a productivity of 10x or even 100x.

Once online publishers know how widely each item of information is utilized, they can determine the average productivity for all their metadata. As they find additional possibilities using metadata to insert information in content, they will be able to raise the average productivity of their information.

Spending on the development of metadata capabilities should be considered both part of marketing expenses and customer retention expenses. Because metadata transcends and integrates functional silos, the budget for developing metadata should be ideally be shared by various operating units.

Metadata will influence performance (KPIs) across the organization. For example, metadata helps prospective customers discover interesting content and thereby helps bring in more marketing leads. Cost-per-lead is commonly defined as the total marketing spending divided by the total leads. The contribution of metadata to marketing success would be reflected in that metric. But retaining customers involves different metrics such as customer lifetime value. To keep existing customers happy, enterprises invest in self-service and customer education content that is supported by metadata. These are part of retention costs that include customer support, billing, promotional incentives. Cost attribution is difficult when the uses of metadata are so wide.

Compared to the overall spending on marketing and customer retention, spending on metadata capabilities will only be a small fraction. The expense of metadata capabilities needs to be understood in the broader context of the business functions metadata supports.

Publishers may find it helpful to think about building metadata capabilities as a series of incremental projects, involving discrete focus areas and add-ons, rather than as a big purchase or initiative that require unrealistic financial justifications. As small wins are demonstrated, executives will feel more confident about the business case based on specific scenarios rather than across-the-board outcomes.

Who pays to build metadata capabilities can be a political issue. As noted in Chapter 3, metadata doesn't get created when it's considered an "unfunded mandate." When organizations allocate cost in a stovepiped manner, it can be hard to budget for metadata. Such practices hurt overall profitability. The most successful companies consider profitability at the company level, rather than at the divisional level. Tim Cook, the CEO of Apple, comments on how divisional P&L thinking fosters silos and hurts overall profitability. "We don't have 'divisions' with their own P&L. We run one P&L for the whole company."[66]

Another approach to building a business case for metadata is to consider the value of information delivered via metadata in important customer scenarios. The financial value of metadata can be seen by focusing on how it can influence revenue-associated events and track metrics associated with these events. We will examine some common scenarios shortly.

How metadata can improve revenues

For many organizations, revenues are the most single important measure of how successfully an organization is performing. While metadata does not *directly* influence revenues, it does influence revenues *indirectly*.

Consider a simplified picture of a company's revenue pipeline. It can be broken into three parts:

1. Recurring revenue from satisfied (retained) customers (*Baseline* expected revenue)
2. Incremental new revenue from sales to new or existing customers (*Current* revenue growth beyond the baseline)
3. Potential revenue from new leads (representing *future* revenue beyond expected growth).

Some revenue is the result of current activities of the enterprise, some is related to future activities, and some is linked to past activities. Because revenues are linked to different time periods, enterprises need to track both leading indicators and trailing indicators.

One of the biggest challenges to increasing revenues is connecting with customers who don't know about a brand, and with whom the brand doesn't have any relationship. To use marketing jargon, the challenge is to attract "visitors" and convert them into "leads." Leads are potential revenue: if they decide to buy, they will add revenue. Potential revenue from new leads depends on attracting new visitors. "Reach" — the number of visitors exposed to a brand's information — can be a leading indicator of potential revenue.

Metadata influences revenues at different stages of the customer lifecycle. Some of the ways it can enhance revenue include:

1. Aiding discovery of products
2. Making products more desirable
3. Making information about products and services personalized and relevant
4. Helping customers customize products they purchase
5. Helping customers understand and be interested in the value of products and services
6. Making product functionality more useful and competitive
7. Resolving customer problems more quickly.

The bigger take away for executives is that metadata can make customers more willing to buy. It delivers crucial information to buyers.

Viktor Mayer-Schonberger, a professor at Oxford University, argues that firms must be prepared to let go of their habit of competing on price.[62] Numerous price comparison websites exist, where buyers can check out the prices offered by different sellers. But Mayer-Schonberger argues that price is an inadequate indicator of what's best for consumers. Buyers want the ability to compare features, not just prices. That's where metadata is so powerful. It allows buyers to compare features of different brand products sold by different sellers. How all that information stacks up against competitors will influence how likely customers will buy from a firm.

By offering better, more complete information about products, metadata can support additional revenue at different stages of customer interaction, from awareness to consideration to purchase:

- Improving the **click-through rate** of customer discovery journeys, by better matching what information is sought with what is offered
- Improving **landing page conversion**, by adjusting information elements based on performance
- Improving the **conversion rate of product information**, through the completeness and richness of product descriptions (especially important in B2B), or through personalization and configuration (important in the desirability of consumer goods and services)
- Improving **margins**, so a firm can command price premium relative to competitors. Firms selling services can differentiate themselves from competitors by highlighting what's special or unique that they offer.

Metadata is an important element in the customer experience. It supports both understanding and desire. Metadata helps customers understand what they are buying, and therefore pique interest in it.

Most any product or service comprises many factors can work together to deliver an experience. It's often hard to know what matters most to consumers, and at what stage these factors most matter.

Metadata can help firms optimize their product experience, so it is more transparent and easier to track and manage. Metadata can reinforce brand positioning, transforming it from a vague idea or promise into something more concrete and verifiable. For example, many insurance companies make brand promises about their reliability. Those that highlight ratings by third parties (such as AM Best or Fitch) in their metadata will make their brand messaging more factual and credible (see Chapter 14 on the promotion of information using metadata).

---

[64] This issue is sometimes referred to as the problem of "generalization" — the tendency towards and risks of discounting situational factors that influence outcomes.

[65] It can still be valuable to manage this information within metadata for many reasons such as ease of updating and tracking, even if it is used only once at a time. This is a simple illustration of productivity, not a complete one.

[66] quoted in Teet, *The Silo Effect* (Little Brown 2015), p.64

[67] See his book, *Reinventing Capitalism in the Age of Big Data* (John Murray, 2018)

Improving product discovery with metadata

Metadata helps to surface information that customers are seeking. Better product discovery creates revenue opportunities. Metadata helps customers discover what a firm has for sale several ways.

One scenario is known as longtail search, where the customer knows precisely what they want. They specify several product characteristics (brand, model, price, for example) in order to retrieve information relating to products with those parameters. Metadata enables customers to discover products that match specific parameters (see Chapter 11 on search discovery).

Another scenario is when customers are looking to confirm that a product is in stock in a local store. They want to confirm that a product is available from a specific store outlet. Metadata can link together information about products, store location, and inventory holdings.

In both these scenarios, metadata helps to make the sale. Metadata can get information to buyers immediately, so that they don't lose interest or choose a competitor. It makes shopping easier and more precise.

Yet another way metadata helps customers select product is by supporting images. By selecting images, customers don't need to rely on text to indicate interests or needs. Pictures can serve as an input or stimulus for customers to indicate what they like or need. Metadata connects a visual representation of a product, such as a photo, to detailed information about the product. Metadata frees customers from having to use "keywords" to describe items explicitly.

Business-to-consumer platforms can use metadata to provide customers with suggestions and fine-tune them. Metadata provides structure to information that supports techniques such as "conversational commerce" or quizzes that probe a buyer's readiness or preferences. Firms can refine their recommendations, by starting wide, showing what's most popular, and then tailoring options to show more specific items. Metadata can make shopping less tedious when users no longer have to specify ranges or literal values. Customers instead can use everyday language for concepts such as "rugged" to indicate what they'd like. They can see an example, and say they want something cheaper, or smaller. IT systems can use metadata to recognize examples that match those requirements without asking users for an exact price or size. Metadata provides the precision so that shoppers don't have to worry about being precise themselves.

Attracting audiences (and prospective customers) using metadata

Most online publishers want to increase their *reach* — the number of visitors who encounter a firm's content. Metadata can help online publishers improve their reach.

Content plays many roles: it attracts prospective customers, informs them, and answers questions they may have prior to making purchases. Metadata helps match the right content with the right audiences.

In contrast to the discovery scenario, where the customer is actively looking for product information, in the attraction scenario the customer becomes interested in the product as a part of the larger process of learning about a broader topic of interest.

Online publishers can use metadata to attract people who might be interested in what a firm offers, even if these people aren't specifically looking for it. Such attraction is the basis of content marketing.

Metadata can help to connect broader topics with more specific product information. The pathways connecting users with topics is known as attribution. By looking at how metadata connects different kinds of information, online publishers can understand the relationship between customer segments, the topics of greatest interest to them, and their products.

Customer journeys illustrate how metadata helps connect different people with different kinds of content. Each customer journey can involve interaction between four dimensions:

1. **Customers** (defined by segments): the clusters of people who have common interests
2. **Content themes** (defined by topics): the preoccupations and interests of segments
3. **Product categories** (defined by brands and entity types): how segments think about solutions
4. **Specific products** (defined by product properties): how a segment prioritizes goods and services for sale.

In a typical attraction pattern, a customer starts by having a general interest in a topic relating to some issue in their life, such as being fit and healthy. On further exploration, they become interested in a category of products they think might be useful, such a kind of exercise equipment. Finally, they become interested in comparing specific products within the product category.

Consider a specific customer journey. People who are "empty nesters" (their children are grown and have left home) may have an interest in content relating to retirement planning (theme). As part of their reading about retirement, they become more interested in insurance products that are relevant to their life stage. Finally, they become interested in a specific product: catastrophic health insurance.

In a different customer journey, the parents of teens might be interested in reading about vacation ideas. They become interested in packages relating to the outdoors, and ultimately decide to explore booking a lodge somewhere.

In such customer journeys, metadata provides value attracting and connecting at different stages. It can help online publishers understand variables and promote high-interest information. It helps them know:

- The motivations of customers according to their exploration of themes
- How to how to best connect with certain audience segments
- The importance of theme to a product category
- Whether a product category is part of the discussion about a theme
- The importance of product features to the product category
- Customer priorities relating to specific solutions.

Personalizing information using metadata

Many firms believe personalization is financially valuable. Metadata can make content more relevant, and valuable, to customers.

Personalization involves modifying generic content to display information of special relevance to a reader or audience segment.

Metadata provides publishers with the ability to tailor information to specific users and groups. Metadata helps determine *what* information to personalize and *where* to personalize it.

Content personalization is possible with a wide range of content types. How valuable is personalization? Online publishers should consider the value of showing more specific content compared to showing generic content. They need to consider the value they can realize by *not* showing generic content.

Metadata enables the display of dynamic content. For example, metadata can support customizing content based on search terms.

Personalization may entail the simple matching of information with users, such as when users from a certain geographic region are shown content related to that region.

A more granular form of personalization could swap information about product attributes (features, prices, etc.) to match customer attributes and audience location attributes. For example, an insurance company could display information for a specific age group, or for residents of a specific location. This may be done based on customer eligibility, perceived interest, or other considerations.

The most sophisticated matching is dynamic, where the content changes according to additional information that becomes known about users. For instance, a user's content choices when exploring information can indicate a user characteristic such as their goals or where they might live. That user characteristic, once known, can influence the subsequent content displayed.

It's important to recognize that while personalization can be associated with the use of metadata, the two concepts are distinct. Personalization doesn't necessarily require the use of metadata — for example, some automated marketing systems change photos and messages based on data prediction.[68] And the benefits of metadata extend well beyond personalization. Personalization can be a strong rationale for implementing a metadata program, but probably shouldn't be the sole rationale. Personalization is not necessarily the killer app for metadata, but it can certainly deliver revenue benefits. Personalization will be explored more in Chapters 9 and 11.

Customizing products using metadata

Marketing success depends on what is known as the "customer-product" fit. How well the customer feels the product fits her needs will to a large degree determine her willingness to purchase the product.

Customized products can sometimes command higher margins, especially when customers feel they've been able to build their perfect product. Customers expect choice, and many products and experiences for sale are made to order. Customers want to specify specific details of the products they buy, to choose the options available.

Granular metadata can allow customers to dive into specifics, which makes the product more appealing. Metadata changes how customers explore products and services, by shifting the focus toward tangible factors. Customers can explore the dimensions that most interest them, and are free from thinking about product categories or model names. They can do product and feature comparisons, slicing and dicing information in multiple ways.

Customers may use metadata to explore the possibilities available. They may do faceted searches, showing and hiding possibilities available according to different parameters. Metadata can help present different visualizations and cost estimates of possibilities.

Metadata can make products more desirable by supporting product configuration. When reviewing product options and ordering, customers use metadata to specify their preferences. Online publishers offer configuration options for the ordering many kinds of products and services, including customizing the features and trim of new cars or bicycles, redesigning kitchens, and vacation planning. Configuration has long been available, supported by backend databases. But metadata standards offer more flexibility to customers, who no longer have to log into a portal. When product configurations are expressed using standard metadata vocabularies, customers can revise them over time on different devices. The configurations can be sent through email and shared with others.

Offering more than competitors doesn't automatically result in more sales. But if consumers perceive a gap in what's available, they may choose options they feel offer them more.

Supporting customer education and interest using metadata

Customers buy products to do jobs for them. They need to understand how a product fits in the context of their life or work. Consider vacation planning. It provides a good example of how metadata can help educate customers about possibilities, realize their goals, and cope with constraints.

Suppose someone is looking into visiting a place for a vacation. They may be interested in location-related features of a town, or amenity- related features of a hotel. Information about features is available in metadata. Metadata can indicate to visitors what features are available, and whether they are included in the base price, or require additional fees. A customer may want to know, does a hotel have a sauna, and if it does, is it included in the price of the room? Sites can even aggregate information from different vendors to allow customers to understand options more readily.[69]

Online publishers can use metadata in the content to track what topics are of interest to customers, and what is the depth of that interest. In the case of vacation information, publishers might be interested in knowing how many people looked into the sauna information.

Historically, ecommerce vendors have bundled features into packages in tiered prices. These practices were sometimes opaque to consumers. It was hard for customers to understand what the additional costs of each tier offered them. Now customers can get more detailed information to compare features from different vendors. Vendors who provide more transparency can gain an advantage over competitors who hide fees or aren't explicit about what's included.

Enhancing product functionality using metadata

Product functionality relates to what consumers can do with a product. Enhancing the lifetime value of products to customers can build long-term customer loyalty.

Historically, product information existed in two separate places. Some product information existed in a file within the product itself, for example, the basic instructions and help information. Outside of the product existed more detailed information or supplemental information that was created after the product was made. These might be instructional videos, reference materials, or troubleshooting guides. To know how to use a product, the user needed to consult different places.

Increasingly, the boundary between product and information is disappearing, as all product information exists in the cloud, and the product acts as an interface to this information. This opens up new possibilities to extend the range of information available *about* the product that's available *through* the product. Brands can offer enhanced, bonus content to make using the product more enjoyable. It also allows more remote control of the product through other interfaces.

Metadata can connect information between different devices or platforms that a customer uses. Some scenarios where metadata facilitates how users can access information include:

- Cross-device access, when one app (such as on a smartphone or smartwatch) controls or monitors aspects of another product (perhaps a smart speaker or thermostat).
- Device-agnostic access to products (same product or service can be accessed from different kinds of devices, such as a phone or in-car entertainment system).
- Sharing products or services within families or households (account-based services, where different family members have own profiles and preferences).
- Providing online information relating to a non-digital, physical product.

Metadata helps to bridge a customer's offline and online experiences. For example, a buyer of a canned good might use their phone to scan a bar code on the can. This could access nutritional information about the product, as well as recipes for using the product.

Resolving problems more quickly using metadata

Retaining customers depends on keeping them satisfied. Metadata can connect information about an owned product with diagnostic and help information. Metadata makes products more responsive.

Metadata vocabularies are addressing more scenarios relating to automation. Standards are also being developed for the Internet of Things (IoT), a technology that will likely become more important in customer service scenarios in the future. (IoT is discussed in more detail in Chapter 12 on external channels.)

---

[68] Such changes "reskin" the content to make it look more appealing without changing the core information.

[69] For a discussion of the relationship of tourism and hospitality metadata, see http://ontologies.sti-innsbruck.at/acco/ns.html

PART II. APPLICATIONS AND BENEFITS OF METADATA STRATEGY

Part II looks at the many benefits that metadata standards can deliver. It provides a wide range of potential goals for a metadata strategy. Some applications are being implemented widely by different publishers, while some are still very new and their potential has yet to be fully uncovered. Some chapters will cite many examples when those are available, while other chapters will be more focused on possibilities when the application is not yet widely used.

When setting goals for their metadata, online publishers will find themselves using metadata standards in one of three ways.

Nearly all publishers start using metadata standards for a single purpose, typically to support their search engine optimization.

Once publishers are comfortable with using metadata standards for SEO, they may explore other applications. For example, they may also use the standards to support interaction design functionality, to increase the reuse of information, or to support a new channel such as voice. These publishers have moved from single-purpose metadata to multi-purpose metadata.

Finally, some publishers may transition from having metadata that's multi-purpose to having metadata that's general-purpose. They will use external standards for all their web operations, and will be able to get a 360 degree view of how their online information is performing.

The more different ways a publisher can use their metadata, the more benefits they will derive from their strategy.

CHAPTER 9: HOW METADATA MAKES CUSTOMER EXPERIENCES SEAMLESS

nformation overload is a common symptom of poor metadata. When customers must look at too much information, they experience friction.

People often want less information because the information is difficult to access and process. Sometimes less information is required, especially when what is wanted is higher quality, more relevant information. But the *quality* of information alone doesn't determine the friction experienced. When and how the information is encountered is equally important. Experience is *personal*. Metadata helps make information more personal, and cohesive.

Online content needs metadata in order for it to become seamless to customers. Metadata helps connect the right information with the intent of the customer. Customer experience depends on the satisfaction of customer goals — and these goals are often connected to specific information. Customers make choices about what information to pursue, what to pay attention to, what information to use later, and what information to share. Through these activities, the information is no longer alien, but personal.

"Personal content is content that the user has a relationship with. Content becomes personal through creation or use."

-- Nokia Research

When customers choose what information to look for, to notice, and to refer to later, these activities entail effort on their part. Much of that effort is not visible to the online publisher. Yet the effort required by the customer etches a lasting impression that can shape how much they want to be involved with a brand.

Nokia Research developed the GEMS model of content use. The GEMS model helps online publishers understand how each customer interaction with online information can influence whether the experience is seamless or not.

- *G* is for **Get** (or acquire) which includes tasks such as receive, create, capture, purchase, and trade.
- *E* is for **Enjoy** (or consume) which includes tasks such as edit, listen, view, read, and recall
- *M* is for **Maintain** (save or collect for future use) which includes tasks such as organize, archive, rate, and annotate.
- *S* is for **Share** which includes tasks such as send, publish, give, show, and sell.

The value of the GEMS model is that it highlights the range of actions consumers can take with online information. These actions involve specific information that customers want to use.

Metadata and product evaluation

"Buyers want to know the specifics of what they are buying — specifications, quality, reliability, workmanship, guarantees, and much, much more."[70]

-- David Sarokin and Jay Schulkin

Economists classify goods into three categories according to how buyers evaluate information. The categories are search goods, experience goods, and credence goods. Each has relevance to how metadata can support the customer's evaluation of products online.

Search goods are products that are easy to evaluate without having seen or experienced them. Product evaluation involves finding products that match the features being sought. Many purchase decisions involve finding products with specific characteristics, especially if the brand is already known. Much online search involves finding products with brand names and certain properties, and buying them. Metadata is critical to successfully finding the right product in these situations.

Experience goods get their name because it is harder to assess the quality and characteristics of the product or service prior to being used. Experience goods can be supported through metadata. A good example is a vacation. Content can preview the experience, by showing photos, linking to location information, suggesting transportation options or restaurants to explore. All those connections are made possible through metadata.

Credence goods are products or services that are even harder for customers to ascertain the utility or value, especially in the short term. Examples of credence goods include vitamins, education, car repairs, and some forms of medical treatment. When buying credence goods, customers rely on third-party evaluations, such as expert opinions, and information relating to the reputation of vendors. Transparency is important for these goods, as is linking to relevant third party information sources, such as accreditation organizations, awards bodies.

Metadata can even integrate information relating to all three dimensions: tangible parameters (search), experience, and reputation (credence).

The *Washington Post* notes how the restaurant and retail review site Yelp is providing a range of information about health care facilities, including the experience and reputation. "You can now look up ER wait times, hospital noise levels and nursing home fines on Yelp."[71]

Metadata can seem like it is "in the weeds" — low-level background details that aren't directly connected to the primary goals of a customer. Some content marketers suggest that customers don't care about boring details, they are interested in impressionistic stories. I disagree. Often the detailed information captured by metadata is the basis of the story the customer tells to himself or herself. Metadata reveals the characteristics of a product.

Parents may wonder: Is this toy safe? Sometimes it is hard to know, because the needed information isn't accessible.

> *"Each ingredient that goes into a toy has its own complex backstory."*[72]

-- David Sarokin and Jay Schulkin

Historically, detailed information was put on the packaging of products. Today, when customers order online, they can't see the packaging. They must rely on metadata to tell them about the product. The metadata has replaced the information on the packaging.

The era when products were commodities has passed. Products today exist in great variety. Customers are the ones who decide what characteristics are important.

Consider shopping for produce, such as fruit. Until recently, the shopping experience would involve glancing at a pile of apples, and if they weren't rotten, buying a few. But even apples come in different varieties. Some are good for baking, others for eating. They may be ordered online now.

Even the in-store shopping experience for fruit is relying more on metadata. A supermarket I visited in Italy presented detailed information about the properties of lemons for sale, such as their ecological footprint, and their nutritional values. (Figure 9.1)

Figure 9.1. An electronic display above lemons for sale in an Italian supermarket provides detailed, real-time information about the fruit. Source:

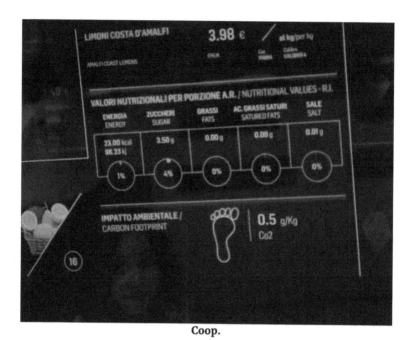

Coop.

The customer experience is not limited to shopping of course. Shopping is just one step in the customer journey.

Customers interact with information two ways. On one side information is pushed to customers: the system delivers content in anticipation of a customer need. On the other side information gets pulled by customers: they indicate what information they want.

Metadata supports the customer experience from high-level goals to low-level tasks. Customers start with high-level goals when exploring information or interacting with a brand. They decide which tasks they need to do to realize their goals. Tasks involve a series of actions. Each level of experience depends on information described by metadata.

[70] David Sarokin and Jay Schulkin, *Missed Information* (MIT 2016), p. 29

[71] See https://www.washingtonpost.com/news/to-your-health/wp/2015/08/05/coming-to-yelp-a-bigger-dose-of-data-on-health-care-facilities/

[72] David Sarokin and Jay Schulkin, *Missed Information* (MIT 2016), p. 92

Customer goals and metadata

Customers have various goals that metadata can help with:

- Find information quickly
- Monitor information and feel in control
- Plan activities
- Integrate information and get details
- Understand the connections between different things.

A customer's journey involves a series of steps. By looking at the goals of these steps, we can see how metadata can influence whether a customer is happy or annoyed. Metadata, far from being a technical detail, influences the emotional experience of customers exploring content.

Too often, customers spend most of their energy collecting information from different sources and trying to make sense of it all. It involves considerable friction they are keen to avoid.

In some cases, the customer goal is to solve a problem they have with a product or service. The customer often wants a "don't make me think" kind of experience. They don't want to view long texts or videos to learn how to diagnose their problem, or hear detailed instructions on how to resolve it. They want to have their problem resolve automatically, or at least as automatically as possible. This is a low interaction scenario. Metadata can support pushed communications. The vendor can send a message to a customer describing the problem, and then offer a choice of how to resolve it. The item is out of stock: Do you want to cancel, or wait 4 weeks? Status and actions are easy to indicate in metadata, as we will discuss in the next chapter (Chapter 10).

Recommendation engines are a sophisticated example of using metadata and code to push choices to customers for them to decide. They can do this by evaluating the similarity of content items to items that a user (or people similar to the user) have liked.

In other cases, the customer's goals are more experiential. They aren't trying to minimize content. They want to find content that makes them feel wiser and more in control. Metadata empowers customer choice.

Metadata helps customers feel in control of a situation. Customers want to be kept informed and be able to monitor the status of something in real time. They want to observe progress in an activity and perhaps be alerted if there are any significant changes. A familiar example that relies on metadata is flight status information. (Figure 9.2) This information is portable, able to move from web to email to cards on your phone. It can show if a flight will arrive on time, and notify if a flight is delayed or canceled.

Figure 9.2. Flight information relies on metadata. Metadata standards allow the same information to be delivered to different channels. Source: Google Assistant.

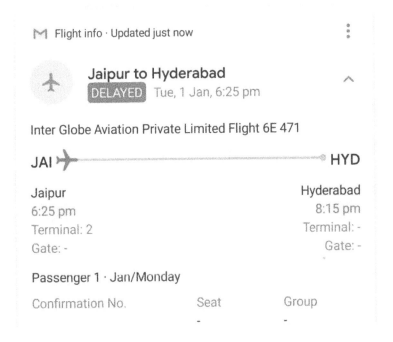

Your flight departs soon ✈

≋ Haze 23°C

M Flight info · Updated just now ⋮

✈ **Jaipur to Hyderabad** ∧
DELAYED Tue, 1 Jan, 6:25 pm

Inter Globe Aviation Private Limited Flight 6E 471

JAI ✈ ⸺⸺⸺⸺⸺⸺⸺⸺⸺⸺ HYD

Jaipur	Hyderabad
6:25 pm	8:15 pm
Terminal: 2	Terminal: -
Gate: -	Gate: -

Passenger 1 · Jan/Monday

Confirmation No.	Seat	Group
-	-	

Metadata can help customers to better prepare for the future. Customers rely on information to plan activities, such as a vacation. Their planning is more interactive and helpful when the information is described by metadata.

The customer wants to explore possibilities: for example, what's available? Some tasks associated with this goal are to find and view examples of options, and to prioritize these options according to different criteria. Specific actions include collecting and listing options, and filtering, sorting and ranking them. Metadata is vitally important in these activities.

Metadata also lets customers have a better sense of whether they would like something they haven't yet experienced. Customers may want to try something out, to imagine it. Their task can involve configuring something based on different features. Actions can be to add or remove items, and to view lateral links of related features. Vacation planning, mentioned earlier, is an example.

Customers want to connect and integrate information. Customers don't like silos. They embrace services that can help them transcend such silos, especially ones that don't compromise their privacy. We see evidence of this: there's more family or household sharing of accounts, and private groups on different platforms. Metadata can support groups of people interact with and integrate information.

Metadata allows information to be available at a tap. For example, smartphone apps can link to information stored in a knowledge graph. Bing is one of several IT companies that offers its Knowledge Graph to other developers making apps for customers.

Customers also want to learn. They want to understand stuff they use and enrich their knowledge. Metadata helps them discover content to view, but it can do more. Standards are emerging that provide frameworks for learners so that they can move through content in a structured sequence according to their existing knowledge and proficiency. This is a big step up from the "list of links" approach available via hypertext that required learners to decide which page link was most appropriate to view next.

An example of how metadata can support learning is the Profit Project (Figure 9.3). Funded by the EU, the Profit Project is "a platform promoting the financial awareness and improving the financial capability of citizens and other financial market participants."[73] It utilizes adaptive techniques to improve financial literacy. Leveraging the capability to explain the association of information about related items, the project has at it core a knowledge graph of financial concepts so that learners can connect different financial events.

Figure 9.3. The EU's PROFIT project uses semantic technology to provide financial literacy information to EU citizens. Source: Project Profit.

Metadata helps customers understand. It can answer: What makes two things similar? Sometimes such questions can be difficult to answer. If you like a wine, but want to try a different wine that might be similar, how do you choose? Generally, we rely on existing categories to help us spot similarity. Categories are a top-down way of considering information. Categories force users to choose a category, then look for criteria within that category.

The human capacity to make distinctions using categories can be overwhelmed by the number of potential categories available. "Things that are 'hard to categorize' are hard to like" notes Tom Vanderbilt.[74] Top-down categories look simple but can be frustrating to users who aren't thinking about their needs in terms of a predefined category.

If choosing a vacation destination, a prospective traveler might not have a specific category in mind, such as "adventure travel in Southeast Asia". Instead, they might have preferences or curiosities about different aspects of a vacation. They want to approach the task from the bottom-up.

Properties can provide users with "scaffolding" to create and understand categories from the bottom-up. Customers can consider different dimensions and build our own categories, for example: "good rock-climbing sites located near interesting ancient historic monuments." Properties can highlight similarities between entities that might not otherwise be apparent from a top-level category. Categories divide; properties connect.

---

[73] http://projectprofit.eu/

[74] Tom Vanderbilt, *You May Also Like* (Simon & Schuster 2016)

How metadata makes content more relevant

Publishers are aware of the importance of relevant content. Yet relevance is rarely a binary property where content can be classified as either relevant or not relevant. Even if all the content is high quality, not all of it will be relevant to everyone. Relevance depends on context: for whom, when, and for what purpose. Metadata parameter-izes information, and provides software with clues to help decide what specific content is most relevant in a given context. Metadata makes sure the details are relevant, so the content as a whole is relevant.

Unstructured information results in *TMI*: Too Much Information. The information can't be manipulated by the user. Metadata lets the user decide what specific pieces of information are most relevant. Metadata gives the user editorial control over their personal content experience.

When there is lots of information, about hundreds of products, for example, computer scripts can help to simplify the information into more manageable chunks. Computer algorithms use metadata for several key tasks:

- **Prioritization** (rank according to pre-defined criteria) used in search, Q&A, and some timelines
- **Classification** (group information based on common features) used when scoring content according to similarity or reputation
- **Association** (determine the relationship between two entities) used to predict related topics that aren't directly connected.
- **Filtering** (include or hide information based on given criteria) used in filters and feeds.

Working with algorithms, metadata provides customers with the curation of information relevant to their needs.

Providing the right detail using metadata

Metadata allows customers to modulate the amount of content they see. A core goal in content strategy to deliver the right level of detail to audiences — not too much, and not to little. Customers frequently feel that the information they encounter is fragmented and hard to absorb. They may find the steady drip of curt alerts or data hard to follow. Conversely, they may be overwhelmed by a massive explanation that is encyclopedic.

Metadata can support an immersive perspective about a topic. Immersive visualizations can allow users to move through time and/or space to explore data.

When users view a digital map, zooming in or out, they see different levels of detail. They are manipulating metadata parameters to access the detail they are most interested in. The principles used in displaying maps can be applied to other forms of information. A label can be moused over to reveal details. Tapping on the current stock price reveals the stock performance over the past 12 months. Customers can even change multiple parameters and see how the values vary, such as when using multiple sliders.

Figure 9.4. Augmented reality apps are becoming more popular. The information they present can be sourced from metadata. Source: Smartify.org.

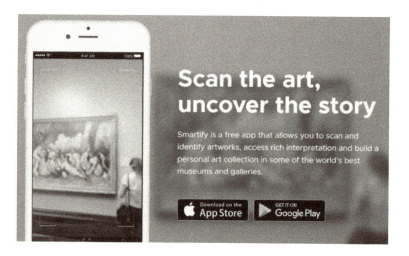

Augmented reality (AR) allows metadata to be overlaid on a view of a physical environment (Figure 9.4). AR is most commonly used in navigation and location-description use cases. Because the investment to code an immersive framework can be high, publishers will want the ability to use a range of metadata that can be feed into an AR framework, and be able to use information in AR that can be re-used to support other use cases.

CHAPTER 10: CONTENT METADATA TO SUPPORT INTERACTION

M etadata helps users do things with information, such as find the perfect movie (Figure 10.1). Metadata is essential to making content interactive. Metadata can let users:

1. Locate and specify information
2. Experience information in different ways
3. Act on information on any platform, or any channel.

Figure 10.1. When searching for a film, users may interact with metadata such as actors' names, film categories, and IMDb ratings. Source: Searchkit.

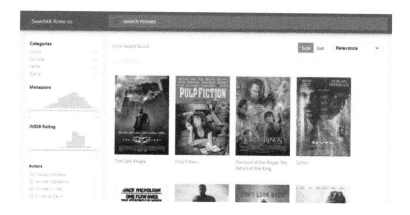

When publishers use standard vocabularies for their metadata, they can offer a wider range of options for users to interact with information. By using standard vocabularies, existing information is not coupled to specific applications, and can be available everywhere it is needed. This allows users to interact with online information independently of the specific app or platform they may be using.

Metadata and the UI: Supporting choices with information

Users expect up-to-date and relevant information. They also want choices about the information they view and are able to act upon. Publishers need to link available information in their metadata to different user interfaces their customers are using. External standards can help publishers keep these activities in synch with each other.

Figure 10.2. The values for many UI elements can be directly populated by the same metadata used for SEO and other scenarios of use. Source: Google.

The structure of metadata, representing the relationship of different information, is mirrored externally by the structure of the user interface, which arranges informational elements within a hierarchy. UIs are increasingly composed of widget elements that are building blocks for screens. Publishers can integrate metadata with these building blocks, so that information in metadata is injected onto a screen element. The presentation layer (the UI) is supported by a data layer (the metadata). Both layers convey meaning: one layer conveys information visually, while the other layer represents the information as code.

To be useful to users, interaction must be informative. The purpose of interaction is to provide information that supports the intent of users so that they can find or choose what they want or need.

UIs can become more informative and offer greater choices when UI elements get "bound" to metadata representing useful information. Metadata can be bound to common UI elements such as:

- Breadcrumbs
- Dropdown options

- Buttons that have variables

    o For example, *Buy Now for* Product.price (where Product.price is a variable)
- Ratings

- Option values

    o Checkboxes
    o Radio buttons
    o Toggles
- Steppers
- Time pickers
- Data tables.

When metadata is used populate the text of UI elements, the information on the element is more up-to-date and precise than if the UI element were "hard coded" in the label.

The most flexible way to bind metadata and UI elements is by using external vocabularies such as schema.org. The code used for UI widgets can be aligned with the standardized descriptions used in the metadata. Information that appears in any user interface is described consistently.

Being one with information: interactive data

Users will often want to explore an entity according to its properties and values. They may want to focus on one or two properties and find out what the values of the properties are.

Maps illustrate how metadata enables information interactively. A location on a map is a pair of values: one for the longitude property and the other for latitude property. Many different entities can be associated with locations: businesses, parks, parking lots, etc. Locations are metadata-rich, full of connections to associated information.

If a customer wants to know what businesses are near a location, they view a map and choose the location area. Behind the scenes, metadata is connecting the business and location information being displayed.

Maps are also a good illustration of information that needs to be portable. Map-related information may be sourced from different places and needs to be available to different platforms, each of which will have their own user interfaces.

Google has provided an example of how standard vocabularies make information more portable, and work with UI frameworks. Google offers a UI framework called the Polymer web component framework (Figure 10.3). It recommends using schema.org metadata written in the JSON-LD syntax to populate information displayed in reusable widgets, such as maps, in their UI framework. Google notes that using the schema.org vocabulary to create interactive features can save developers effort:

"Avoid repetition and ensure data consistency, by reusing the same data snippets to populate different widgets as well as inform search engines...We can achieve this by using the schema.org standard and the JSON-LD format for our data...Reuse the same data structures to inform the UI as well as the search engines...about the exact meaning of the page's content."[25]

Figure 10.3. Data on interactive maps drawing on metadata in JSON-LD. Source: Google.

Google makes the case that "JSON-LD and Web Components work really well together. The Custom Element functions as the presentation layer and the JSON-LD functions as the data layer that the custom element and search engines consume. This means you can build custom elements for any schema.org type, such as schema.org/Event and schema.org/LocalBusiness."[76]

Metadata encoded in JSON-LD can work with other interaction frameworks, not just Google's web components. In some cases, a few tweaks to the file are recommended to make the file easier to use for front-end developers.[77]

---

[75] Ewa Gasperowicz, "Creating semantic sites with Web Components and JSON-LD", https://developers.google.com/web/updates/2015/03/creating-semantic-sites-with-web-components-and-jsonld

[76] "Easier website development with Web Components and JSON LD" https://webmasters.googleblog.com/2015/03/easier-website-development-with-web.html

[77] These tweaks involve abstracting away the @ prefix symbol through 'aliasing', and converting properties that could exist in multiples into arrays, to bring more consistency. See "Publishing JSON-LD for Developers", https://datalanguage.com/news/publishing-json-ld-for-developers

From reading to doing

Users typically seek out information to support tasks. While reading a cookbook can be fun, making the recipes is generally a more rewarding experience. Cookbook recipes are composed of information about ingredients, and steps (actions) about those ingredients (Figure 10.4). Metadata standards are beginning to focus on how to represent actions that people or objects take.

Figure 10.4. Information wants to be acted upon. Metadata can also represent actions. Source: RecipeScape research project.

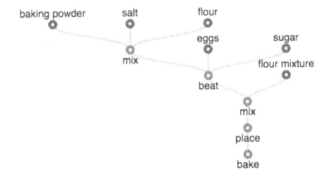

Presently, people interact with content largely on screens. Buttons present a potential action. A classic case of a non-semantic button is one that's labeled "submit". The user has filled in some details on a form, read some instructions, and is told he or she needs to tap the button for the server to receive the information. The experience doesn't make the user feel in control. The developer needs to write code to act on whatever information has been submitted. The user may get a confirmation that says "successfully submitted." It's not a very satisfying experience.

Users don't want to "submit" to computers. They want to take action and have computers do things for them. They want their buttons to be a bit smarter.

The schema.org vocabulary can express a range of common actions users want to do. Schema.org introduced actions in 2014 and now has over 100 actions available (Figure 10.5). By standardizing these actions, which are commonly linked to entities and properties also described in metadata, it can be easier for developers to make functionality available.

Figure 10.5. Some of the actions available in the schema.org vocabulary. Source: Schema.org.

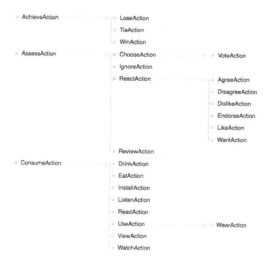

Traditionally, actions were written as custom functions or scripts. The actions available depended on what app or platform the customer used. Now the specification of actions are being standardized, which allow them to become independent of platform and technology.

Figure 10.6. Buttons can be bound directly to schema.org metadata. The pause button can be bound to the schema.org SuspendAction .

When defined as metadata, user actions become information. Suppose a student plays the audio of a lecture that is stored in the cloud. The student may pause the lecture at several points. The student could get information about where she paused the lecture, to review these parts again later. The professor could learn how often the lecture was paused, and at what points.

Because actions are device-independent, users can start a process on one device, and finish on another.

Somewhat counter-intuitively, *actions* in the schema.org vocabulary are a type of entity.[28] Actions can have properties such as status, and start and end time. These properties indicate what information is needed to perform an action, and what information is generated as the result of an action. Actions connect to other related entities. Users can listen (ListenAction) to different entity types such as podcasts or music. Conversely, an entity type may have different potential actions associated with it. For example, users can do different actions relating to a movie. They can read about it or they can watch it.

By formalizing the kind of action, the schema.org vocabulary lets app developers to use metadata to indicate the kind of action that's associated with a link or button. For example, if the user is exploring content to decide on a video to watch, they could be either reading a summary about the video, or watching a preview of the video. If the user notices an image thumbnail that highlights content about the video, they will likely want to know if the content is text summary or a video preview. The user may see an icon noting the type of content (text or video); schema.org's actions metadata indicates what the icon means. Google explains how actions make available different kinds of options to users: "To send users to an information page, use a *view action*. To send users directly to the content so they can watch it, use a *watch action*."[29] The correct icon can be generated automatically based on the actions metadata associated with the content.

By using actions, publishers can provide deeper context around entities. This is especially useful within apps, where the user doing tasks but doesn't have easy access to related contextual information. Google provides an example of how uses an action in Android apps to provide users with more information:

"Improve the assistant user experience by providing content-related references related to the current activity. You can describe the app content using the common vocabulary defined by Schema.org through a JSON-LD object. [For example,] a music app provides structured data to describe the music album that the user is currently viewing."[80]

Actions are related to two distinct kinds of entities:

1. Actions that relate to entities that are content or media (movies, songs, etc.)
2. Actions that relate to entities that are physical things, events, places or people that are described by content.

Actions relating to both kinds of entities can be enriched by additional contextual information.

---

[78] Actions are similar to verbs, just like many properties seem like verbs. But actions can have properties that qualify the action similar the way that adverbs or prepositions qualify verbs. Because actions have properties, they are considered entities.

[79] https://developers.google.com/search/docs/data-types/tv-movie

[80] Google, "Assistant", https://developer.android.com/training/articles/assistant.html

Actions as tasks

Actions can be tracked and aggregated. They can provide a picture of how users are reacting to content.

Let's consider a scenario where actions can be useful. A professional association is organizing a conference. It will get proposals from speakers and will want attendees to indicate which proposals they are most interested in. Once the proposal is accepted, it will need to track the planning of the talk. When the conference is held, it may want to let attendees provide feedback for the event. These different tasks can all be handled by actions in the schema.org vocabulary.

When considering a proposal, the conference organizer could use the AssessAction. This action has a range of options available, depending on how participants are encouraged to express their preferences.

Conference attendees can indicate overall preferences, with actions available to:

- Choose (a theme)
- Vote (for favorite topics)
- Ignore (if indifferent)
- Want (an option).

The organizer could also use the ReactAction to get reactions to specific proposals, using actions such as:

- Agree (with a decision)
- Disagree (with a decision)
- Dislike (a format for a session)
- Endorse (a speaker)
- Like (a format for a session).

When planning the conference sessions, the organizers might use the OrganizeAction, which has sub-types. AllocateAction could be used to manage speaker proposals, using actions such as:

- Accept (the talk description)
- Assign (for review)
- Reject (the talk description).

The PlanAction could be used for scheduling, which includes actions to:

- Cancel
- Reserve
- Schedule.

With these kinds of prioritizing actions, the action can be linked to a status property that may have an enumerated value associated with it. So if the action is to cancel, the status could say canceled. These actions can be utilized in all kinds of communications: forms, email messages, calendar notifications, and event announcements. Actions enable a seamless dialog between the organization that is responsible for publishing the information and the many individuals who are making choices and checking for updates.

Actions open up a new range of possibilities in content design. Sometimes content promotes actions, and sometimes actions generate information that prompt new content. Actions can play either a primary role or a secondary one.

Online publishers can utilize metadata actions in different scenarios:

1. Where information *triggers a task* (action) for the user to take, such as prioritizing.
2. Where information prompts an *elective action*, such as when the user learns about an event and decides to book a ticket to the event.
3. Where actions trigger a desire to *consult support-information*, such as the when user gathers information as part of planning
4. Where *actions generate fresh information*, so that content provides notifications about actions, for example, tracking the status of a delivery.

CHAPTER 11: SEARCH DISCOVERY AND PERSONALIZATION

S emantic search is the most common application of semantic metadata, which within the search community is referred to as structured data.

The role of metadata in SEO is widely known. The specifics of SEO are constantly changing, and are discussed in detail in online sources. This discussion will not repeat information available elsewhere, but will focus on strategic dimensions of metadata in search.

Search has evolved from primarily indexing strings of text, to indexing available metadata. Text remains important, but metadata is becoming more important. Publishers that implement semantic metadata report improved audience engagement. Natural language processing is also improving in search, so the historical reliance on keywords to signal the topic of text is diminishing.

Search historically has been about retrieving a list of results, the search engine results page (SERP). Google and other search engines are now building additional services that utilize search metadata to support other user needs. Publishers can take advantage of these services provided they follow with search engine guidelines.

Eventbrite, the events listing website, illustrates how metadata supports different user tasks. Eventbrite uses schema.org event metadata to support user queries in Google search as well as Google maps. A Google case study notes that "enriched search results often include advanced interactive features, which lets users perform certain actions (such as viewing event details) while still in Search. For example, if a user searches for 'concerts in Denver,' an immersive-event discovery experience appears in markets where the enriched event search is active."[iii]

Search discovery involves several distinct activities:

1. **Locating relevant content**: Getting more precise information, and avoiding ambiguities that can arise from text.
2. **Previewing relevant content** worthy of looking at: De-contextualizing information, lifting it from the original source.
3. **Connecting relevant content together**: Presenting relationships, suggesting related material, showing related entities.

It's been widely remarked that search is now more about providing answers than providing links. Links are primitive information. Webpage links imply a relationship between two webpages, but audiences don't know how links are related without reading each and every one of them. Results are ranked according to relevance that is largely based on the content's generic popularity, rather than contextual factors.

As search queries use more natural language, search engines aim to understand user intent and the concepts being sought. Search engines interpret the query by examining the meaning of the words (and sometimes other contextual information). The matching the query with the right content is based to a large extent on metadata.

Metadata is especially beneficial with "long tail" queries that relate to specific things or details. For example, someone might search for a product with very specific properties.

For publishers, structured metadata provides more predictability in how their information will be seen. Unlike text-crawling, structured metadata gives publishers an idea what content will be selected, and even some control over how it is presented. It brings predictability to how third parties use the information, compared with web scrapping.

Structured metadata can allow for different visual configurations that displays information. Search engines provide templated formats to display information relating to certain topic domains, such as events and recipes. Google even provides a "Rich Cards" report in the search console that allows publishers to verify that they have they've included the requisite information.

In the future, Google and Bing are likely to offer more "verticals" (content types associated with a specific topic domain), which will highlight certain properties, display images, and sometimes present actions that are available.

Structured metadata also changes of the role of images in search discovery. Images can become a gateway to detailed information. Users increasing click on images to get to information they are seeking. Structured metadata can be used to describe entities in images. With image search, a publisher can add metadata related to the image. If the image represents a product, a recipe, or a video, an image preview can also indicate associated information. If a photo of a cupcake is shown, a badge indicates if the image relates to a recipe for cupcakes or a video about cupcakes. A photo of a product can be presented with key information to surface beside the image.[82]

Figure 11.1. China's Baidu search engine draws on and extends the schema.org vocabulary. Source: Baidu

The role of standard vocabularies in search is not limited to Google and Bing. Yandex in Russia uses schema.org metadata in its search results. Baidu in China also draws on an extended version of the schema.org vocabulary (Figure 11.1). For companies that sell in China, or partner with Chinese suppliers, the schema.org vocabulary provides the basis of a common set of terminology to describe information.

Figure 11.2. Wolfram Alpha provides the ability to search for product attributes. Source: WolframAlpha.

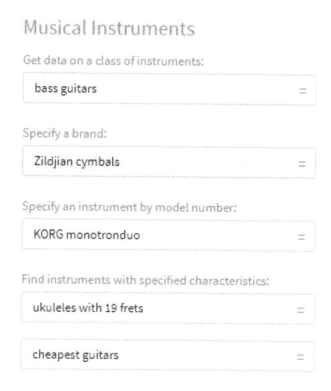

As information described with standard metadata vocabularies becomes more ubiquitous, other search services and appliances can query the same information. Wolfram Alpha is an example of such a service (Figure 11.2).

The changing nature of search: the example of job postings

Job searches provide an example of how search is changing. Historically, job seekers needed to visit different job listing websites such as Monster or Indeed, and search their databases individually. But now they can use a search engine to discover job openings that might be listed on many different websites. They perform a federated search, rather than searching a centralized database.

Federated searching allows for comparison of information across different sources, such as job roles or locations. Federated search also enables the aggregation of information across sources.

Search engines can retrieve job postings from different sources, who all use common metadata in the posting.

Metadata standards give firms with vacancies the flexibility to post jobs on own website, or post on a third-party site such as an applicant tracking systems (ATS), job boards, or job distributors. All these sources are equivalent from the search engine's perspective.

One benefit of search engines is that they provide specific ways to prioritize information. For job searches, they prioritize what's newest. Google reports that the job website ZipRecruiter has benefited from Google's bias toward freshness — how new a published item is:

> "Online job seekers want to see new job listings as soon as they're posted, but don't want to waste time on ones that are outdated, but not yet removed. ZipRecruiter was pleased with the accuracy and freshness of their job postings in Google Search results."[83]

Job hunting provides another use case for search engines: as a vehicle to aggregate information, not just locate a single record.

Aneesh Chopra, the first White House Chief Technology Officer, helped create and promote the schema.org Job Postings vocabulary.[84] Chopra notes that metadata about jobs can be aggregated to develop insights useful to employers, training providers, and governments. "Signaling job titles, job locations, and required skills and credentials, online job postings are powerful indicators of labor market demand." He notes:

> "The labor market would benefit from a collaborative data governance strategy that mitigates the influence of data monopolies—in which a few companies have unparalleled access to job postings—and that enables a more seamless exchange of high-quality real-

time data. The broad adoption by employers of an open data standard would make online job postings better sensors of real-time labor market demand."

However, the ability to aggregate job postings is challenging:

"Inconsistent publishing formats are akin to mismatched fire hoses and hydrants; the incongruence stymies the flow of the information. By comparison, a consistent data standard makes it easier for third-party applications to find, parse, and utilize content regardless of where it is published."

Chopra sees vast potential for analyzing the voluminous information relating to job postings. While he has been successful in getting some properties included in the schema.org vocabulary, he would like even more granular information to be available. He asks: "What are the fields -— salary, location, hours, education requirements, and skill keywords -— that should consistently define job postings?" The question suggests that additional detail (properties and enumerated values) could be available to describe job titles, and job and educational credentials. These properties currently are free-text values.[85]

---

[81] "Eventbrite Case Study", Google, https://developers.google.com/search/case-studies/eventbrite-case-study

[82] "Google Image Publishing Guidelines", https://support.google.com/webmasters/answer/114016?hl=en

[83] "ZipRecruiter Case Study", Google, https://developers.google.com/search/case-studies/ziprecruiter-case-study

[84] See http://schema.org/docs/about.html

[85] Aneesh Chopra and Ethan Gurwitz, "Modernizing America's Workforce Data Architecture: Using Open Data Standards to Enhance the Quality and Availability of Online Job Postings", August 2017, American Progress, https://cdn.americanprogress.org/content/uploads/2017/08/11081348/WorkforceInfrastructure-report.pdf

Personalization

Personalization is different from targeting, such as found in pay-per-click ads, or Facebook promotions. Targeting tries to find audiences that match existing content. Any modification of the content is superficial; it is not based on structured metadata.

Personalization starts with the user, whomever they may be. Personalization modifies what is shown to the user based on what is reliably known about them. Personalization changes the information, according to what information is most relevant.

Bharat Arand of Harvard Business School notes the limits of targeting: "Targeting has become easier but has not delivered on its tremendous promise."[86] Targeting is unreliable because it doesn't really tailor the content to user needs. It tries to force existing content on segments, some of which are based on sloppy data profiles.

Personalization in some respects resembles a form of predictive search. Computers can match or configure information based on specific parameters that users don't need to explicitly specify. Either user data predicts content preferences, or content usage data predicts user preferences for other things. These two forms of personalization relate to known users, and unknown users respectively.

For an example of how metadata can support a known user, we return to the example of eBay. EBay customers can be loyal, and interested in specific kinds of items. They may enjoy browsing through listings. But given the size of eBay's offerings, browsing can be fatiguing.

EBay first tried to introduce personalization without much metadata support. Buyers could "follow" a seller, for example. "That was a lot to ask of a casual customer: to curate their own feed," said Bradford Shellhammer, EBay's lead for personalization.

The tech website *Recode* noted:

"The main advantages eBay has over everyone else — including Amazon — are rare items you can't find anywhere else. This differentiator for eBay is useless, however, if the right customer can't easily find the right item for them — or have it appear in front of them serendipitously."[87]

EBay's Shellhammer notes that "the majority of visits to eBay don't start on the homepage." EBay decided to deliver personalization by drawing on structured data properties. Shellhammer said eBay is looking to Netflix as a model for personalization and recommendation done right."[88]

While personalization can be very effective when the user is known, many publishers don't know who the user is. Publishers need to consider how to tailor content to unknown users. There is a growing resistance to online tracking, and concern about privacy. Europe's introduction of the General Data Protection Regulation (GDPR) is one sign that data collection will be restricted in many scenarios.[89]

Aram Zucker-Scharff of the *Washington Post* explores this issue in a provocatively entitled article, "Personalization without people: What happens when no one can track consumers?"[90] "Publishers need to take a look at the new generation of tools that can provide the data needed for personalization on-page without ever tracking a user." He notes: "Metadata standards are improving and adding detail." The challenge is to find "new ways of telling the story about a story could bring about a revolution in personalization."

The key is basing personalization around the known characteristics of the content, rather than the presumed characteristics of the person looking at the content. "What can we build on using enhanced metadata? Geographic coordinates could drive a set of recommendations even more relevant than attempting to geotarget the user."

Zucker-Scharff believes that online publishers need to let go of their attachment to tracking, and embrace the power of metadata in content:

"Owners of this process will need to consider personalization on a variety of factors that describe form, format, key ideas and digital objects. They'll have to build out a framework on how articles connect to each other that will describe small universes of content. A site that takes full advantage of metadata structures can promise a richer experience for readers, viewers, and listeners than any provided through cookie-based tracking, an experience based on in-the-moment intent."

Zucker-Scharff concludes: "We have the technology and industry pressure to deploy successful alternatives. Understanding, expanding and adapting the use of detailed metadata across the web will build better media companies and a better open and well-connected internet."

In the future, personalization will rely more on content metadata. Personalization solutions that ignore content metadata will be at a disadvantage.

[86]Bharat Arand, *The Content Trap*, p. 262

[87]Jason Del Rey, "eBay is overhauling its homepage again to personalize recommendations for each visitor", *Recode*, Mar 20, 2017, https://www.recode.net/2017/3/20/14971600/ebay-new-homepage-redesign-recommendations-personalization

[88.]*Ibid.*, also Bradford Shellhammer, eBay, "Rethinking the eBay Homepage", https://www.youtube.com/watch?v=SB4p1qEdviY

[89]The California Consumer Privacy Act of 2018 is another example of growing restrictions on the collection of user data.

[90] "Personalization without people: What happens when no one can track consumers?" https://digitalcontentnext.org/blog/2017/11/14/personalization-without-people-happens-no-one-can-track-consumers/

CHAPTER 12: CHANNEL FLEXIBILITY AND SILO-RESISTANCE

By following metadata standards, publishers are better prepared to deliver important information to new platforms.

Publishers worry about getting content on various platforms for several reasons. New platforms keep emerging, some of which become popular with certain audience segments for certain scenarios. Not all new channels turn out to have momentum — interactive magazines being an example. But the general trend is toward more fragmented content consumption. The computer browser will always be an important channel. Yet it won't be the dominant one for many scenarios.

Consumers access content through multiple channels. They often start in one channel and continue in another. Metadata can make such information hand-offs possible. Microsoft uses schema.org metadata to let users work on tasks as they move from voice interaction to email.[91]

> *"Thirty years ago, the then-futuristic Jetsons' loyal maid Rosie spoke to the kitchen appliances to help with producing her grocery list, cooking dinner, and cleaning the kitchen. Today, Rosie from the Jetsons is*

metadata personified."[92]

-- Myles Peacock

Companies can gain a competitive advantage when they support convenience, offering content *where* it is wanted: in the car, in the kitchen, or on a device. They are more competitive when they provide the information in a *format* desired: as a narrative, as a dialog, or as an interactive.

Expanding into new channels allows information to be used in new ways. Browser-based web content has largely been focused on reading. In other channels, the emphasis is more on doing. The old expectation that you could create complete and finished content once and publish it everywhere is no longer true. Different platforms have different contexts, which means that the content needs to be different. Publishers face the temptation to develop specific content for each new channel, since new channels have new requirements. While it is true that requirements differ, one should also be mindful of the commonalities of different platforms. The underlying information will be the same on each platform. Which is where metadata brings more flexibility.

Metadata standards make delivering information to different channels easier. Not all channels rely on external metadata standards. When they expect custom metadata, more silos emerge. But more channels are using external standards. Publishers that adopt external standards will find that they have more options. Let's look at how different channels are using external metadata standards.

Epub ebooks

Epub is a W3C standard for ebooks. Ebooks based on Epub are starting to replace PDFs as the vehicle to distribute longer-form content. For example, the OECD uses Epub to distribute reports, and IBM uses Epub for documents. Since Epub is built from HTML, it can contain metadata.

Epub is especially well-suited for bundling educational content. Epub has specific metadata properties that are helpful for indicating educational criteria:

- `educationalAlignment`: indicates it is part of an educational framework.
- `educationalUse`: such as 'assignment' or 'group work'.

- `interactivityType`: whether it is 'active', 'expositive', or 'mixed'.
- `learningResourceType`: for example, 'presentation' or 'handout'.
- `timeRequired`: the approximate or typical time it takes for the intended target audience
- `typicalAgeRange`: age range of the intended audience.

Another great feature in ePub is its accessibility metadata.[93]

---

[91] "Cortana can extract contextual information from email messages and put it to good use, like automatically tracking a flight based on a confirmation email. Just markup your data according to Schema.org, using our markup tester for quick validation, and insert that data into your email message." See: "Allow users to automatically track key information they receive in emails, like flight confirmations." Microsoft Bing, https://www.bing.com/partners/tools#RegisterCortanaActions

[92] Myles Peacock, "The New Brand Narrative: Story-selling Metadata", Sept 25 2018, https://www.martechadvisor.com/articles/machine-learning-amp-ai/the-new-brand-narrative-storyselling-metadata/

[93] See: "Schema.org Metadata Integration Guide for EPUB 3", https://idpf.github.io/epub-guides/schema-org-integration/

Mobile apps

Customers get all kinds of information via mobile apps.

While people focus on only a handful of apps, the ones that get used are important. Apps are useful where customer loyalty and transactional behaviors need to be supported.

Users don't like to switch apps unnecessarily. Individual apps can be considered as silos. Apps should be connected using metadata.

On easy way to avoid app changing is to push information to a feed on the user's main screen. This is the approach of card UI, "cards" that are presented on screen. Cards can display information that's encoded with metadata standards.

Figure 12.1. UI cards can draw on metadata to support user interactions, as this example of Microsoft Flow illustrates. Source: Microsoft.

 Microsoft Flow

Pending approval

 Requested by **Miguel Garcia**
m.garcia@contoso.com

Date
submitted: 06/27/2017, 2:44 PM

Details: Please approve the awesome
               changes I made to this fantastic
               document.

Link: [Link to the awesome
               document.pptx]
               (http://awesomedocument)

Approve ∨   Reject ∨

An example of card UI working with metadata standards is the Microsoft Flow app — a smartphone app used in enterprise settings (Figure 12.1). Microsoft Flow can display cards displaying metadata using the MessageCard type in an extension of schema.org.

Another metadata standard relevant to mobile apps relates to app linking, which links web content to mobile apps.[94]

"App Links is an open standard to deep link to content in your app. When someone using your app shares content to Facebook or another App Links-enabled app you can create a link that makes it possible to jump back into your app from that piece of content. App Links work by adding metadata to existing URLs on the web so that they can be consumed by your app."[95]

Facebook notes: "Apps that link to your content can then use this metadata to deep-link into your app, take users to an app store to download the app, or take them directly to the web to view the content. This allows developers to provide the best possible experience for their users when linking to their content."[96]

---

[94] https://developers.facebook.com/docs/applinks

[95] App Links Overview,
https://developers.facebook.com/docs/applinks/overview
[96] Facebook, "App links reference",
https://developers.facebook.com/docs/applinks/metadata-reference

Messaging apps (bots)

Messaging apps have become common. While these bots vary in their technical approach, some are using external metadata standards to supply information in responses.

Facebook Messenger is a bot that lets people pay for products. Online merchants such as eBay are connecting their schema.org-defined product information to Facebook Messenger.

Many bots perform queries, much like search queries entered in a search box. The software fetches information described within metadata, and converts the information into a human-friendly format.

Figure 12.2. How Google uses schema vocabulary for query patterns. Source: Google.

Type	Example Query Pattern	Example User Query
$org.schema.type.Date	read my sms from $org.schema.type.Date:my_date on sms pro	read my sms from april 1st on sms pro
$org.schema.type.Number	blink the flashlight $org.schema.type.Number:number times	blink the flashlight five times
$org.schema.type.Time	read my sms from $org.schema.type.Time:my_time on sms pro	read my sms from 5 pm on sms pro
$org.schema.type.DayOfWeek	show me my meetings on$org.schema.type.DayOfWeek:day_of_week	show me my meetings on Tuesday
$org.schema.type.Color	turn on the $org.schema.type.Color:my_color strobe light	turn on the red strobe light

Google Assistant provides a "query pattern" (Figure 12.2) that utilizes schema.org metadata.[92] If a user asks: "Set temperature to 70 degrees Fahrenheit" this gets translated into a query pattern encoded as:

```
set temperature to $SchemaOrg_Number:num
degrees$SchemaOrg_Temperature:
```

Similarly, if they ask: "Show Italian restaurants", the pattern is:

```
show $SchemaOrg_servesCuisine:my_cuisine restaurants
```

Google also provides content-based actions that use information described in schema.org. They can consume schema.org recipes. "Users can follow your recipes through rich cards presented in the Google Assistant and learn about your content on the Assistant directory."[98]

---

[97] See "Query Patterns",
https://developers.google.com/actions/reference/rest/Shared.Types/QueryPatterns
[98] "Content Actions - Recipes",
https://developers.google.com/actions/content-actions/recipes

Voice apps and voice bots

Google Assistant provides voice interaction as well as text interaction. Voice interaction is also central to Amazon's Alexa, Apple's Siri, and Microsoft's Cortana.

Amazon's Alexa has become popular with customers within a short time period. When Alexa started, it relied on a custom set of properties. Since then Amazon has embraced external standards. It is cooperating with Microsoft to improve the interoperability of Alexa and Cortana. Amazon has also developed an ontology for Alexa called "The Alexa Meaning Representation Language" which incorporates and extends schema.org standards (Figure 12.3). Amazon notes: "The Alexa ontology utilized schema.org as its base and has been updated to include support for spoken language. In addition, using schema.org as the base of the Alexa Ontology means that it shares a vocabulary used by more than 10 million websites, which can be linked to the Alexa ontology."[99] Amazon's adoption of schema.org is another example of the value that external standards offer even to the largest of digital content publishers.

Figure 12.3. Alexa's Ontology. Source: Amazon.

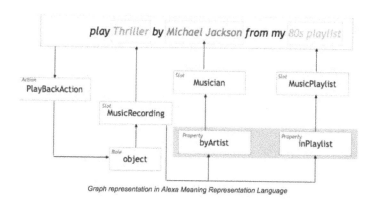

play Thriller by Michael Jackson from my 80s playlist

Graph representation in Alexa Meaning Representation Language

The Alexa Skills Kit supports SSML tags to indicate the pronunciation of words. SSML is another metadata standard useful for content in multiple channels as more content is read aloud.

Voice bots are commonly are built from APIs and kits. These tools don't necessarily expose standards-based metadata to developers. But the service may consume data that is represented in standards-based metadata. For example, both Google and Microsoft consume structured data from a person's email to present services.

Four kinds of information defined by metadata are used consumed by voice bots:

1. Information from knowledge graphs
2. Information from web pages encoded in schema.org
3. Information from open data references such as IMDb
4. Information embedded in personal messages such as emails

Figure 12.4. Metaphacts offers wikidata skills for Alexa. Source: Metaphacts.

Voice bots make possible new kinds of applications. For example, wellness applications can have a dialog with a user. Voice bots are also well-suited to coaching applications.

Search queries are an obvious application for voice bots, but voice interaction presents unique issues. Voice bots are "command line interfaces" — the user must say with precision what they want. Voice interaction doesn't afford the opportunity to scan or browse. So, recommendations need to be on target.

Metadata standards can improve the delivery information in voice interfaces, according to an academic research team that developed the "Slugbot" prototype for Amazon-sponsored Alexa prize.[100]

The Slugbot research project examined the kinds of information that's needed to support conversation. The research team looked at various user intents such as "to provide opinions, give or solicit information, contrast two possibilities, request the system to perform an action, and more."

The Slugbot team noted the benefits of relationships captured by ontologies that define related entities. "These types of relations can be used to instantiate the expansion relation, which basically captures moving to strongly related subtopics."

The team concluded: "Structured data can be easier to formulate into system responses and can often more easily handle on-topic follow-up questions, but is more limited in scope" since users might change topics abruptly.

The research team noted that integrating data from many sources is important to provide complete answers. Standardized metadata is important to transcend silos of information, and to allow information from different sources to be combined. "It is rare for a single resource to aggregate all the information that might be useful, so SlugBot must be able to leverage information and integrate information from multiple sources."

To support more human-like dialog, conversational designers should not presume people always have a specific information need. People seem to enjoy undirected chats about topics that interest them.

---

[99] http://aclweb.org/anthology/N18-3022

[100] See "Combining Search with Structured Data to Create a More Engaging User Experience in Open Domain Dialogue", https://arxiv.org/abs/1709.05411

In-Car entertainment

In-car entertainment is expected to become an important channel in the future. Currently, different platforms and automakers are developing alliances that will shape the use of standards in this channel. In-car entertainment will combine aspects of voice interfaces and mobile apps.

IoT metadata

The Internet of Things (IoT), which allows for device-to-device communication and interaction, is expected to grow in importance. There are efforts to develop metadata standards for IoT applications. A "Thing Description" (an extension to schema.org) has been created to describe different equipment or appliances parameters.[101]

Each IoT device represents another channel to manage. IoT devices generate data (known as telemetry), can process data, and can accept remote commands. Devices have their own metadata, indicating their ID, type, model, revision, date of manufacture, and hardware serial number.

With IoT, people will be able to communicate and interact with their environment. Examples of applications include:

- Personal data metadata (for example, light intensity exposure) that could be combined with other reference data (for example, the daily UV index)
- Bluetooth beacons (providing URIs for physical locations, or for fixed or movable objects) that can be linked to descriptions.

Machines have had the ability to post or get data for a long while. What's new is that machines gain the ability to act on data when it is described with semantic standards. The use of standard vocabularies shifts the emphasis from exchanging data, to helping devices understand the meaning of data.

A team at Siemens describes the benefits of **"semantic interoperability"**:[102]

"The integration of two or more physical devices should not only happen at the level of the data exchange but also understand the meaning of exchanged data. Instead of mere interoperability, the IoT devices are required to achieve semantic interoperability. Only then, it would be possible for machines to discover devices relevant for an added-value service, and further to understand their capabilities, to integrate and process their data, and to ultimately create a new value."

An IoT will be important for businesses with customers who want to interact remotely with their product and service — for example, by using an app to set a burglar alarm. Customers can also receive alerts: an air conditioner could trigger the sending of an email to its owner that its filter will need replacement.

[101] On the schema.org's vocabulary relationship to IoT, see "IoT Getting Started", https://iot.schema.org/docs/iot-gettingstarted.html

[102] "Shaping Device Descriptions to Achieve IoT Semantic Interoperability"

Email

Email is so familiar that we may not notice that it is getting smarter. Publishers sending emails can use the schema.org vocabulary to highlight important information in an email.[103]

Figure 12.5. Schema vocabulary supports actions relating to email. Source: Postmark.

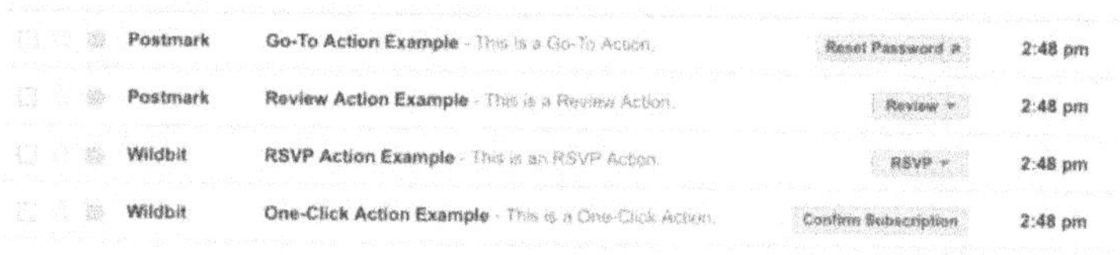

	Postmark	Go-To Action Example - This is a Go-To Action.	Reset Password ⇗	2:48 pm
	Postmark	Review Action Example - This is a Review Action.	Review ▾	2:48 pm
	Wildbit	RSVP Action Example - This is an RSVP Action.	RSVP ▾	2:48 pm
	Wildbit	One-Click Action Example - This is a One-Click Action.	Confirm Subscription	2:48 pm

Structured metadata in email can prompt users to take an action (Figure 12.5). For example, an invitation sent by email can ask for an RSVP (Figure 12.6). Google and Microsoft email clients are using this functionality, and other email clients could also start using actions as user awareness of the feature increases.

Figure 12.6. Schema.org vocabulary supports actions relating to email.
Source: Postmark.

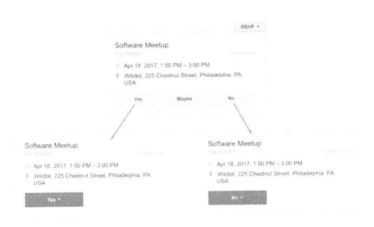

Google's Gmail supports schema.org actions (for more on actions, see Chapter 10.) Gmail lets publishers add a range of actions, such as:

- An RSVP Action for events
- A One-click Action for single click actions
- A Go-to Action for more complex interactions
- Interactive cards (for flights).

Microsoft explains how they use schema.org actions in both email and voice applications. A publisher can:

"send flight and reservation information in an email, which Cortana can extract and use to expose a related skill (such as track flights). Once you receive an initial flight confirmation email that contains the required markup, Cortana can automatically track updates and other changes to the flight from that point forward. No subsequent notifications are required."[104]

---

[103] See "Increase user engagement with actions in emails",
https://developers.google.com/gmail/markup/

[104] https://docs.microsoft.com/en-us/cortana/data-markup/structured-data-markup

Smart Home Devices

Connected devices can access metadata to enhance functionality. An example is the Niam, a high-end audio equipment maker. It sells a hard disk music player that can look up track information utilizing MusicBrainz metadata.

Google Assistant supports a range of home devices:

- Camera
- Dishwasher
- Dryer
- Light
- Outlet
- Refrigerator
- Switch
- Thermostat
- Vacuum
- Washer.

Actions for home devices at the time of this writing don't support the schema.org vocabulary, but this possibility seems likely in the future, especially as more appliances get touchscreen displays and have cloud-connected audio.

Physical world

How can metadata connect with physical things that are in our environment? How can people get more information about a building they see while traveling? If they encounter a physical object and want to know more about it, how can they retrieve more information?

Physical things need identifiers. While famous objects such as the Hope diamond or the Empire State Building have digital identities thanks to their entry in Wikipedia, less famous object such as the bus stop outside your home do not have an online address. Every item that could be described by metadata needs an online address — its own unique URL.

One big step in this direction is an initiative by GS1 to give products their own URI, which provides much more information than the basic GTIN barcode. The URI indicates the GTIN, Batch/Lot, Serial Number and Expiry Date.[105] This will allow people to scan a box of medicine or food to see if there is any recall information about it, or get additional information about the sourcing of ingredients.

The big task is matching computer identifiers with physical things so that people can get more information about an object. To return to the example of the bus stop, the user wants to know what bus routes will stop at a location, when they will come, and where they will go. They need to relate information about buses and travel routes to a specific object.

The user needs a way to identify an object, so he or she can get more information about it. This can be done through an image-recognition app such as Google Lens, or with RFID. Steve Macbeth of Microsoft, who has been active in the development of schema.org, believes that getting unique identifiers for physical things will be important. A simple solution could be to put a QR code on a physical label that's on or next to a thing in the world.

---

[105]   "GS1   Web   URI   Structure   Standard",
https://www.gs1.org/standards/Digital-Link/1-0

CHAPTER 13: REUSING INFORMATION

Publishers focus considerable attention to the creation of new information, even though much of their content involves reusing information. Sometimes publishers don't even know what information they have already discussed in their content.

> *"What facts are contained in this content? Today, it would take a person reading the content to figure that out. That level of granularity of information is simply not available."*[106]

-- James Powell and Matthew Hopkins

Content strategists are increasingly concerned with how to reuse content. But they rarely talk about how to reuse information that appears in content. It's important to distinguish reusing information from reusing content. Content is a unit of meaning — a larger message to convey. Content, whether in the form of explanations or diagrams, contains information. Online publishers can reuse information by reusing blocks of content (through what is known as *transclusion* or *content assembly*, Figure 13.1). Or they can reuse specific information without reusing the finished content.

Figure 13.1. Illustration of the transclusion process, where a content block (B) is reused in other content (A, P & Q). Source: Wikipedia.

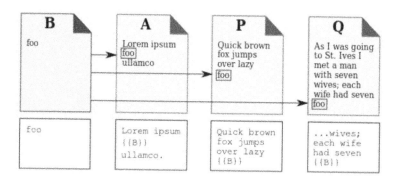

The easiest way to think about the relationship between content blocks and information elements is to consider wikipedia. Wikipedia pages are made up blocks (templated modules), which support both the reuse of content, and the reuse of information.

Sometimes more than one page will need to talk about the same material in the same way. Wikipedia allows multiple pages to include material for another page — the reuse of content. "When two pages need to discuss the same material in the same way, they can share a section. This involves creating a third page and transcluding that page onto both pages."[107]

Wikipedia pages commonly include an "infobox" module that contains information (Figure 13.2).

Figure 13.2. Example of part of a Wikipedia infobox describing an organization. On the left side are metadata properties sourced from wikidata. Some of the values on the right side are metadata entities in wikidata. Source: Wikipedia.

The content block (the infobox module) is populated by metadata (wikidata) (Figure 13.3). These metadata properties populate the information (values) presented in the infobox illustrated above.

Figure 13.3. Some of the wikidata properties that can populate an infobox about organizations. Source: Wikipedia.

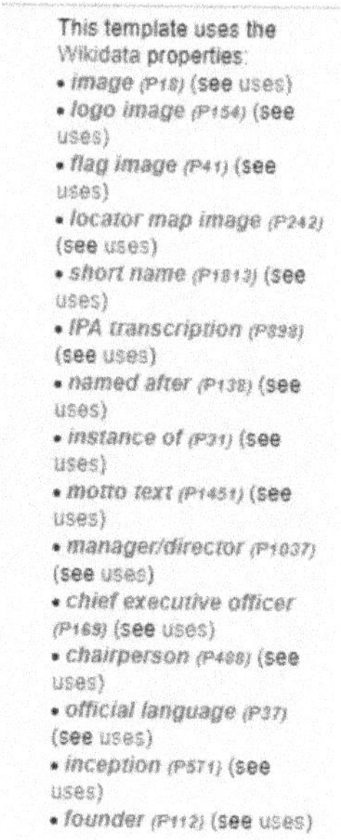

This template uses the Wikidata properties:
- *image* (P18) (see uses)
- *logo image* (P154) (see uses)
- *flag image* (P41) (see uses)
- *locator map image* (P242) (see uses)
- *short name* (P1813) (see uses)
- *IPA transcription* (P898) (see uses)
- *named after* (P138) (see uses)
- *instance of* (P31) (see uses)
- *motto text* (P1451) (see uses)
- *manager/director* (P1037) (see uses)
- *chief executive officer* (P169) (see uses)
- *chairperson* (P488) (see uses)
- *official language* (P37) (see uses)
- *inception* (P571) (see uses)
- *founder* (P112) (see uses)

The same metadata properties that populate the organization infobox can also be used to populate other modules. In other words, the specific information can be reused in different contexts.

It's easiest to reuse content when the information within the content doesn't change. The meaning stays the same, in whatever context the content appears.

When the information changes, the meaning of content shifts. The question arises whether the content is still talking about the same thing, or whether the subject of the content has changed. If the price changes, we assume the content is still talking about the same product. If the name changes, we infer the content is now talking about a different product.

Publishers have a strong motivation to reuse and manage granular details. These details can appear in many places: in different content, in different apps, in different channels, combined in different ways for different audiences. It pays to reuse information. It can save time and can reduce errors that could arise from re-keying or pasting the information from other places it is used. Publishers can centrally update values for an entity.

Information can be reused a range of ways, through:

1. **Content variations**: where the same information is shown in different presentations, for example, showing some or all properties related to an entity, or in a different format.
2. **Value variation**: showing changes in values over time, or showing high and low values.
3. **Information recontextualization** or remixing: showing the same information in different contexts, beside other information that is related in various ways
4. **Information repurposing**: using the same information to support distinctly different purposes.

Information can change on two levels. An entity (thing) has many potential properties (dimensions), each of which has many potential values. An entity (a description of a thing, location, person) can vary according to the properties it has, and the values of those properties.

Metadata identifies facts so they can be reused. It bridges the world of databases with the world of sentences, narratives and other content blocks that convey meaning. Information and content can both vary:

- Factual information stays the same, but the content using information varies (*both property and value reuse*)
- Factual information stays the same, and the content using information stays the same (*evergreen content — no reuse potential*)
- Factual information changes, and the content using information varies (*perishable content*)
- Factual information changes, but the content using information stays same (*property reuse only — no value reuse*)

Often content involves rearranging existing information. Publishers can tell new stories with the same core facts.

For example, as I write this book I presently live in the city of Hyderabad, India, which is represented in Wikidata by the identifier Q1361.[108] There are various other facts associated with Hyderabad that are available in Wikidata: that it was founded (P571) in 1592, that it has a population (P1082) of 9.3 million, that it is the capital (P1376) of Telangana state (Q677037), that it was once part of (P131) the Mughal Empire, that it is 500 meters above sea level (P2044), and that it has an airport code (P238) of HYD. This information could all be combined into an article focused on Hyderabad. Or only select items of information might be used as part of an article focused on broader or tangential topic, such as big cities. When entities have standard properties, they can be compared to similar entities in content easily.

Online publishers reuse certain factual information with regularity. They typically hold that information in a database, but not always. Databases can hold factual information, which includes information that is routinely revised such as prices, as well as information that doesn't change, such as the specifications of a product. CMSs can connect to databases, which can supply specific information that is injected into the content. For example, a .NET CMS will connect to a .NET database, while a PHP CMS would generally be connected to a PHP database. CMSs and databases are often joined together by the platform programming languages, rather than standard metadata vocabularies. Information described by vocabularies, in contrast, is platform-independent. Information described by standard metadata can be used by different applications, to support different use cases.

All kinds of content, from product descriptions to maps, involves variables: bits of information that change according to what information is requested. One of the most common ways publishers reuse information is by using variables within content templates. The template provides the organizational structure of the content presented to audiences, such as where to put headings and tables. The template can be filled in with text. But if some part of the text needs to change depending on circumstances, this text can be identified as a variable. This construction means that one template can present many variations. Tables are the most obvious form of a template populated by variable data, but many other kinds of templates use variables.

A variable built from external metadata standards might appear in code as $schema.book.name — which would indicate that the variable is the name of a book according to the schema.org metadata standard. Within a page template or an app, the variable signals: Put the relevant information here.

Mobile apps also use variables extensively. Again, a template design can present different information that is injected as variables. A common example is an app that displays the weather — the template provides a structure, where the data is displayed in the app changes. The same information can support different templates, which might be designed for different devices. The same metadata can also be used in interactive scripts, such as chatbots. A single set of metadata allows information to be used in any context.

When presented to audiences, the variable will sometimes appear with a label beside it, explicitly indicating what kind of property it is. That label can be different from the property name used in the metadata vocabulary. Other times the variable is placed within a sentence, heading or a paragraph, and the kind of property is implied to the user through the context.

Design considerations: Reusing properties, and reusing values

Content designers need to consider two dimensions of information: properties and values.

Property reuse happens at the template level. Reusing properties keeps the structure of content consistent, and allows content variations. A single template will generally present the same properties for all content built from the template. The properties appear as a "block": they appear together.

Fixed blocks of properties and values that get reused multiple times. An example would be an address block for a store location.

But even within templates, there can be some variation in which properties are displayed together. A property might not display in some contexts because:

- It is not a priority
- It is not relevant in some circumstances
- There is no value, so there is no reason to show the property.

By reusing blocks of properties, templates signal that information in the content is about related things.

But a single property can appear in different content templates. Different content types, built from different templates, will nonetheless share common properties such as the title or creator.

Property reuse indicates "include this kind of information here" but it doesn't tell us whether we are reusing the same information used elsewhere, or are using different information. We want to consider how information within the content will vary.

When information reuse involves reusing values, content designers need to consider how reusing factual details will relate to the context they are used. Different values sometimes indicate different entities. Other times, different values can refer to the same entity, if the value changes. If content talks about a product, but the name of the product has changed, we assume the content refers to a different product. If the content refers to different prices, it may be that price of the same product has changed.

Different kinds of values change at different frequencies. Values may be constant, or may be constantly changing. Content writers tend to think of variables as numbers, which of course can change. The temperature will change, while your name normally remains the same. But it is a mistake to think of text as fixed and numbers as variables. The value of number pi is a constant. The value of United Nations Secretary General's name is a variable, since there are many people who have served in that role.

Broadly, we can distinguish two kinds of values: persistent values and dynamic values.

With persistent values, the information is reused. The goal is factual consistency. Constant values are important when managing master data. Generally, a property has a persistent value. Comparing the values allows audiences to see how similar or dissimilar entities are. Content designers often reuse persistent values when certain information is required, but may have a secondary role. A classic example is what's known as "boilerplate" copy, such as disclaimers.

With dynamic values, the information is variable, the goal is factual timeliness. Here the focus may be a single entity has changed, rather than on comparing two entities.

More specifically, values have different characteristics within the persistent and dynamic groupings:

- Persistent (fixed)

  o **Canonical** record (immutable — write once only) : Can never be changed, such as a product ID
  o **Versioned** (rewritable): Will stay constant will long period, but will change periodically (such as the name of the current CEO)

- Dynamic (fluctuating)

  o **Random**: Can't anticipate value (for example, title of today's most popular article)
  o **Oscillating**: Value moves back and forth within a range (for example, an average rating)
  o **Cyclical**: Cycling through a limited number of allowed values (for example, indicating a "state" such as order status)
  o **Accretive** Values appended to other values (such as lists)
  o **Conditional values** Value depends on context (for example, nearest store).

Dynamic values are not persistent: they change over time. A property will have many values, though generally not at the same time. These values are dependent on time or another contextual dimension such as location.

Dynamic values aren't reused the same way persistent values are. With persistent values, the information can be copied from a source and placed into different content. With dynamic values, the information can exist in only one place, and needs to be delivered on demand at the time of publication to assure that it is timely.

Conditional values provide the possibility of changing what properties are displayed in different contexts, and what values get displayed for a given property.

No matter whether the values are persistent or dynamic, all content discussing the same entities should always show the same values for properties addressed at a given point in time. All the content, regardless of channel or platform, needs to present consistent factual information.

---

[106] James Powell and Matthew Hopkins, *Librarian's Guide to Graphs, Data and the Semantic Web*, (Chandos Publishing, 2015) p. 66

[107] "Wikipedia: Transclusion",
https://en.wikipedia.org/wiki/Wikipedia:Transclusion

[108] Wikidata entities begin with a Q, while properties begin with a P.

Knowledge Graphs

One of the most sweeping cases of information reuse is offered by knowledge graphs. Knowledge graphs were recently added to the Gartner "Emerging Technologies Hype Cycle", which will likely bring more attention to them.[109]

Knowledge graphs store a massive amount of information, and connect different facts together. They are similar to an ontology, but are often on a larger scale. The information included knowledge graphs is often sourced from information that has been published using metadata standards.[110] Knowledge graphs can themselves be built upon standard vocabularies, though not all are.

Knowledge graphs can be internal (which are called enterprise knowledge graphs), or they can be externally available.

The IPTC, a trade association for the news industry, has developed a knowledge base to track the relationship between concepts in the news. They note:

"Increasingly, news organizations are using entity extraction engines to find 'things' mentioned in news objects. The results of these automated processes may be checked and refined by journalists. The goal is to classify news as richly as possible and to identify people, organizations, places and other entities before sending it to customers, in order to increase its value and usefulness. This entity extraction process will throw up exceptions — unrecognized and potentially new concepts — that may need to be added to the Knowledge Base."[111]

The IPTC Knowledge Base workflow illustrates how Knowledge Graphs develop (Figure 13.4).

Figure 13.4. Content is scanned to find concepts. When they don't exist yet, the concept can be added to the knowledge base. Source: IPTC.

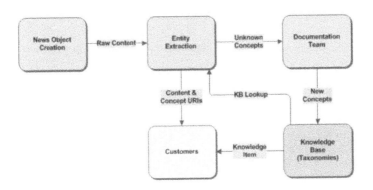

Most online publishers probably won't create their own knowledge graphs. But knowledge graphs are becoming increasingly important in everyday content, especially by search engines and social media platforms. They are becoming the source and record of much factual information. Many voice interaction platforms, where users can ask questions, rely on knowledge graphs to provide answers. Even if organizations don't build their own knowledge graphs, their information is likely to be incorporated in knowledge graphs built by other organizations.

Externally accessible knowledge graphs can represent general information, or domain-specific information.

An example of a domain-specific knowledge graph is the Thomson Reuters Knowledge Graph, which covers company information.

Externally accessible knowledge graphs aren't "open" in the sense they are free for anyone to use. Some knowledge graphs are available for consumers to access within a product. Other knowledge graphs are geared toward developers, who can access them through an API. The knowledge graphs themselves are generally proprietary, but they utilize information harvested from published metadata that utilizes widely-understood external standards.

A growing number of technology companies offer general purpose knowledge graphs in various forms. Some examples are:

- Bing's Knowledge and Action Graph (formerly Satori)
- Google Knowledge Graph

- Facebook's Entity Graph
- WolframAlpha
- Watson Discovery Knowledge Graph (IBM)
- DuckDuckGo.

Consumers may get information supplied by knowledge graphs and not be aware of its source. Both Google (Figure 12.5) and Microsoft offer their Knowledge Graphs as APIs, which can be integrated within customer-facing applications made by others.[112]

Figure 13.5. Google offers developers a widget that lets users search its knowledge graph. Source: Google.

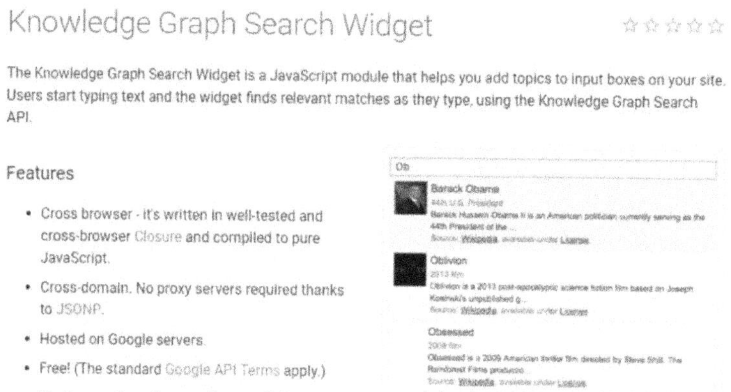

Bing pitches the benefits of its Knowledge and Action Graph to publishers: "Tap into 21 billion facts, 18 billion action links, and over five billion relationships between more than one billion people, places, and things. You can then use this info in your app to stop sending users to their browsers for more information."[113]

	Domain-specific	General purpose
Internal use	Enterprise KGs	Proprietary (e.g. Facebook's Entity Graph)
Externally accessible	Specialized KGs (e.g. Thomson Reuters)	Comprehensive (e.g. Bing and Google)

Because many customers will get information either directly or indirectly from these services, publishers will want information about their companies and products represented on knowledge graph services.

Unfortunately, most companies that create knowledge graphs are not very explicit about where all their information comes from. But a few knowledge graphs have provided a glimpse of how the acquire their information.

DuckDuckGo states: "Our instant answers come from a variety of sources, including Wikipedia, Wikia, CrunchBase, GitHub, WikiHow, The Free Dictionary — over 100 in total".[114]

Facebook has an internal knowledge graph that manages entities discussed within the Facebook community. A Facebook engineer explained:

"One of the early choices we made was selecting Wikipedia as the canonical set of things we would match against. We evaluated a few other data sets, but realized that the power law distribution of connections meant that in an edge-weighted sense, Wikipedia was at least as good (and often better) at representing the things users had included on their profiles as the other data sets, especially when it came to languages other than English. Plus, Wikipedia is open and constantly improving".[115]

A common theme in knowledge graphs is that Wikipedia is a core source of information, which is accessible as metadata through DBpedia. Wikidata, another member of the Wikipedia family, may also be an importance source.[116] Publishers will want to cross-reference information they publish with DBpedia and wikidata identifiers.[117] This will improve the likelihood that their information will be discovered and incorporated in various knowledge graphs.

Knowledge graphs represent the ultimate form of information reuse. They can answer an unlimited range of questions about any topic, and be accessed through any channel.

[109] Gartner places knowledge graphs slightly ahead of flying autonomous vehicles in terms of readiness and expectations, for what it's worth.

[110] Knowledge Graphs represent information about entities that are covered by the knowledge graph. It is a form of curation (see Chapter 16). This information is collected from many different sources. At times, information from different sources may be in conflict, and needs to be reconciled. While some information is collected using machine learning, it is easier to collect when the information is expressed using metdata standards. The information is likely to be more reliable as well when is it already structured with metadata.

[111] IPTC, "NewsML-G2 Guidelines: Knowledge Items",
https://www.iptc.org/std/NewsML-G2/guidelines/#knowledge-items

[112] See "Knowledge Graph Search API" at
https://developers.google.com/knowledge-graph/, and "Bing: Bing the Knowledge and Action Graph",
https://www.bing.com/partners/knowledgegraph

[113] https://www.bing.com/partners/knowledgegraph

[114] DuckDuckGo, https://duckduckgo.com/api

[115] Eric Sun, "Under the Hood: The Entities Graph",
https://www.facebook.com/notes/facebook-engineering/under-the-hood-the-entities-graph/10151490531588920/

[116] While extensive and freely available, these sources also contain some noisy data that needs to be vetted for clarity and accuracy.

[117] This can be done using sameAs to link to another ID elsewhere.

CHAPTER 14: SMART PROMOTION OF INFORMATION USING METADATA

Businesses and other organizations want to get their information in front of people who might be interested in it. To do that, they need to promote their information. Promotion differs from discovery, where the audience is actively looking for information. With promotion, the publishing organization is trying to raise awareness of information that audiences might not be explicitly looking for. In other cases, audiences may be interested in the information, but are not looking for it from a specific source.

Marketers tend to think about promotion as a campaign, or as a dialog, often on social media. They build awareness through postings, targeted ads, and other marketing tactics. Metadata is not normally used in traditional promotion.

It's possible, however, to utilize metadata to support awareness goals. Online publishers generally focus on directly promoting their content, and don't consider how metadata can indirectly support disseminating key information and messages that appear within different kinds of content.

Metadata makes information easier to exchange. As a result, the more widely metadata is used, the more widely information is exposed to audiences in different channels.

Promoting one's own metadata

Why might an online publisher promote their own metadata? Publishers can use metadata can build a critical mass of awareness about certain facts. Promotion may be passive if the publisher chooses not to publicize that it is disseminating these facts through metadata — the facts just start to appear more frequently within different content. Alternatively, publishers can actively promote dissemination, by publicly announcing that others should pay attention to certain kinds of facts. Both passive and active promotion can build awareness, but they differ in the level of attention expected.

Marketers like to emphasize to consumers a product characteristic they excel at, or that is of special interest to a specific customer segment. A company that makes gluten-free deserts will want to emphasize that it "contains no gluten". They can promote this information in metadata, by stating gs1:NutritionalClaimTypeCode-FREE_FROM_GLUTEN . Metadata can help build awareness of that message, and so customers start to pay closer attention to gluten-related statements in online information.

Many companies and organizations like to publicize certifications or recognition they've received. These bragging rights are sometimes important to consumers. They often are presented as evidence of a product or firm's quality. They include ratings, awards, accreditation, certification levels, and so on. Using the GS1 Web Vocabulary, publishers can indicate whether a product:

- Has a certification
- The certification agency
- The certification standard
- The certification value.

Such details can enhance consumer perception of a brand. Metadata can play other roles to promote information that can enhance brand positioning. Metadata can be used to highlight the heritage of a brand. Is IBM's Jeapardy-beating "Watson" AI system named after a Sherlock Holmes character, or a former IBM executive? If a company has a connection to some famous place or person, people might be looking for information about that place or person.[118] Metadata can highlight the connection: the company was founded by a famous person or the company is located in a famous place. Metadata can also highlight a famous trademark (brand logo) and define what the trademark means.

Online publishers can use metadata standards to get factual information about their organization into the "commons," so others can use this information in new ways. Organizations can contribute information to a range of community information projects including Wikidata that utilize metadata standards that enable the reuse of information. When facts about an organization are easy to access and repurpose, it increases the likelihood that others will be talking about these facts.

Figure 14.1. MusicBrainz URIs are widely used content to connect information relating to music. Source: MusicBrainz.

Uniform Resource Identifier

URIs can be constructed by prefixing the MBID with the address of the MusicBrainz server and the entity type, for example Queen's URI becomes http://musicbrainz.org/artist/0383dadf-2a4e-4d10-a46a-e9e041da8eb3i9, and Bohemian Rhapsody's URI becomes http://musicbrainz.org/recording/ebf79ba5-085e-48d2-9eb8-2d992fbf0f6d9.

An example of pooled metadata is MusicBrainz.[119] MusicBrainz is a community-contributed database of information about music albums that is available as a metadata service (Figure 14.1). Both individuals and publishers can contribute information to MusicBrainz.

MusicBrainz creates URIs to identify musical entities. The BBC has used these IDs, and also contributed data to the MusicBrainz project. Ticketmaster, Universal Music, Amazon, and Spotify all utilize the data. Given the wide use of MusicBrainz information, online publishers that work with music-related content will want to contribute their information to the MusicBrainz pool of data.

When musicians have standard IDs for their music, people can connect to the music (and related information about the music) in new ways. Developers are building services on top of MusicBraiz IDs. An example is AcoustID:

"AcoustID is a project providing complete audio identification service, based entirely on open source software. It consists of a client library for generating compact fingerprints from audio files, a large crowd-sourced database of audio fingerprints, many of which are linked to the MusicBrainz metadata database using their unique identifiers, and a web service that enables applications to quickly search in the fingerprint database."[120]

The MusicBrainz example raises a broader point. Publishers should make efforts to get key information about their organization and products into publicly accessible knowledge graphs. The best way to do that is to use "canonical" URLs and identifiers in metadata, so statements about one's organization and product can be discovered and connected to the knowledge graph.

Each knowledge graph will make its own judgments about what "facts" to incorporate. Publishers are frequently frustrated when they see information in knowledge graphs they consider incorrect and wonder where the information came from. If a publisher fails to assert facts about itself using standard metadata vocabularies, it runs the risk of being ignored, or even having competitors steal the limelight by having their competing assertions incorporated in a knowledge graph. More users are asking queries online such as "Who is the first...?" or "Which is the biggest...?" How facts are presented in metadata matters.

---

[118] For example, a company can be related to a city or town in a knowledge graph through a point of interest. The town of Corning, New York has as a point of interest the Corning Museum of Glass, and is headquarters to Corning Inc.

[119] While not positioned as a knowledge graph, MusicBrainz shares some aspects of one. It is used in Google's Knowledge Graph.

[120] "AcoustID", https://acoustid.org/

Promoting the reuse your metadata by others

Some commercial organizations are encouraging other publishers to use their metadata. Getting other publishers to reuse one's metadata can help spread that information and build authority.

Thomson Reuters, the business information publisher, is one firm doing this (Figure 14.2). To track the many companies and directors who appear in their content, they have created a series of identifiers called Thomson Reuters Perm ID (Permanent Identifiers).[121] Thomson Reuters allows others publishers to use their IDs in their metadata through a "free and open license." Such sharing helps to link external content to Reuters content.[122]

Figure 14.2. Thomson Reuter's PermID is freely available metadata identifying corporate entities. Source: Thomson Reuters.

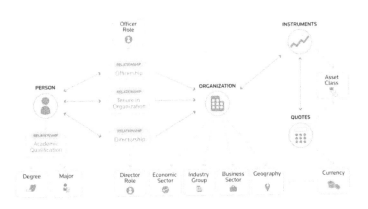

An even more extensive example is the scientific publisher, Springer Nature. Springer Nature is interested in getting researchers to use their content. This content is related to various research projects, topics, conferences, and events. Their goal is to help others understand the wider context of their content.

Figure 14.3. SciGraph provides metadata that others can reuse. Source: Springer Nature.

Springer Nature SciGraph is a database of metadata about scientific research, containing a billion metadata statements (Figure 13.3). It links data about organizations, events, concepts, and publications.

SciGraph provides freely available data that let users explore the relationships between authors, institutions, locations, fields of study, funders, conferences, research grants, citations, clinical trials, and patents.[123]

Why would Springer Nature create all this metadata and give it away for free? The metadata helps to promote their content. It not only makes content more discoverable, but it also makes the content more valuable, providing new insights for researchers. Researchers may become more interested in the content when they see the connections. And they will want to explore the metadata because it is not only focused on information within the article content. The Springer Nature SciGraph embodies one of the best features of standardized metadata: it is multipurpose.

[121] "PermID", https://permid.org/

[122] Thomson Reuters also uses a freemium model, where basic metadata is CC-BY 4.0, but extended metadata is CC-NC 4.0, meaning that commercial users need to pay a license to use the extended metadata. "Open PermID Terms and Conditions", https://permid.org/terms#organizations

[123] See "Springer Nature platform now holds a billion metadata statements", https://www.researchinformation.info/news/springer-nature-platform-now-holds-billion-metadata-statements

Increasing the visibility of specific dimensions of a topic

To increase awareness of an issue, a company or organization can encourage others to address a specific factual indicator related to the issue in their content. A publisher can promote the use of properties or values that either they've created, or that they advocate. Such promotion gets others focused on following indicators related to issues that the publisher cares about for either policy or marketing reasons. An example would be when appliance or machinery manufacturers promote awareness of "kitemarks",[124] or various energy efficiency ratings. Civic or environmental groups might promote awareness of indexes such as the air quality index (AQI).

Another scenario would be a prize committee that wants to encourage recipients to publicize their winning a prize. Winners who publicize their accomplishment simultaneously promote awareness of the prize. Third-party publishers may be interested in aggregating all people or products that have won a prize.

If an individual or firm has won an award, that's only meaningful to others if they have heard of the award before. The winner of the award has an incentive to publicize that they won the award, and have that event cited by others. When the award is cited using metadata standards, the profile of the prize increases.

Metadata can be used to publicize information about a new concept by combining two or more properties. For example, a "design prize" can be indicated as an "award" conferred by an "awarding organization". The GS1 Web Vocabulary has a property gs1:awardPrize that covers an award or prize given to the product.

---

[124] "Kitemark", https://en.wikipedia.org/wiki/Kitemark

Advocating that others reuse other publisher's metadata

It may not be obvious why a publisher would advocate for the use of metadata that was created by other publishers. Yet metadata becomes more powerful and useful the more people who use it. Online publishers can have an incentive to expand the availability of third-party metadata about a common topic. They can benefit by encouraging others to use metadata that they use themselves. Online publishers can benefit by advocating wider use by others of existing metadata standards.

More detailed metadata can deliver new audiences to information. Metadata defined by external standards can be combined from different sources, which adds detail and richness to information. The ability to integrate information from different sources is synergistic. Different information properties can be be combined for a more complete profile, and different values can be added together to provide more complete information.

A good example of how different parties can share mutual interests is provided by a tourism-related case study. The case study relates to tourism in the Tyrol region of Austria.

A regional tourism board is responsible for marketing the region on behalf of its members. While hotels are direct competitors, all have a common interest in promoting regional tourism. Likewise, regional tourist sites and cultural events are complements to hotels. Sites and events depend on tourists staying at hotels for ticket sales and entry fees, while tourist hotels depend on these activities to draw guests. Significantly, the prospective visitor has an interest in seeing an integrated view of offerings available. They are planning their visit around a time period and will want to know what room availability coincides with specific activities happening during the time of their visit.

Visitors don't want to deal with different silos of information, needing to visit individual websites powered by separate databases. They want to use a portal or app to get all the information they seek in one place. Standard metadata vocabularies could combine information from different sources, "enabling data query from distributed sources, topical or location based data integration, matching of service providers and requesters, as well as transactional web services for tourists."[125]

A research team at the University of Innsbruck (based within the Tyrolean region of Austria) has explored the possibilities of using semantic metadata standards to combine tourism-related information from different sources. When assessing the current state of systems, they encountered many silos, nothing that "a lot of data [is] stored in the databases of proprietary software and served with an API."

They faced the task of how to combine information that is sourced from different sources. By describing the information from each source using a common metadata vocabulary, all information would be visible on search engines, and could be pulled into a portal to support common transactions.

The research team developed a proof of concept that explored what is needed to convert data in different local databases into a common format. Their research continues on ways to break down silos in the local tourism sector. The Innsbruck research team concludes:

"More than just for increasing online visibility on search engines, a semantically annotated content of touristic service providers within a region could contribute to the tourism information system of the region. ... [W]e believe that the seamless interoperability among organizations which is still an issue in the tourism industry can be solved by semantic web technologies including semantic annotations."[126]

The tourism sector is one of many where firms can collaborate to promote related information. Competitive and complementary businesses can collectively benefit when their information is integrated and made more easily available to users. The Tyrolean tourism example shows the importance of metadata standards to enable the sharing of information across firms and sectors.

---

[125] Z. Akbar, et al. (2017) "Complete Semantics to Empower Touristic Service Providers". In: Panetto H. et al. (eds) *On the Move to Meaningful Internet Systems*. OTM 2017 Conferences. OTM 2017. Lecture Notes in Computer Science, vol 10574. Springer

[126] Akbar Z., et al., *ibid.*

CHAPTER 15: USING METADATA FOR CURATION AND RECOMMENDATIONS

C uration may sound artistic. Most online publishers consider it a labor-intensive activity. It has lost much of its buzz in recent years. But curation, when used with metadata, can be a serious strategy to increase content engagement. Curation can attract attention from target audience segments. And curation can be a way to extract more value from existing content.

Sources to curate

Curation is an approach, not a product or a content type. Curation can take many forms. Online publishers can act as a curator of information, and they can facilitate the curation of their information by others.

Curation can integrate information from multiple sources relating to specific topics. Metadata can provide a mechanism to match sources and topics. For example, the BBC has curated UK regional news using metadata properties such as coveredBy and createdBy. Different sources of information specialize in covering different regions. The BBC curated these different sources to offer greater breadth and depth in its coverage of regional news.[127]

Curation can integrate different types of information about a common topic. For example, a source may want to integrate data relating to a company from a CrunchBase database and link it to articles about that company.

Some firms curate publicly disclosed information, by aggregating it and cleaning it up. Public Now does this, and then distributes it as a NewsML feed.[128]. Its goal is to find high-value information that could be actionable for an investor.

In addition to bridging fragmented information, curation can select information based on its importance to readers. Online publishers can even curate their own content, selecting highly specific content for a targeted audience on a targeted theme. When curating one's own content, curation may involve shifting the delivery channel, such as gathering content of interest from websites, and then distributing it by email to newsletter subscribers.

Metadata can help other publishers discover and curate one's content and information. Metadata assists with automated curation. The host will get content from others, through APIs, feeds, or by crawls, and look for metadata that match profiled topics of interest. Even though publishers have a limited ability to influence the precise choices in automated curation by third parties, their use metadata will improve their visibility and the opportunities to get additional exposure.

Audiences face an endless stream of information that's available. From their perspective, these feeds are a firehose. How can they not miss something they want to see, without being distracted by information that is not as important?

The relevance of material assembled depends on the purpose of the curation. Online publishers may approach curation in various ways:

- Defragging: consolidating different kinds of information
- Thematizing: collecting similar items
- Alternative perspectives on a topic
- Notability.

---

[127]Jeremy Tarling, "coveredBy and createdBy: using linked data for editorial curation" *Medium*, https://medium.com/@jeremytarling/coveredby-and-createdby-c1a622e5d6f4

[128] https://www.publicnow.com/home

Defragging

For the first approach, we will borrow the term "defragging" from the field of computer storage. Defragging means to "reduce fragmentation ... by moving separated parts into a contiguous location."[129] Curation can transcend the fragmentation of information, by assembling related information in one place.

Curation offers values when linking two different types of information together through common metadata identifiers.

An example of a defragging approach to curation is offered by Thomson Reuters. Information about companies exists in different formats. Some of it is text that can lack structure, while other information is highly structured financial data. Thomson Reuters curates information by using a metadata property called PermID. They note:

The ability to move seamlessly between textual content and the relevant numbers adds huge value. By integrating content from Thomson Reuters, you can use the PermIDs embedded in our data to allow users to go directly from the companies, instruments, people, and events found in unstructured content to relevant data on financials, estimates, prices, officers, deals, and more".[130]

---

[129] "Defragging" definition in Wikidictionary

[130] Thomson Reuters, "Reduce The Cost Of Linking Unstructured Content To Financial Data",
https://financial.thomsonreuters.com/content/dam/openweb/documents/pdf/financial/intelligent-tagging-search-brochure.pdf

Thematizing

Thematize is a technical term that means "to make something (such as an idea) a theme or framework".[131] It captures one of the functions of curation: finding connections for content that's related to a theme. Curation looks for what's similar, not what's the same. Economists refer to similar items as "complementary goods".

> "*Algorithmic curation is definitely getting better, but it won't have a discerning taste or a unique point of view.*"[132]

-- Michael Bhaskar

Themes can be selected by audiences, or by publishers. Themes are often more subjective in character. For example, fashion trends get named but can be hard to define. But specific items of clothing, hairstyles, or colors, can be palpable examples of a fashion trend, and help to give it concreteness.

Similarly, curation allows the collection of information and content that is similar, and the characteristics of the examples in the collection can be better understood through metadata.

Metadata can facilitate curation by audiences. The best-known example is Pinterest, whose "pins" utilize schema.org metadata.

Pinterest gathers content that is assembled under a *user-defined* category — the Pinterest "board". Boards often feature different entities which have specific properties defined in schema.org. For example, a board on party ideas could have different kinds of products, which could be associated with a party, potentially even non-traditional ones. These can be shared with followers through a feed. That forms a graph between topics, entities, properties, and people. The curation of content can allow the aggregation of metadata to reveal insights. Pinterest is able to report on food trends based on what their users pin.

An example of *publisher-defined* curation is provided by Europeana, the EU-based arts consortium. Europeana relies extensively on metadata about artworks to promote discovery by audiences of similar items:

"Europeana offers visitors 'Similar Items' to encourage them to move between related pieces of information and find out more about artifacts, based on their own interests. For example, searches on Mona Lisa now turn up tens or even hundreds of results. Europeana also offers an 'Explore' button and hosts dozens of online 'Exhibitions' to encourage further discovery."[133]

---

[131] "Thematize" definition from Merriam Webster, https://www.merriam-webster.com/dictionary/thematize

[132] Michael Bhaskar, *Curation*, p. 114

[133] "Real-Time Graph Search of Millions of Artworks Powered by Neo4j", https://neo4j.com/case-studies/europeana/

Alternative perspectives

Everyone has an opinion, though no person's opinion will necessarily be complete and fully accurate.

Figure 15.1. Quora saw an opportunity to improve the curation of its topics by using metadata standards. Source: Quora.

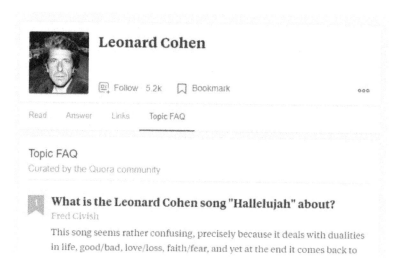

Numerous websites solicit user opinions about products, restaurants, and music. Quora focuses on factual questions that can relate to any topic. Quora hosts user-contributed questions and answers that are curated around topics, which could be the James Bond film series, kittens, Chicago, or Leonard Cohen (Figure 15.1). These topics are mapped to Wikidata (Figure 15.2):

"The mapping of topics to Wikidata will let us improve the quality of topics by giving us more signals about what the topics are about, letting us be more sophisticated in how we use topics to personalize your Quora experience."

Figure 15.2. Quora topics are mapped to Wikidata. Source: Wikidata.

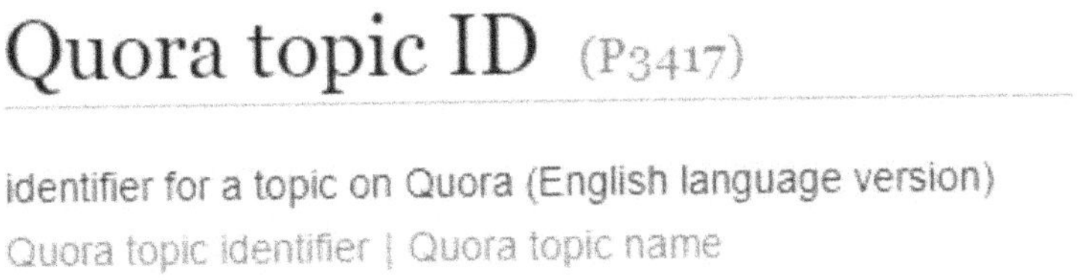

Quora topic ID (P3417)

identifier for a topic on Quora (English language version)
Quora topic identifier | Quora topic name

Quora notes that Wikidata metadata helps them curate the topics more effectively: "The relationships in Wikidata provide Quora with information that will allow us to fill in missing details about topics" which includes "relationships between topics, such as parent topics, that let us fill out structured information about each topic and identification of duplicate topics, particularly topics labeled with obscure acronyms."[134]

---

[134]   "Announcing   Wikidata   References   on   Topics",
https://blog.quora.com/Announcing-Wikidata-References-on-Topics

Notability

> *"Good curation helps the new, the unexpected; bad curation just confirms what you already want."*[135]

-- Michael Bhaskar

With so much information continuously available, curation helps with "parsing vast amounts of noise for the signal" to facilitate "discovery of the long tail of content."[136]

Event-centric curation is a common approach. Online publishers provide highlights of events that may unfold over a period of time, and will sometimes connect these events related entities.

A basic purpose of curation is to select what's important. When audiences face the prospect of too much information, curation is a way to not only isolate relevant content, but to package together information that is related, so that the package is more than the sum of its parts.

As Zeinab Abbassi of Columbia University notes that curation is a tool to help audiences tame the firehose of information they encounter daily:

"Users have limited time to sift through contents in their stream. The curation function by the aggregator then must take this into account by choosing a relatively small set of contents that followers would find most interesting."[137]

---

[135] Michael Bhaskar, *Curation*, p. 209

[136] Quotes from Michael Bhaskar, *Curation*, p. 217 and p.225

[137] Zeinab Abbassi et al "Distributed Content Curation on the Web", *ACM Transactions on Internet Technology (TOIT)*, Volume 14 Issue 2-3, October 2014. http://www.eurecom.fr/~loiseau/W-PIN%2BNetEcon2013/papers/Abbassi.pdf

Recommendation engines

Whereas curation represents the choices that a publisher considers most interesting, recommendations represent choices that the publisher thinks are most relevant to a specific person in a specific context.

The challenge of recommendations is making them personal. That requires connecting many different pieces of information together. Recommendations engines are pervasive, but many of their recommendations don't feel truly relevant.

To improve the relevance of recommendation engines, some online publishers are exploring the use of linked data and graph databases, which connect different pieces of information expressed in metadata. EBay is among those investigating this approach.

Figure 15.3. EBay's Shopbot provided recommendations on Facebook messenger, by utilizing metadata. Source: eBay.

EBay's "ShopBot" is a shopping recommendation engine that uses linked metadata stored in a graph database to provide product recommendations (Figure 15.3). ShopBot draws on schema.org vocabulary metadata that eBay created as a result of its "Structured Data Initiative." The bot allows customers to specify what they want via text, voice, or photo search.

EBay uses graph software "because existing product searches and recommendation engines were unable to provide or infer contextual information within a shopping request." Connecting product metadata to the user's context is important to make relevant recommendations. According to eBay's Chief Product Officer:

"Consider the information implied within the phrase, 'My wife and I are going camping in the Lake District next week, we need a tent.' Most search engines would just react to the word 'tent' – so all that additional context regarding location, temperature, tent size, scenery, etc. is typically lost, though specific information is actually what informs many buying decisions."[138]

The example of tent shopping shows how recommendation engines need to consider all the contextual information, not just react to a keyword, as is done by most chatbots today. The ability of metadata to weave together different dimensions associated with a user need improves the relevance of the recommendation measurably.

After a two year trial, eBay announced it was stopping the ShopBot feature on Facebook Messenger, but would be incorporating its features into Google Assistant and other apps (Figure 15.4).

Figure 15.4. EBay's Shopbot provided recommendations on Facebook Messenger, by utilizing metadata. Source: eBay.

The evolution of eBay's recommendation engine shows that technology and channels are in constant flux. But solid metadata can allow online publishers to pivot when required.

---

[138] quoted in Emil Eifrem, "Creating The Most Sophisticated Recommendations Using Native Graphs", https://www.cbronline.com/opinion/creating-sophisticated-recommendations-native-graphs

CHAPTER 16: IMPROVING OPERATIONAL COORDINATION USING METADATA

The way that many web teams coordinate their activities is not based on a shared awareness of common needs. Communication is accomplished through a relay. Web teams have an ongoing series of person-to-person chats about issues that are often loosely defined. They hold serial conversations about work to do. But frequently these conversations are focused on specific tasks that can seem unconnected to the work of other teammates. Fortunately, there's a solution to this task fragmentation. Teams can improve their coordination by using metadata. Web metadata can provide a common language to define and track outcomes in web work.

Most online publishers under-utilize metadata in their operations. Instead of treating metadata as a shared language, they treat metadata as having only a limited role. They view metadata as serving a narrow technical function, such as helping with their SEO visibility or tracking the date when a content item was created. While metadata supports those tasks, it can serve a much broader role. Metadata can connect content to the activities and goals of an organization. It can help web teams understand how content is performing. These insights are useful to everyone on a team, whether they are involved with editorial work, technical work, or analytic work. Metadata can improve operational coordination, by providing a common language for everyone to use.

Operational silos exist in different guises. They may be disconnected groups of people, incompatible information, or disconnected IT systems.

Silos are storage containers, originally for storing corn or other grains. A couple of synonyms for silos are repositories and warehouses. We often find these terms being used by data architects, who talk about "data repositories" and "data warehouses." Such containers may contain useful information, but they are cut off from the rest of the company, accessible to only a few people, who need specialized knowledge to understand and act on the fine-grained information.

Silos are more than hypothetical problem to guard against. They are hindering the operations of many publishers. According to a survey of business users by one metadata management tool vendor, the majority of users indicated they had the following problems:[139]

- Can't use metadata for impact analysis and/or to facilitate integration (*61% agree*)
- Can't connect all types of metadata – e.g., technical, business, operational (*54% agree*)
- Find it hard to ensure access and collaboration across all data stakeholders (*59% agree*)
- Can't see an integrated view across metadata for all data sources (*56% agree*).

The survey highlights the kinds of problems that business organizations face. Tools can help with overcoming these problems, but technology by itself won't solve these issues.

Developing a common worldview

To escape the pull of silos, all stakeholders involved with online information should be moving in the same direction, and have a common frame of reference. They should coordinate what they are working on, supporting each other, and not working at cross-purposes.

Coordination is hindered when information is:

1. Described in different ways by different teams that need to work with each other

2. Held in different systems that are not accessible to everyone.

Organizations can coordinate more effectively when they follow a common way of classifying and describing things, what is referred to as a *schema*. Like the word silo, schema is another word of Greek origin. According to Merriam-Webster, a schema provides a "structured framework." A schema involves a "particular organized way of perceiving cognitively and responding to a complex situation."[140] The schema that the organization uses influences how work gets done.

When there's no common schema, it's harder to work together and get tasks done. Different silos within an organization think about information in different ways. These include terminology problems, scaling problems (granularity of properties and values tracked), and missing metadata (differing priorities about the importance of metadata). These have their origin in the different worldviews of different stakeholders, and are manifested in the different systems these people use to perform their work.

Different worldviews can arise from:

- Different but related lines of business doing parallel work
- Different geographies doing parallel work
- Different functional roles performing related work.

Metadata can be used to bridge different cultures within an organization. To accomplish that, organizations need to harmonize publicly-facing content delivered to customers with internally-facing information used to run the business. They need common semantics. They should use external vocabularies that are already available.

Opportunities for common metadata exist across business functions, both "front stage" customer tasks and "backstage" support tasks. These include:

- Product information (IDs, naming, properties)
- Orders (confirmation numbers, order status)
- Invoices (billing and payment information)

- Services information (descriptions, start/end times, locations, pricing), including more specifically

   o Information related to financial services
   o Information related hotel services
- Location information of outlets (e.g., for tourism, restaurants)

- Event information (for entertainment, education, and other services).

For example, when customers buy goods or services online, they will want to know about their order status. This information is processed by backend systems that are used by logistical staff working on inventory and delivery. The customer will access this information by accessing their account portal or receiving an email. All this order status information can be described by the schema.org OrderStatus entity type, which can indicate:

- OrderCancelled
- OrderDelivered
- OrderInTransit
- OrderPaymentDue
- OrderPickupAvailable
- OrderProblem
- OrderProcessing
- OrderReturned.

Even if the staff handling these issues don't directly interact with customers, their actions affect the customer experience. It is important that information is consistent for all parties involved.

Content is needed to explain the order status, which must coordinate with a process to fulfill the order. If a team realizes there is a problem with orders (such as returns or cancellations), they may want to look at content relating to order status to see if anything can be improved.

Let's return to an item that's for sale online. Is it in stock and ready to ship? The inventory management database indicates that it is, but customers want to see that information in their search results in Google. If a competitor shows that the item is in stock on Google but you don't show that, the competitor might get the business. Sellers need to get the information stored in an inventory management database (which talks about "SKUs" rather than GTINs) into standards-compliant web metadata that Google can use. That requires good integration across their operations.

External metadata vocabularies may not provide the granularity needed in every case. But they should be used where possible, to link the public web content to other activities. IDs can provide a bridge between the two worlds. In some domains, such as autos and health, specialized vocabularies are now available.

External metadata standards can help organizations in the execution of tasks. It can support tasks involving:

1. **Coordination** (tracking the same goals)
2. **Collaboration** (working toward the same goals)
3. **Interoperability** (exchanging information)
4. **Integration** (using common systems).

---

[139] Irene Polikoff, "Polling Results: Feedback from companies across industries on what they can't do with their metadata management tools. Do you agree?" (TopBraid survey), https://www.linkedin.com/pulse/polling-results-feedback-from-companies-across-what-cant-polikoff

[140] "Schema", https://www.merriam-webster.com/dictionary/schema

Coordination

Businesses need to coordinate their operations across different groups and functions. These operations include:

1. Project execution, such as building new functionality or adding new content types
2. Process routines, such as workflows
3. Planning, goal-setting, and prioritization.

Most business activity is coordinated around time. Project managers reconcile different streams of activities and look at dependencies between them. One stream says they need some other input in order to start or complete their activity. The different activities seem related only in time. They lack semantic description.

Metadata makes it possible for different functions, with different goals, to coordinate their activities by referring to a common reference. This is important because often different functions will be working on tasks related to a given project output at different times. After the handoff, the discussion stops. The party handing off is already working on a different task.

Metadata bridges the mental models of different teams. "Teams" refer to various groupings of staff who have common responsibilities. Teams come in many types: informal, temporary, or permanent. They can be project-oriented; functional, defined according to expertise; accounts-based, related to products or P&L reporting; or geographically-based. In some cases, larger teams will be formally designated departments or divisions of an organization. Teams can be diverse in their makeup but need to work toward common goals. They need to think about objectives using a common frame of reference. Metadata can help teams have a common frame of reference.

Metadata can help teams diagnose problems. Consider a web team that supports a website that sells products. Potential customers use search engines to locate information about the kind of products that the firm sells. An SEO team member makes sure that the key features of products are visible in search results. The editorial and design team members make sure the content presented is compelling. An analytics team member measures how many views every page receives. The technical team makes sure that content is delivered responsively and smoothly. Despite everyone's good efforts, for some reason one of the products isn't selling well. On many project teams, this situation would trigger a series of discussions and brainstorms about what's not working and why.

Now suppose everyone working on the project was able to discuss their work and responsibilities in terms of a common frame of reference. Discussions would be easier, especially when the team is responsible for a large volume of content. Metadata can offer a common reference for everyone. The web content relates to a specific GTIN, which is indicated with metadata (a GTIN is the product code that is found on product packaging). Although few customers care about GTINs, GTINs are very useful as content metadata. Customers search for names and features of products. They find content about products with these names and features, and each product has a GTIN. GTINs are linked to product names and product features in the metadata. Every content item about a product is associated with a GTIN.

The analytics team members can track how well content is performing according to GTIN. They may notice that while customers seem to be interested in information associated with a certain GTIN, they aren't convinced by certain content that features that GTIN. It turns out that whenever customers see a certain photo of the product, they are less likely to buy it. Apparently, they don't like the color yellow, which was the background color in the photo showing the product. No problem, however. The product manager and editorial staff check their Digital Asset Management repository to see if there are other photos available of the product. Fortunately, all these photos are tagged with GTINs, and a photo of the product with a different background color is found. The alternative photo is pushed to the website, and the problem is fixed.

In this example, the culprit was editorial (background color). But in a different scenario, the content could have a technical problem, such as video with a glitch, or an SEO issue, such as missing values. Whatever the issue, common metadata descriptions allow all web team members to coordinate their discussions.

Collaboration

The potential for coordination extends beyond communication tasks. Suppose an organization hosts events for customers in different cities. They may create content about specific event locations. They are also interested in monitoring business results of events in different locations. When this information about locations is described with standard vocabularies, both content writers and event planners are better able to collaborate to review data to decide the best locations for future events. Content reporting metrics and business reporting metrics can be aligned and compared.

Few web teams have team-wide discussions about the metadata used in their content. Metadata, when discussed, is most often a topic of a side conversation, not a team conversation. For many team members, metadata is a problem for someone else to deal with. That attitude can create a blind spot for teams and can hinder their overall effectiveness. That attitude, that metadata is someone else's worry, hinders opportunities for collaboration.

Collaboration needs to happen at different levels:

- High-level goals everyone is working toward
- Mid-level goals that vary by function
- Tactical issues that require joint resolution.

Even within the content domain, there are different functions that require collaboration:

- Planning
- Developing
- Managing
- Delivering
- Assessing.

Because different staff are working on different phases of content, it can be hard to follow how all these separate activities connect together.

One way to improve collaboration is by planning around goals in addition to planning around tasks. Each member of a project team should ideally understand the common goal they are working toward, and how they are individually contributing to it. That goal is not just the delivery of a project, but more broadly it is the purpose of the project. Metadata helps to bring visibility to critical customer-facing information that is necessary for a project to realize its purpose. As teams design, build, and test, they will iterate their planning to incorporate new insights. They will refine their understanding of what data values are most important to their business or organization, and will make sure these data values are adequately represented in the metadata.

Metadata can help teams understand how published content is performing, so that content is effective and delivering value. The insights gained looking at the performance of published content will provide useful feedback for cross-functional teams to plan future content as well.

Interoperability

Interoperability refers to coordination at the process and systems level. Large organizations have many systems and processes. These tend to be "connected and distributed." They need to link, reference, and exchange data with each other.

On the process level, standardized metadata can help support cross-domain interoperability: how different groups of stakeholder refer to information.

On the systems level, metadata standards can support the exchange of information between systems, such as:

- Marketing Resource Management
- Product Information Management
- Enterprise Resource Planning.

Metadata standards make information interoperable: facilitating the sharing of information, and coordination of tasks using common information. As noted earlier when discussing standards, the concept of interoperability doesn't mandate that all parties use the exact same terminology labels. But it does require that all terminology used in different systems and processes can be mapped to a common standard, so that information can be shared across different groups. It provides a way to translate different labels into a common language. Fortunately, mapping how different terms are equivalent and related is possible using a SKOS-defined thesaurus. RDF data can connect different sets of information to present a richer graph of information.

Metadata schemas support interoperability and make information more useful, by providing:

- Vocabulary: terms used for properties
- Rules: whether the term is used properly (the values are correct)
- The ability to make statements about things
- Support for query: the ability to find out.

Interoperable metadata provides *disambiguation* of different terminology labels. It can indicate distinctions that are important to different stakeholders, such as broader and narrower terms, and can show how different labels overlap.

When organizations adopt external standards for metadata, their information can exist on different systems yet remain accessible. Such standards can support federated searching, where different sources are searched together at once.

[141] SKOS is a basic metadata vocabulary used to create thesauri and taxonomies.

Integration

Standardized metadata by itself doesn't trigger operational or systems integration. But should an organization decide to pursue such integration, standardized metadata will be needed.

The choice of whether or not to integrate will depend on many business factors. Systems integration may not be required nor will it necessarily be the best solution. Some use cases benefit from centralized systems, but others don't. Centralized systems require that all users can understand how to use them and are able to. Small centralized teams might find centralized systems easier to use than large distributed teams would.

When systems integration is desirable, metadata helps make it possible by getting everyone to follow a common framework defining entities, properties, and values.

One significant scenario arises when one firm acquires another, or two firms merge. In such cases systems integration is imperative. The costs and efforts associated with system integration can be monumental when each is following their own custom metadata standards. Post-merger integration costs are reduced when the parties are following external metadata standards.

Another scenario where metadata can help web teams better integrate is by enabling the re-use of content and re-use of designs. Publishers already have a lot of content, but may want to present it differently. They might want to put their location information in a map or put events into a table or a timeline. Teams will have more flexibility when they have content that predictably follows metadata standards. Existing designs can accommodate new content that is structured using standard metadata vocabularies. The emerging area of web components and semantic metadata standards complement each other and can offer important synergies.

Operational agility

More organizations consider agility as a prerequisite for operational excellence. Agile IT has been a driving force for the past 15 years. Now agile marketing and agile UX have followed.

Web teams that follow agile practices are very good at prioritizing around available resources. What they need is more visibility into prioritizing according to goals and outcomes. This includes better ways to connect their different activities in a coordinated manner. Metadata can help teams get more from their resources, and help them connect content with goals and outcomes.

Agility requires a foundation. That foundation doesn't emerge organically; it must be designed and planned, so that it can be built over time. Some agile teams assume that data they need will be available when they need it. That only happens when their tools allow the team to access data they need from other systems and sources. The ability to leverage outside data resources depends on interoperability, which is enabled through common metadata standards.

Standards-based metadata supports agility. Consider the difference between common JSON syntax, widely used for custom metadata properties, and standard-compliant JSON-LD. JSON is "inherently a schemaless message format" that can result in "JSON property soup," in the words of Paul Wilton.

External standards can shape whether operations are marked by coherence or by entropy. Wilton notes that "simple, clean" proprietary data models evolve and become "mess and complexity" because "developers are left to their own devices" and make changes "on an *ad-hoc* basis."[142] Proprietary data models tend to decay quickly and awkwardly.

External metadata vocabularies can help teams do things faster. A developer working for the Southern Cross Health Society, a New Zealand insurer, shared his experience on the schema.org community Listserv:

"Schema.org saved us a month! Yes, this is actual feedback from the agile team developing a new wellness product. Schema.org not only provides a direct, timesaving, 'dictionary' style reference to the data we have mapped in the core insurance system; but it provides a first-order model for all the key elements of /Person, /Organisation, etc."[143]

Common vocabularies make information and systems more "plug-and-play" ready. Standard vocabularies help all players know what information is available. Such standards reduce the documentation required to explain the metadata. Documentation is a big productivity drag for APIs and other IT specifications.

External standards help teams implement projects more quickly. By sticking with standards to define properties and values, developers don't need to read the documentation as much and can get on with development work. Content teams planning new projects have the ability to "slot-in" information where needed more easily.

Another way metadata standards can accelerate product development is by associating content metadata (the information layer) with the user interface (the experience layer). Metadata standards can integrate with UI libraries to bind information. The integration of UI component and metadata can make it faster to deploy new apps to customers.

A common model accelerates development by clarifying what is available to work with. In the case of Southern Cross, utilizing an existing model eliminated time previously needed for specification work:

"Schema.org helped us way beyond data mapping and models. The structure of Schema.org, as a massively peer reviewed, Internet ready, semantic 'model' saved so much specification time."

A major benefit of semantic metadata (metadata based on external standards using the RDF data model) is that it is extensible.

A shared, common model can allow teams to do a wider range of things with information. Having a common model can support concurrent engineering approaches to projects. Agility is closely associated with flexibility. And external standards make information more flexible.

Most content that's published online is fixed, in terms of its purpose and how it is used. The information doesn't change, and the content is defined by a fixed template.

Content reuse was addressed in the chapter on reusing Information . Let's consider how reuse relates to agility and flexibility.

When content is reused, generally the purpose of the content will be only slightly different, if at all.

But content, and information within content, has the potential be reused and repurposed in many ways. Templates define chunks of content that are used together. Templates reflect the purpose of the content, such as who the content is for, and what task the content supports. Different templates support different content goals, though they may share certain elements with one another. Templates also incorporate information variables, such as values that are used within text or tables. Metadata allows the recombination of content chunks and information variables.

Online publishers may want to:

- Use a slightly different mix of content or information for the same purpose (using the *same template*)
- Use existing content or information for an alternate, known purpose (using an *existing alternate template*)
- Use existing content or information for a novel purpose (there's *no template yet*).

Metadata promotes greater flexibility by making content and information *multipurpose*. Information defined with metadata can be available for all kinds of purposes, including ones not yet anticipated. Multipurpose content is similar to software code. A developer creates some code to solve some problem for an application. Another developer realizes she has a similar problem and reuses the code — even though her problem isn't exactly the same one. Likewise, information created for one purpose can be repurposed to support new use cases. With metadata, the details are extracted from the content and are independent of the specific presentation in the content. Chunks of content, such as summaries, can also be defined by metadata standards, and be available for reuse in different scenarios.

Online publishers need the ability to use existing content and information in new contexts. They encounter new use cases that content needs to support.

Metadata standards help to make content future-ready. Standards can connect pieces of information in novel ways that haven't been anticipated. While planning for future needs is always valuable, some needs can't be fully anticipated. But when information is described using standard metadata vocabularies, content can be repurposed for new scenarios.

---

[142] Paul Wilton, "Publishing JSON-LD for Developers", https://datalanguage.com/news/publishing-json-ld-for-developers

[143] David Gibson Southern Cross Health Society https://lists.w3.org/Archives/Public/public-schemaorg/2018Feb/0008.html

CHAPTER 17: DISTRIBUTED PUBLISHING AND THIRD-PARTY CONTRIBUTED CONTENT

Metadata standards are helpful when organizations delegate some or all responsibilities to other parties to contribute or publish content. This situation arises when organizations have a dispersed structure, or when they act as a host for content contributed by others.

Distributed publishing occurs when different units affiliated with an organization publish independently without a central editorial review. This is especially common with very large organizations having a federated structure. Many multinational corporations need to *coordinate* or *provide guidance* about some aspects of content and information, but must permit local units to publish as they deem appropriate.

Distributed publishing: the Australian government case

From the earliest days of online content, the Australian government has used metadata standards to improve online content availability. The Australian government isn't a single publisher, but comprises a federation of many government websites run by different government organizations. The governance challenges are enormous. The Australian government developed a metadata standard called AGLS to coordinate distributed publishing.[144] For nearly 20 years, the AGLS metadata standard has been used to classify services provided by different organizations within the Australian government (Figure 17.1).

> *"A good rule to follow is 'If it's worth publishing online, it's worth AGLS metadata'."*

-- AGLS Usage Guide

The AGLS metadata strategy adopts an existing standard and builds upon it. The government adopted the widely-used Dublin Core metadata standard, but added additional elements that were specific to their needs (for example, indicating the "jurisdiction" that the content relates to). While existing standards covered most of what was needed, the government identified a few areas where existing standards didn't provide needed coverage. The Australian government's approach is perhaps the earliest example of an organization extending an existing metadata standard (an approach that's now becoming more common). In the case of AGLS, the Australian government implemented an existing standard (Dublin Core), extended it with additional properties, and subsequently got the W3C to recognize their extension.

The AGLS strategy addresses implementation at various levels in different ways. The metadata standard provides a way for different publishers to describe their content consistently. It ensures all published content is interoperable. Individual publishers, such as the state government of Victoria, have their own government website principles and requirements, but these mandate the use of the AGLS metadata standard. The common standard has also promoted the availability of tools to implement the standard. For example, Drupal, which is widely used for government websites in Australia, has a plugin that provides support for adding the metadata to content. Currently, over 700 sites use the plugin. But AGLS is not limited to Drupal. Because AGLS is an open standard, it can work with any CMS. An AGLS plugin also exists for Joomla.

Australia's example shows that a well-considered metadata strategy can provide benefits for many years.

Figure 17.1. The AGLS Metadata Standard provides a detailed usage guide to assist publishers to implement the AGLS Usage Standard. Source: AGLS Metadata Standard.

AGLS Metadata Standard
Part 2 – Usage Guide

Version 2.0
July 2010

[144] See "AGLS Metadata Standard", http://www.agls.gov.au/

Third-party contributed content

Another common situation is when organizations host content contributed by others. They need to make sure that content submitted conforms to standards, so that information is easily findable, and can be integrated with content submitted by different parties.

EBay is a good example of a publisher that hosts content submitted by different parties. Before they introduced metadata standardization, different sellers used their own descriptions, which resulted in an idiosyncratic content that couldn't be integrated or found easily.

EBay decided to require all vendors to submit a product ID in their listings (similar to the barcode you might find on product packaging). With an unambiguous identifier, they could build a catalog of products describing properties in a consistent way.

EBay provides vendors with a "tool" that can access a catalog of all the information eBay has about the billions of items for sale on eBay. In eBay's words:

"We're using barcode recognition technology that identifies the UPC code and maps the same product you're holding in your hand to a match in our catalog. From there, you're taken straight to the listing page with all the information auto-populated. Now, you can get your new condition items up for sale in about 10 seconds."[145]

By linking a product code to other information, eBay can take advantage of structured information using the schema.org standard.

---

[145] See "Building eBay's Simpler Listing Flow" https://www.ebayinc.com/stories/news/ebays-new-feature-lets-you-list-items-in-seconds/

CHAPTER 18: SMART CONTENT PRODUCTION BY UTILIZING METADATA

Metadata identifies information within content and describes what the content is about. Both these features of metadata can help make the content creation process smarter.

Metadata can improve the author experience — but only if the right metadata is available, and if it can provide information that authors would find helpful when creating content. The author experience is still a relatively neglected area of content management. Yet it is crucial to the productivity of content creation.

Metadata can help online publishers improve their publishing process in various ways. It can support automation, reducing manual oversight and tasks, and provide intelligence, adding insights into the content creation process. Online publishers can become more efficient and more effective by utilizing metadata in the content creation process. Metadata can augment research, writing, and the review of content.

"Metadata strategy [is] increasingly important as content ecosystems incorporate more machine intelligence, and content moves through autonomously."[146]

-- Rachel Lovinger *Razorfish*

Creating content is widely perceived as a craft activity, the product of the mental efforts of an individual or small team. But while imagination and originality will always be needed, many aspects of content production are routine and laborious. Given the scale of content that organizations must produce, they can benefit by embedding *intelligence* into their supporting content production systems. The value of using metadata during content creation is not limited to efficiency. Metadata can also help add value to the editorial depth of content.

Organizations tend to follow distinct production workflows based on the nature of their content and how many people contribute to it. General-purpose content platforms such as CMSs don't yet include much in the way of smart production. The potential for more intelligent tools is greatest in more specialized tasks that involve managing specific information. By focusing on generic needs associated with the broadest market, CMS vendors have neglected many opportunities to make content production smarter.

Even though smart content production is not yet mainstream, we can see some emerging trends that suggest how metadata may be used in content creation in the near future. Marketing automation and journalism automation are two areas that have smart content creation tools that take advantage of metadata. Other content publishers can learn from the experience of these early adopters.

Metadata can provide three benefits to content creation:

1. Reducing the time required to create content
2. Reducing the cost to create content, such as labor and review costs
3. Enhancing the value of the content.

Time to create content: a faster turnaround time

Speed is of great concern to most online publishers, especially those that create a high volume of content that may have a short shelf life. Metadata can help authors put together content more quickly. In some cases, metadata can support the automation of content creation.

Two sources of inefficiency in the content creation process are:

1. Recreating content that exists already in some form
2. Hunting down related content that exists.

Metadata makes it easier to reuse existing content and assets. It can help authors when they need to search for content that was created earlier. Metadata can help authors make sure have rights to use assets in different contexts.

Depending on the setup, metadata can be used to have existing content found automatically (*auto-retrieved*), or have existing content is placed automatically (*auto-populated* content).

Another area where metadata can help authors work more quickly is by finding related content that can be integrated or referenced. For example, when creating an article on a topic, the system can note other articles about the topic that a writer might want to link to within their text (*auto-suggested*).

Metadata also makes the gathering of assets less confusing for authors. For example, many companies have several related brands or products, and it can be easy for content producers to confuse photos or text related to them.

Content automation reduces time. As one vendor explains the role of metadata in content automation:

"The author creates reusable content components that are not tied to a specific document or format. Because every document uses reusable components, no one has to keep track of updates to multiple documents, and metadata enables downstream systems to automate how the content is output."[147]

---

[146] Rachel Lovinger, "10 Things I've Learned in 10 Years as a Content Strategist", https://www.slideshare.net/rlovinger/10-things-i-learned-in-10-years-as-a-content-strategist-66787884

[147] *Content Automation For Dummies*, Quark, p.12

Reducing the cost to create content

The cost to create content is reduced when content is handled efficiently.

Metadata can facilitate the gathering of content and information from different parties. In some organizations, assets may not be centrally stored. Distributed files, stored on different IT systems, can be located through their metadata. Common metadata allows the federated search and retrieval of information and assets.

Metadata lowers the future cost of content by making content more reusable for the future. Autotagged content (such as autotagged images) makes content more versatile, ready for future needs. Live content, such as streaming feeds, live Q&A, and events, are examples of fresh content that can be reused later, provided that adequate metadata is added to the content so that the content becomes discoverable and repurposable.

Metadata can support better workflow integration, reducing labor intensity. Metadata can be linked to approvals and reviews (who needs to see, and when). In some large organizations, a directory of SMEs can be cross-linked to topics, so that collaboration and review are enabled. Workflows can designate specific metadata properties that trigger an automatic review by legal or compliance teams.

Metadata also reduces the effort of ingesting content from other sources, such as social media.

A widely cited example of how metadata can improve the efficiency of content creation is "automated journalism." Automated journalism is an approach to writing formulaic articles using structured data — information described by metadata. In journalism, these processes are being used to create stories relating to sports and corporate earnings.

The *Columbia Journalism Review* notes the relationship between automated journalism and metadata (which it refers to as structured data): "The key drivers of automated journalism are an ever-increasing availability of structured data." It adds: "Automated journalism cannot be used to cover topics for which no structured data are available and is challenging when data quality is poor."

Metadata allows online publishers to reuse information in different ways. "Algorithms can use the same data to tell stories in multiple languages and from different angles, thus personalizing them to an individual reader's preferences."[148]

[148] "Guide to Automated Journalism", *Columbia Journalism Review*, https://www.cjr.org/tow_center_reports/guide_to_automated_journalism.php

How metadata can add value to content

Metadata can help authors make content more valuable to audiences.

Some good examples of how metadata can add value to content creation are emerging from online newsrooms, which are pioneering practices that can be adopted more widely by web publishers.

The journalism website, *Nieman Reports*, describes new tools that use metadata to provide "richer" content:

"The tools support news organizations in their push to develop new storytelling formats that highlight the relationships between news events and help provide readers with richer context. Most of these efforts require large amounts of detailed metadata that can help link together stories that have in common people, places, or ideas. Adding metadata is a frustrating task for most reporters, who are typically more concerned with crafting their story than dissecting it. Automation is a way to expand the use of metadata — without putting an extra burden on reporters and editors."[149]

Metadata can provide authors with contextual help. It can support suggestions about related content, instead of making the authors look for material. Systems could use metadata to make suggestions about different angles for addressing a topic, based on relationships to other topics, or association of topic to audience segment.

Through contextual linking, metadata can help authors get related data to incorporate, or get media assets to illustrate content. Having a unified set of metadata description that covers all types of content helps online publishers integrate video and graphics into a story easily.

Metadata also promotes spin-off content. If one theme attracts interest, publishers can create more detailed material that builds on it.

Reuters' "Lynx Insight" product provides another example of how metadata can support "suggestions, facts and contextual background." Lynx "can augment human journalism by identifying trends, anomalies, key facts and suggesting new stories reporters should write."

Reuters notes how information can be tailored to address specific use cases:

"Down the road, Lynx Insight could be extended to sports data — supporting previews and wrap-ups of matches, or creating injury reports, or league rankings - or to any other field that would benefit from data-driven story authoring. It can also help in the creation of more customized or personalized content — for example, it could be used to power market reports tailored to individual users."[150]

Automated journalism offers an approach that can be applied to other kinds of content besides journalistic content. Potential applications include formulaic web content, such as email notifications, and content that involves the detailed comparison of information, such as product comparisons. Online publishers have an opportunity to examine their workflows to identify labor-intensive tasks and consider how metadata can be used to automate these tasks.

---

[149]   "Automation   in   the   Newsroom",   *Nieman   Reports*, http://niemanreports.org/articles/automation-in-the-newsroom/

[150] Reginald Chua "The cybernetic newsroom: horses and cars", *Reuters*, https://www.reuters.com/article/rpb-cyber/the-cybernetic-newsroom-horses-and-cars-idUSKCN1GOOZ0

CHAPTER 19: SEMANTIC ANALYTICS AND USER CONTENT CONSUMPTION

W eb analytics haven't been very sophisticated about using metadata. Most analytics focus on tracking web pages, rather than tracking metadata variables. Those that track variables have mostly relied on tracking custom "tags". Fortunately, new solutions based on an approach called semantic analytics are moving beyond the limitations of tag-based web analytics. Semantic analytics offers online publishers insights about how people relate to specific things mentioned in content. Until recently, these kinds of insights have only been available to large-scale social media platforms such as Facebook (see the chapter on metadata and content strategy). Because the semantic analytics approach is new, and publisher case studies are not yet widely available, this discussion will focus on the potential applications of semantic analytics, and how they differ from conventional web analytics.

Limitations of standard web analytics

Content analytics look at how content is performing, and why content performs as it does. Google analytics is the most widely used tool. Web analytics tools provide very useful information about visitor journeys and behavior. They are often geared to tracking conversions or other metrics. They generally aren't focused on measuring the characteristics of the content. Weak metadata capabilities prevent such measurement from being possible.

Most web analytics track visitor behavior and page views, but they track content characteristics according to only a few parameters:

- Titles
- Authors
- Section
- Tags
- Publication dates.

These characteristics aren't ideal. Titles may not be informative, and can't be generalized easily. Sections are too broad. Tags give some indication about the topics discussed in the content, but tags aren't very granular.

The limitations of tags can be seen by looking at the capabilities of Parse.ly, one of the most sophisticated analytics tools. Parse.ly is used by many leading news publishers. It provides a view of content performance according to CMS tags.

By clicking on a specific tag, editors can see:

- Stories with that tag
- Authors who wrote stories with that tag
- Referrers sending traffic to posts with that tag
- Campaigns driving traffic to posts that tag
- Social interactions with to posts with that tag.[151]

While helpful, this data is still superficial. The tag gives only a high-level picture of what the content is about. The analytics only give a broad sense of topics that are popular. One would need to read all content having the same tag to understand why the performance varies among similarly tagged items.

Topic tags may be adequate for headline-driven, short-life news articles. But for content where readers are seeking specific information, tags aren't sufficient. More granular metadata is needed.

Content strategists want to be able to answer basic questions such as:

- What kinds of information are included in the best-performing pages?
- Was there a difference in performance of two similar pages if one included details another lacked?

It is possible to get answers to such questions. But first, we need to talk about another kind of tag, which is used with web analytics tools.

---

[151] "Tags", Parsely help, https://www.parse.ly/help/post/3359/tags/

Measuring user events and behavior with Javascript 'tags'

Analytics examine audience behavior. They do this by focusing on visitors, and on sessions. Visitors may new or old. They may visit only once or may return often. Each short visit could be part of a longer series of activities, which could culminate in a significant event such as the submission of an online order.

Visitors and events are the currency of analytics.

Analytics tools provide the means to measure how audiences react to content. They do this using another kind of "tag" — an event tag, which is not metadata, but a piece of Javascript code. These tags track events such as when users click, tap, scroll, and submit information.

Although potentially confusing, event tags (used by web analytics tools) are not the same as topic tags (used by content management systems). Event tags measure user behavior. They can measure whether users successfully completed a goal, but they don't tell us what the user's goal was — for example, what information the user was interacting with.

Web measurement tools can be broadly be divided into Tag Managers (which allow the tracking of specific behaviors) and Analytics packages (which report on behavior overall). Generally, these tools focus on reporting user behaviors such as form submissions, rather than content characteristics. This makes it difficult to understand broader patterns in content performance.

It is important to distinguish the measurement of webpages from the measurement of content. Analytics packages are primarily geared toward measuring webpages. They consider the webpage as the essential unit to measure, and then break down the page into structural components, such as links and buttons. That data, while important, doesn't indicate the content of the webpage. One can compare the pageviews of two webpages, but one doesn't know if the content is similar or different.

Analytics track on-page activity. A webpage has different characteristics that online publishers may want to monitor. They are valuable for measuring single pages but can be limiting if trying to measure the performance of categories of content. Standard web analytics commonly provide filtering by user behaviors, but not by content characteristics.

Analytics packages track generic events such as pageviews. It is possible to define "custom variables" to track specific elements within a page. These might be DOM elements on a webpage, which can be used to track events such as whether users viewed a video embedded within a webpage. But when configured appropriately, analytics packages can also track content according to metadata within the content. This allows content to be filtered by metadata description, and for content with common metadata descriptions to be looked at as a category.

When analytics packages are able to track and measure metadata properties and values, it is capable of semantic analytics — measuring content according to its meaning. Specifically, it is now possible to track schema.org metadata within tools such as Google Analytics.[152]

---

[152] For a discussion of how to set up, see Mike Arnesen, "Semantic Analytics: How to Track Performance and ROI of Structured Data" https://moz.com/blog/semantic-analytics

Measuring content with semantic analytics

Analytics packages by default track generic events. They track page views, but not views of content about specific entities. It is possible to inject structured data into Google Analytics. Online publishers can customize their analytics so that the metadata markup in their content is intelligible to Google Analytics. Consider it as the marriage of analytics and SEO.

The role metadata in analytics has parallels to how metadata is used in an online search. In both cases, the metadata is indexing information. Metadata helps users search content according to parameters (what audiences are seeking from content). Analytics is tracking parameters (what audiences are doing while viewing content, or after viewing content). All that's needed is to match search parameters with tracking parameters.

In an online search, customers have questions for which they seek answers (information). Metadata describes key information in the content and can surface it in response to a search query. Does that information meet their needs? Are readers motivated to explore more related information, or do they exit and look at other sites? Online publishers can check the performance of content containing this information. If they find many people search for certain information, but that the content addressing that information does not result in hoped-for behaviors, then the publisher knows what kinds of content aren't performing well.

Online publishers can filter content according to metadata parameters and see how performance differs.

When analytics track specific behaviors, in conjunction with specific metadata properties and values, the combination can be quite powerful.

The marriage of metadata and analytics allows online publishers to learn what's popular. Metadata indicates how content varies. Analytics tell us how performance varies. Semantic analytics reveals how variations in content affect the performance of content. When semantics are included in analytics, it provides insight into how content varies. It then can answer the question of how different content varies in how it performs according to different criteria.

Metadata becomes another kind of variable in analytics. The online publisher can set a trigger to capture if visitors watch videos about a specific topic. These would be "custom dimensions" in Google analytics.

Online publishers have the option to customize their analytics programs to track metadata using a tag manager. But semantic analytics packages are also becoming available. SchemaApp, a tool that lets online publishers add metadata markup to their content, offers the ability to track metadata properties associated with a URL:

"You can import the details of how you describe your content with schema markup into your analytics. With Google Analytics, you get a URL and the associated traffic; with Semantic Analytics you have details about that URL that you can then use to see trends.[153]

Drilling down into content metadata

Metadata offers the ability to discover very granular details of information mentioned in content. Publishers can look at at the details to develop better attribution about the performance and influence of content.

The first step in understanding semantic analytics is to know what information is in your content. Larger publishers may have a hazy understanding of this. Before they can set up automated tracking of metadata, they will need an understanding of what metadata they have available to track.

Few online publishers are used to querying their own metadata to see what relationships are there. This can be done by running SPARQL queries.[154] Publishers can use SPARQL to analyze the entities associated with the content. Online publishers can look for all content containing a specific entity type, any content where the entity has a specific characteristic, or only content that matches very specific criteria.

Figure 19.1. SPARQL can locate information according to entity type. Source: British Museum Researchspace.org.

It is easiest to understand how this works by looking at a graphic user interface that queries semantic metadata. The GUI for the British Museum (Figure 19.1 and Figure 19.2) shows how different entities can be queried together to locate specific content.[153]

Figure 19.2. SPARQL can search for values associated with an entity type. Source: British Museum Researchspace.org.

Once the publisher can see what combinations of entities exist in their content (Figure 19.3), they can then begin to track different aspects of the performance of this content. This inquiry may also prompt the publisher to consider adding more metadata to their content if they feel that more detail could be useful. For example, the may want more a granular breakout of entity types, and decide to declare additional, more specific entity types in their metadata.[156]

Figure 19.3. Results from a SPARQL search on properties, in this case, listing artists who created artworks depicting Mount Vesuvius during the 18th century.

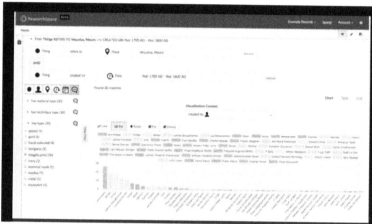

Source: British Museum.

They can evaluate what is mentioned in content and how that impacts its performance. They can see if any comparative information within content is influencing user decisions.

---

[153] "Semantic Analytics", https://www.schemaapp.com/semantic-analytics/

[154] SPARQL is a query language for RDF (semantic) data, similar to SQL used for relational data.

[155] The British Museum's ResearchSpace is a database of art objects described with semantic metadata that can be queried using a GUI. Although the content may not seem relevant to for-profit publishers, the database is in many respects an example of a very sophisticated digital asset managment system.

[156] This can be done in the schema.org vocabulary using the multi-typed entity syntax.

Content parameters in semantic analytics

Any metadata element can be measured. This includes entity types, properties, and values.

Semantic analytics can *compare* the performance of content according to different dimensions:

- Involving **different entity types** (e.g. cars versus motorcycles)
- Describing **different instances** of same entity type (all content discussing product "X" versus all content discussing product "Y")
- Discussing the **same instance**, but some content mentions a certain property (such as price), while other content doesn't mention the property.

Semantic analytics also can look at *combinations* of information, such as content that discusses events and locations together, and compare that to content that mentions events and locations separately.

Performance parameters

The performance is judged according to different criteria. Performance is a big topic and is getting more sophisticated.

Lots of performance metrics can be important. But many of them won't be important for all contexts. Metadata provides critical contextual information to help online publishers decide which performance metrics to focus on. For example, online publishers may not be concerned about repeat visitors for address information, but they will be interested in that metric for their pricing information if it changes often.

Performance metrics relate to:

1. Engagement
2. Actions
3. Visitor paths (user journeys)
4. Visitor type.

Different content can be evaluated according to **engagement**. Common engagement metrics include:

- Duration
- Frequency
- % repeat visitors
- Recency
- Depth of visit
- Click-through rate (CTR).

Different content can be evaluated according to **actions** such as:

- RSS feed subscriptions
- Bookmarks, ratings
- Enquires
- Providing personal info
- Downloads
- Comments.

Different content can also vary by **journey elements** such as:

- Entry page
- Entry type (search, external referrer, direct URL)

- Event – action taken
- Exit page and page exit rate
- Form submissions
- Incoming links (backlinks).

Different content may also appeal to **different visitors**:

- New visitor
- Return visitor
- Repeat visitor.

Combining content parameters and performance parameters

By combining the sophisticated analytics of content properties by querying metadata, and the robust user behavioral data from standard web analytics, detailed insights about content performance are possible.

The URL provides a unique identifier for matching the characteristics and the performance for an item of content. The URL represents distinct page-events that can be aggregated, according to either common content characteristics, or common performance characteristics.

Some basic queries can be filtered through Google Analytics (or another analytics tool). Alternatively, both metadata and performance data can be downloaded into a spreadsheet for more detailed analysis.

Online publishers can approach content performance by either:

1. Specifying content characteristics and then retrieving performance data
2. Specifying performance criteria and then retrieving content characteristics data.

For example, the publisher may want to find content that has certain characteristics such as what entity is mentioned, and then look at performance (the average or range for engagement or action metrics). A content characteristic query might ask: How did content about a certain product do compared to average engagement benchmarks for content about all products?

Alternatively, the publishers may do a performance-based query first. They might ask: What products were discussed in our most viewed content, or attracted the most-new visitors?

Publishers can drill down on characteristics of content to make granular comparisons such as:

- About "X" versus "*not* X"
- "A *not* B" (only mentions A) versus "A *and* B" (mentions both A and B)
- Create collections of content (specific: "A *and* B *and* C" or inclusive: "A *or* B *or* C")
- Property-driven (*any* that has a property of *price* below $Y).

Asset utilization: making content accountable

Another possible use of metadata is to measure the *lifetime* performance of important and widely-used content assets, especially collateral such as photos, videos, and whitepapers that are expensive to create.[157] We can refer to this kind of analytics as *asset utilization* metrics.

> "*Your assets are useless to you unless you have metadata — your archive is full of stuff that is of no value because you can't find it and don't know what it's about.*"[158]

-- John O'Donovan *chief technology officer at The Financial Times*

Content assets are typically stored in a repository. They may be used often, or simply saved for later use. While it has been long possible to track how often an item has been used, it hasn't been easy to analyze the characteristics of which assets are most used, or least used. Asset utilization metrics can track asset use according to various metadata properties. Standardized metadata makes assets more accountable. It can help to answer how valuable an item of content is.

Content can be considered an asset, though not in an accounting sense. Content is like an asset in that it has a cost associated with it, and is expected to deliver value.

Like content analytics, asset utilization considers the characteristics of content. The difference is that asset utilization is focused on how much the online publisher uses content *over time* and *in different contexts*. This is a slightly different emphasis than analytics, which focuses on how different assets achieve specific goals or outcomes. While evaluating content against goals is valuable, it can sometimes cause online publishers to consider the content as having only a single purpose.

When measuring asset utilization, we assume the asset is *multi-purpose* and will be used over time. Asset utilization seeks to track and evaluate the asset's lifetime value. This is far from an exact science, but by using metadata, online publishers can begin to make some critical distinctions between the value of different kinds of assets and be better able to prioritize them.

An important aspect of assets is that they are delivered to audiences within a context. For example, an image or video is embedded within a webpage that has its own characteristics. A whitepaper is downloadable from a webpage. Metadata can help online publishers understand the context (properties) where the asset is used, and where it performs most effectively.

Assets that can be used multiple times for different purposes have a stored value. The asset involves an expense: the costs of producing the asset. The more often that an asset is used, the lower the cost per use. Metadata can help online publishers understand where an asset is used, and how much it is used.

The value of the asset could be defined as its expected contribution to revenues. The more widely an asset supports a business goal, in terms of reach, views, or conversions, the greater its contribution to revenue. For example, a logo is an image asset, but one that is used very widely, and is believed to sway customers.

Asset *valuation* looks at both the cost to create an asset and the incremental contribution to revenues. To estimate these factors, online publishers need the means to track the asset, which is provided through metadata.

Let's consider a simple example, where a firm sells a product. The firm decides to include a professional studio photo of the product on their website. They note the cost of commissioning a photo to determine the expense associated with the asset. They compare how sales of the product perform when using the image and when not using the image. This will reveal the expected contribution of the photo to sales of the product. The use of the photo, the cost of the photo, and the sales associated can all be tracked by the product metadata identifier, such as a GTIN.

For many publishers, the value of content is unknown. The users of DAM systems may have more experience with managing assets, which tend to get reused in different situations. More detailed metadata will help DAMs provide more useful data relating to the value of different assets.

Metadata properties provide a profile of asset. Standard metadata properties can track various characteristics of assets:

- Length (the word count for articles, or the duration for audio and video)
- Format (content type)
- Creator
- Topic (specific entities associated with the asset)
- Content licensing attribution.

Publishers want to know what their best-performing assets are, and well as what their worst performing assets are. That knowledge helps them prioritize what they create.

The performance of assets — the engagement and actions the asset elicits — will be the by-product of two distinct factors:

1. The quality of the asset (overall engagement performance)
2. The placement or positioning of the asset within other content (performance for specific user journeys).

Asset utilization needs to measure two variables: (1) how much the publisher uses the asset in its content; and (2) how much audiences use the asset.

If an asset does not perform well, the publisher needs to determine if it wasn't positioned properly (the context was wrong), or whether the asset itself is weak.

Metadata provides diagnostic data to understand the effectiveness of assets. It can be used to compare performance according to parameters such as asset format, asset length, and who created it (which is possibly relevant if the asset is creative in nature.) When assets appear in more than one context, the difference in these contexts can also be compared, drawing on metadata properties.

Metadata provides granular feedback that helps publishers escape from the trap of "one size fits all" thinking. Context can be important. For example, while it is possible that audiences have a preference or either long or short content, their preference may also depend on the topic and format. Troubleshooting videos need to be short because the audience is likely impatient. Videos that tell stories might be longer if they engage audiences.

Online publishers often face the decision whether to update existing assets or retire them. For example, an educational video or a whitepaper may be offered to audiences over a long time period and may become out-of-date. In general, publishers would like expensive content to have a long shelf-life, so they will explore if updating the content will extend how long the content can be used. Inexpensive content is inexpensive to replace, so there is less incentive to update it.

How many times (how frequently) has an asset been updated? Even this parameter can be derived from metadata. Updating is a cost, but it could also signal the content is valuable. Generally, publishers won't bother to update content that isn't valuable. They may, however, need to update asset more frequently than should be necessary, if they designed the content poorly.

Reuse of assets is generally desirable. Every time the asset is used, the average cost associated with the audience viewing the content declines. But it is possible to overuse an asset, because people tire of it. They may be less inclined to view other content. Reuse is good when presented to different audiences, but reuse can be off-putting when recycled or reused materials shown to the same audience. Tracking parameters associated with the context in which an asset appears can help publishers understand how audiences are experiencing it.

---

[157] There is no formal definition of a content asset. It is generally "evergreen" content that will have a long shelflife and may occasionally be revised if necessary. In addition to images and videos, it may also include audio podcasts and specially commissioned features or graphics.

[158] quoted in the *New York Times* "Innovation Report"

Advanced analytics

Online publishers can apply advanced statistical analysis to analyze their content and assets, and the performance of this collateral. Both R and Python have the ability to retrieve and parse web content metadata, and both have extensive statistical libraries. The possibilities are extensive for those with the requisite knowledge.

CHAPTER 20: REDUCING RISK BY USING METADATA STANDARDS

A well-planned metadata strategy can reduce risks associated with published content. Poor quality metadata carries both financial and reputation risks.

Even if poor metadata does not directly impact revenues, it can affect a brand's reputation. Accurate and reliable information is essential for all brands. When publishers use standard vocabularies that are widely understood, they can signal important information about content that could otherwise result in problems.

An issue has garnered much attention recently is the accuracy of information in the news. As audiences get more information through social media platforms such as Facebook, and online search engines such as Google, they are encountering a diversity of sources, some unknown. They do not always know what information is accurate. This has lead to the problem of "fake news." Many people have blamed online platforms for spreading fake news. Can metadata help curb the problem of inaccurate news?

Timothy Garton Ash, Isaiah Berlin Professorial Fellow at St. Anthony's College, Oxford, thinks metadata can reduce the risk of inaccurate information on the web. In his recent book, *Free Speech*, he argues: "If a user-friendly metadata tag were to become a well-understood norm, we would have food labeling for journalism."[150]

Along with Facebook, Google faced criticism that it was spreading "fake news" — a derisive term for inaccurate or misleading information. In response, Google has worked with schema.org to develop a claims revenue (ClaimReview) metadata.[160] Google hoped that this metadata would be used to fact check claims so that inaccurate information could be flagged. While beneficial to readers, it would also benefit Google, one of the largest global distributors of information, who would be seen as part of the solution, rather than as part of the problem.

However, Google's initial implementation was rushed, and the information Google presented was itself inaccurate, linking to incorrect sources, drawing criticism. The situation led a widely followed journalism blog to announce: "Google suspends fact-checking feature over quality concerns."

The blog noted that Google was "working to figure out how to improve the Reviewed Claims feature before re-launching it."[161] Subsequently, Google has taken additional steps to de-bug the fact-checking process and has been working with journalism organizations to make improvements.

Google's experience suggests two lessons. Metadata can be a tool to reduce risks that incorrect information is presented to audiences. But the metadata needs to be reliable, supported by a well-understood process that has the buy-in from relevant stakeholders.

Poor metadata quality not only hurts brand reputation. In some cases, it can hurt revenues. One widely cited example of how poor metadata can cost money comes from the music industry. "Many collecting societies and publishers estimate that about 25% of music publishing revenue doesn't make it to its rightful owners due to lack of accurate metadata."[162]

Content is an expense that should be managed appropriately. It costs money to create and to deploy. When bought from others, it can entail legal responsibilities.

Content properties that aren't tracked can't be managed. When properties aren't specified or tracked, it can create risks. When publishers ignore issues, problems can arise unexpectedly. Metadata can bring visibility to hidden risks that would otherwise remain below the surface of awareness.

Metadata in prototyping, and proof-of-concept testing

Publishers increasingly want to experiment with new ideas before committing to producing them. Metadata can be used to decide if new products or ideas are worth pursuing. Metadata can support both content testing and functional testing to improve the user experience and more successfully realize business goals.

Existing metadata can help with the design of new templates and applications. Content designers recognize the benefits of using real data in prototypes. This has lead to an approach known as content-first prototyping.[163] Developers can use a simple JSON representation of metadata to feed content prototypes with data in order to see how a webpage would display information to users. Both templates and prototyping software can consume JSON, making it easy to change information in a design. Different presentations of information can be evaluated through formative usability testing to improve the design of the content.

Metadata can also support new functionality related to content. If required metadata is not already available, developers may want to experiment to see how much metadata is necessary to effectively deliver the functionality proposed. For example, metadata is needed to support the functionality in recommendation engines. How much metadata is needed for accurate results? How valuable is additional accuracy?

A publisher could sponsor a pilot project for a recommendation engine for a specific topic. It could judge the accuracy and timeliness of results in the pilot, and check how available metadata influences those results. And for different quality levels, it could test outcomes such as click-through rates and subsequent actions. Such pilots can help determine the sweet spot for the optimal amount of metadata needed to deliver outcomes expected from new functionality. Generally, developers want to keep the complexity of functionality down, to improve ease of maintenance and improve performance.

---

[159] Timothy Garton Ash, *Free Speech* (Atlantic Books 2017), p. 199

[160] "ClaimReview", https://schema.org/ClaimReview

[161]   https://www.poynter.org/news/google-suspends-fact-checking-feature-over-quality-concerns

[162]   http://www.hypebot.com/hypebot/2018/01/why-building-more-rights-databases-wont-solve-the-music-industry-metadata-problem.html

[163] For information about using content in prototyping, see "Content-First Prototyping", *Smashing Magazine*, April 2016, https://www.smashingmagazine.com/2016/05/content-first-prototyping/ and "Priority Guides: A Content-First Alternative to Wireframes", *A List Apart*, http://alistapart.com/article/priority-guides-a-content-first-alternative-to-wireframes

Optimizing keystone content

As noted in the chapter on semantic analytics, metadata can support analytics and improve optimization in general. Yet certain content carries a higher level of risk and needs special attention.

Some webpages, such as product order pages, are critical to a business. A product order page might present three options with different features and different prices. The product manager wants to know what feature mix attracts the most interest at different price points. With metadata, different features can be highlighted in different variations to explore what information seems most important. The testing of content variations, together with the testing of page structure and user journeys, work together in the process of optimization.

Optimization utilizes A/B testing or multivariate testing to determine what appeals to most customers, or to specific customers. Common metrics include the click-through rate (CTR) for specific calls-to-action and conversion rate optimization (CRO) to measure the performance of a page overall.

Currently, most testing of content variations is done by manually. Teams change text-values manually, instead of using metadata to swap information when testing variations. Using metadata to control information variations can be faster and yield more granular insights about which variations deliver the best results.

Preventing asset misuse

Reusing assets is cost-efficient, provided it is done appropriately. But if assets are used incorrectly, it can be costly.

In many cases, a publisher needs to make sure that the asset is used correctly by other parties, such as agencies or business partners. Many digital assets, such as images, videos, and music, have licensing rights. These assets are expensive to create or acquire. There may be restrictions on their use.

Assets can also touch on branding guidelines, and trademarks of partner companies. Sometimes the use of logos is highly controlled, such as when used in social media by a regulated industry such as pharmaceuticals.

Metadata standards can indicate the source of the asset, such as the creator, producer, photographer, or designer. These attributions can be important for the management of the asset. Properties can also recommend how to use the asset correctly.

Rights are covered by different standards, such as the IPTC Photo Metadata Standard. External metadata standards can help with licensing and usage tracking and compliance.[164] Licensing and compliance are intrinsically a multi-party activity. Standards facilitate the tracking and exchange of information relating to these dimensions.

Other examples of rights metadata include:

- plus (Picture Licensing Universal System)[165]
- xmpRights and xmpPlus
- prism (Publishing Requirements for Industry Standard Metadata)[166]
- prl (Prism Rights Language)
- pur (Prism Usage Rights).

---

[164]_"Google Images now displays image credits based on IPTC Photo Metadata", https://iptc.org/news/google-images-now-displays-image-credits-based-on-iptc-photo-metadata/

[165] http://www.useplus.com/

[166] http://www.prismstandard.org

Ensuring regulatory and legal compliance

Many goods, including food, medicine, children's toys, and household tools, are subject to government regulation. Information in content about these goods should be precisely managed. Metadata standards can support the management of regulatory information, to ensure consistency and compliance.

The GS1 vocabulary, for example, has a number of useful properties:

- Regulated Product Name gs1:regulatedProductName
- Health Claim gs1:healthClaimDescription: "a description of health claims according to regulations of the target market."
- Consumer Safety Information gs1:consumerSafetyInformation
- Warning Copy Description gs1:warningCopyDescription: "additional information that outlines special requirements, warning and caution information printed on the package."
- Consumer Package Disclaimer gs1:consumerPackageDisclaimer
- Consumer Safety Information gs1:consumerSafetyInformation.

Versioning can also be important. Metadata can also indicate when something was last updated.

Managing sensitive content

Metadata standards can also help manage disclaimers and warnings, such as content that may be "not safe for work" (NSFW) or not safe for children

IPTC vocabulary has a series of content warnings.[167] These cover situations mentioned in the content about which some audiences will want to be forewarned:

- **Death**, cwarn:death: "The content could be perceived as offensive due to the discussion or display of death"
- **Language**, cwarn:language: "The content could be perceived as offensive due to the language used"
- **Nudity**, cwarn:nudity: "The content could be perceived as offensive due to nudity"
- **Sexuality**, cwarn:sexuality: "The content could be perceived as offensive due to the discussion or display of sexuality"
- **Suffering**, cwarn:suffering: "The content could be perceived as distressing due to the discussion or display of suffering"
- **Violence**, cwarn:violence: "The content could be perceived as offensive due to the discussion or display of violence".

---

[167]Documentation at http://cv.iptc.org/newscodes/contentwarning/

Exposing metadata versus not-sharing information

Some publishers may worry that publishing metadata will reveal sensitive information. For example, some online vendors only reveal their prices after tracking users and deciding what they can charge them. Some companies even try to get customers to put a product in a shopping basket before the price is revealed.

Generally, if a company does not have an intention to deceive, it should not be concerned about publishing metadata. When companies imagine they can control who gets to see their information and when, they make the mistake of assuming they have a captive audience. In practice, audiences will tend to ignore sources that create barriers to getting information.

There may be situations were metadata does not need to be shown, because it could be distracting. Publishers can control the risks of how their metadata is used a couple of ways.

The first way is to indicate the metadata is "no-index" so that search crawlers don't harvest the information. Publishers may want to de-emphasize information on their website they decide they need to keep for archival purposes, but that they don't want to show in current web results.[168]

The second way is to cloak metadata by using custom values. A publisher can use external vocabulary properties with custom values such as arbitrary alphanumeric codes that don't convey the meaning to outside parties. For example, the publisher could indicate the intended audience with a schema.org property for an audience, but use a custom value that reflects their internal segmentation priorities. The code (e.g., XXZ332) could be decoded with a text label in internally-facing systems such as a CMS so that it is easy for authors to understand.

Zeng and Qin cite IBM as an example of a publisher that uses internal classification codes within a standards-compliant framework.[169] For example, IBM used the following metadata in its content:

```
<meta content="CT002v" scheme="IBM_ContentClassTaxonomy"
name="DC.Type"/>
```

The code conforms to HTML syntax standards and uses a Dublin Core property. Yet the actual meaning of the metadata is understandable only to IBM.

The benefit of these approaches is that they still work within the framework of standards. All systems that many need to use the information can identify the appropriate property, since it follows external standards. But the meaning of custom values associated with that property won't be automatically recognized by machines, which prevents third parties from automatically deciphering the information.

---

[168] NB: No-index won't prevent willful webscraping.

[169] Zeng and Qin, *Metadata* (American Library Association, 2016) pp. 84, 115

PART III. TACTICS AND BEST PRACTICES

P art III explores the practical issues faced when implementing a metadata strategy. Publishers will need to consider changes to different parts of their web operations on both the human and technical sides. The chapters provide tips and resources for making sound decisions.

Because publishers vary greatly in terms of their current resources and capabilities, the reader will need to decide for themselves what advice is most relevant to their specific needs. Some advice will be relevant to small size publishers, while other advice will be of interest only to large scale publishers.

Likewise, different chapters will appeal to readers having different responsibilities and backgrounds. Some chapters address technical issues, while other focus on the human side. Readers should feel free to skim or skip areas that are outside of their responsibility.

A successful metadata strategy requires a team effort. It requires cross-functional knowledge. It will be rare for any single person to have expertise in all the disciplines that contribute to a successful metadata program. The program lead should enlist expertise from different disciplines, so that awareness of different needs can develop within teams.

CHAPTER 21: DEFINING SCOPE: ADOPTING AND SPECIFYING VOCABULARIES

A critical part of metadata requirements is deciding the scope of entities and properties to cover. These decisions can involve a range of factors: what information the publisher would ideally like to cover, what information other parties generally cover, and what information would be easy or difficult to include.

In practice, often the simplest thing to do is to follow what other publishers are doing. If an online publisher is behind the curve, and lagging current practices, this is the recommended approach to start with. However, because current practices often fall short of their potential, simply following what everyone else does may not be sufficient.

This chapter will address how online publishers decide what information to include in their metadata. It will highlight some examples of publishers that have gone well beyond current standard practices to realize exceptional value from metadata. However, their approaches may not necessarily be the right ones for other publishers. Every publisher will have different needs and different capabilities. As a result, there is no single best way to decide the scope of metadata.

The fundamental choice online publishers face is whether to rely solely on vocabularies that exist already, or whether to create vocabularies standards of their own. Some ontology engineers (people who design metadata vocabularies) recommend thinking about vocabulary needs as a blank slate, and not to be limited to thinking about needs in terms of what is currently available. There can indeed be great value in starting from a blank slate, so that important requirements don't get overlooked. However, it is also possible that following a blank slate approach can result in unrealistic expectations that are impractical to implement.

At the start of the process, all online publishers can benefit by exploring the scope of their metadata requirements as if it were a blank slate. But only certain publishers will want to rely on this approach as their primary way of defining their metadata scope. Publishers that have a dominant market position in a specialized domain are more likely to need to define their own vocabularies, rather than rely solely on existing ones. For less specialized domains in competitive sectors, existing vocabularies may provide the full coverage that a publisher needs.

As part of the requirements process, publishers document the scope of all the metadata relating to the domain that they talk about in their content. They will often represent the scope in a model, which is sometimes called a domain model. The model identifies the entities and properties that publishers track in their content. It provides a picture of the requirements. To implement the requirements, publishers will draw on existing vocabularies or ontologies, and sometimes supplement these standards with entities and properties of their own.

The scoping process involves both *what* to define, and *how* that can be defined. It involves three distinct activities:

1. **Modeling**: Deciding what entities and properties that a publisher needs to address in its metadata
2. **Mapping**: Identifying existing metadata standards that describe these entities and properties
3. **Developing**: Deciding if some desired entities and properties aren't covered by existing standards, and require the publisher to develop its own vocabulary.

These activities are not necessarily sequential, like a waterfall. Sometimes it makes sense to work on them concurrently.

A common first step is to start with domain modeling: defining the universe of information the publisher wants to cover. This step is especially important when the publisher already knows they want to cover information that is not already well covered by existing metadata vocabularies.

Modeling

A domain model provides a shared description of the information a publisher needs to capture with metadata. It is a visual diagram or graph that can be understood by all stakeholders and that represents the domain of the content: the stuff the content talks about.

The initial sketches of the model will look similar to a "concept graph" that is familiar to many individuals, with bubbles representing concepts that are connected together with links when they are related. The bubbles and lines are labeled to indicate what they represent.[170] It feels natural to draw bubbles to indicate things and draw lines between then to indicate relationships. The drawings or diagrams provide a picture of requirements that stakeholders can see and comment on.

The first step when modeling a domain is to collect input from different sources about the kinds of information that are relevant. This input can be acquired through stakeholder interviews (both internal and external stakeholders), or group ideation sessions. This step will also include an inventory of how the publisher is currently categorizing content: tags, database fields, folder structures, etc. Inputs should be prioritized against some of the requirements known already. All the important information in published content should be identified.

The level of detail in the model will depend on the publisher's goals for metadata. For publishers working in specialized domains, or initiating new projects where no content yet exists, the domain model will start with a blank slate, with many details needed. For routine information domains, or projects involving a straightforward migration of content, publishers will already have a good sense of the scope of requirements.

Michael Smethurst, an information architect currently working at the UK parliament, recommends doing in-depth interviews with subject matter experts, or what he calls domain experts, to fill-in the blank slate:

"Employ a domain expert. Get them to sketch their world and sketch back at them. Concentrate on modeling real (physical and metaphysical) things, not web pages - try to blank from your mind all thoughts of the resulting web site. This work should never stop - you need to do this through the lifetime of the project as you refine your understanding."[171]

The domain model reflects what information *is* discussed in the content (current state), or what it *might* discuss (future state), due to its relevance. In other words, the model should be both retrospective, and prospective. Potentially, the model can become a platform for developing content, providing a detailed map of kinds of information a writer might want to cover in content they are creating.

A subject domain can incorporate different perspectives on a topic. The domain model should reflect both how audiences discuss these topics (the demand side), as well as how specialists talk about them (the supply side). Publishers tend to focus on details in a domain that are not top-of-mind for audiences. Audiences tend to think about domains in a wider context relating to other events in their lives. For example, if a publisher wants metadata to support content discussing insurance for families, it will need to consider terminology relating to major life events such as illness, accidents, inheritance, or divorce, as well as more technical terminology relating to insurance products such as yields and payouts.

Some publishers have an editorial mission that's driven entirely by audience interests. In these situations, the audience perspective of a domain will predominate. Other publishers in scientific or technical B2B (business to business) contexts will focus more on information they need to impart to audiences, and will focus more on modeling their own internal knowledge.

If no content exists yet, modeling will consider things a target audience tend to discuss and would likely be discussed in the content created.

Silver Oliver, an information architect who worked at the BBC, notes that models provide scaffolding for information used in content. With a model, content can be "projected through" it. Publishers can build collections of information on top of the model.[172]

Domain modeling addresses multiple levels of detail. It considers specific items of information, but also considers larger concepts that need to be represented in the metadata. For example, a larger concept might relate to customer service. Thinking about customer service will generate discussion about how a business communicates with customers. The discussion might then focus on specific things customers search for and need answers to.

User scenarios can surface various kinds of information that should be included in the domain model. What questions will information described by the ontology answer? What people, places, and things do you want the content to talk about, and have your audience do things with?

The granularity of the model will depend on which topics are addressed in detail, and which topics are not addressed in detail. The modeling process should distinguish things the publisher *could* mention, from things publisher is *likely* to discuss in detail. Topics that are mentioned occasionally or peripherally can be linked to outside sources of information that can provide more detail.[173] Topics that will be discussed in detail should be included in the domain model. Domain models should reflect the principle to "cover what you know best, and link to the rest." The model should only represent what the publisher will routinely cover.

As the team doing the modeling gathers input, they will want to refine suggestions they've collected. They will want to consider overlapping concepts, look at whether break down or consolidate concept categories, and identify any patterns in relationships.

The refinement process will help to clarify which concepts are entities, and which are properties of entities. It will involve:

- **Naming** things (instances teams will want to track in metadata)
- **Distinguishing** things teams have named
- **Categorizing** things into groups (entity types)
- **Relating** categories to each other (properties).

Modeling is an iterative process. At times it will be top-down, exploring most general concepts first, and then seeing if and how these can be broken down. Other times it will also be bottom-up: looking at specific classes then deciding if they belong to a broader class.

To discover the key concepts discussed in the content — the entities that will be represented by metadata — requirements teams should gather terms for commonly used nouns, considering synonyms and acronyms. Some terms represent examples or instances of a concept, other terms are alternative ways to talk about a concept. When assessing overlapping terms, teams need to identify the core concept represented by different words.

Concepts can be both tangible and intangible. They may be metaphysical or "intrinsic" (subjective, qualitative) concepts or physical or "extrinsic" (objective, measurable) concepts.

Concepts will be related to other concepts. These relationships can be hierarchical, or associative. Hierarchical relationships are for concepts that go from general to more specific. They are "kind-of" relationships. When expressed formally in an ontology, concepts will be classes that contain more specialized entity types.

The modeling process will explore relationships between entities to identify associated entities that are relevant. When a relationship is identified, the team will need to decide what kind of association exists. Some examples of associative relationships are:

- Actions (*created by, used by*)
- *Locations* (located in)
- *How descriptions* (serviced by).

Relationships can be the most difficult part of the model to define. Descriptions can sometimes be vague, too specific or too broad, or difficult to distinguish. It's a good idea to develop definitions for relationships, to understand their scope more thoroughly.

A detailed domain model will indicate what things belong to a domain, what relationships exist between things, and what values are used (enumeration terms).

Domain modeling can produce a blueprint used to build one's own ontology. For example, the BBC followed a domain modeling process to develop metadata requirements, and used the model to create new formal ontologies.

Fortunately, in many cases it won't be necessary to build a large-scale ontology, because existing ones provide most or all of the entities and properties a publisher will need. In fact, most publishers should already be exploring existing vocabularies while they are modeling their domain. They will likely find that existing vocabularies cover many entities and properties they need already. It is often not necessary to specify in detail these common requirements, which are already documented elsewhere.

The granularity of the domain model will reflect how extensive the metadata will be, and how unique it will be compared to other publishers. For many publishers, the model will primarily serve as an informal discussion tool. For some publishers, the model will be a more formal document to indicate unique requirements that will require additional effort to implement.[174]

To know whether other vocabularies meet their needs, publishers need to be clear on their requirements.

---

[170]An approachable introduction to ontologies is the book, *Finding the Concept, Not Just the Word: A librarian's guide to ontologies and semantics.* by Brandy E. King and Kathy Reinold (Chandos Publishing).

[171] Michael Smethurst, "Designing and building data driven dynamic web applications the one web, domain driven, RESTful, open, linked data way", January 29 ,2009, http://www.bbc.co.uk/blogs/radiolabs/2009/01/how_we_make_websites.shtml .

[172] "Linking data in the Enterprise: the road to Olympics 2012", https://www.youtube.com/watch?v=Th4S4y7UcM0

[173] One benefit of metadata is the ability to link to other information, so that publishers are not responsible for recreating information that is already available from other sources.

[174] The formality of the domain model will likely reflect how formal other IT documentation is in the organization. To some degree the best approach will be the one that's the right cultural fit.

Mapping and vocabulary adoption

Once online publishers know what entities and properties they want to cover, they will need to identify external vocabularies that can represent these entities and properties. This alignment is done through a process of mapping.

Each ontology or property vocabulary provides different coverage, which can specify information that can be combined in many different ways. As the largest general-purpose vocabulary, schema.org will likely be the backbone of most online publishers' metadata.

Schema.org provides many or most of the properties that non-technical web publishers will need. Teams should map their domain model to schema.org, and determine what gaps remain.[175] The schema.org vocabulary may even suggest some additional useful terms that weren't included in the original domain model. Despite its broad coverage, schema.org might not provide all the terms needed. For example, a team at Innsbruck University working on tourist sector metadata noted: "Schema.org provides the most common terms to annotate a great variety of entities on the web. But it is a relatively young vocabulary and can't cover all content. That's why we had difficulty mapping" some concepts in their domain relating to tourism in Austria.

In some cases, online publishers can add their own properties and values using the schema.org vocabulary by utilizing certain intangible entities in the vocabulary that permit publishers to define their own terms on an as-needed basis.[176]

Online publishers can supplement schema.org with other standards to cover other properties and entities that are needed. Sometimes another general-purpose standard can meet such needs. Dublin Core, a lightweight and flexible vocabulary, can handle some use cases that are more difficult to accommodate using schema.org.

Online publishers may want to adopt a *high-level* vocabulary to get precise about some things. High-level vocabularies are generic ontologies that are small and tend to focus on housekeeping issues. The Web Annotation Vocabulary is an example of a high-level vocabulary that can be used with other vocabularies.[177]

If an online publisher has a special focus to its content, they might consider a specialized vocabulary relating to a domain. Specialized vocabularies exist for topics such as music and sports.

When adopting a standard, the Open Data Institute (ODI) recommends looking at the license. Who owns the copyright, and what are contributor agreements? These factors may be important if using a standard developed by an industry consortium or other fee-funded organization that controls who is entitled to use the standard.

ODI also advises online publishers to look at the target audience for a standard, and whether it can be extended or customized. Finally, ODI recommends reviewing the maintenance and updating history for indications of how active the standard is.[178]

Extending a vocabulary: the case of Electronic Arts

The experience of Electronics Arts (EA) provides insights into how a well known online publisher adopts an ontology. With revenues approaching $5 billion, EA is one of the largest publishers of interactive games.

EA shared their experience using ontologies at a keynote at the Semantics metadata conference:

"EA has set about changing its approach to the creation, classification, and distribution of digital content. This has entailed structurally modeling and semantically describing the content in EA's ecosystem. This approach has allowed EA to forge an entity-based understanding of available content to provide the right information to the right player at the right time."[179]

Figure 21.1. EA modeled their metadata requirements for exchanging information in relation to stakeholders and platforms. Source: EA.

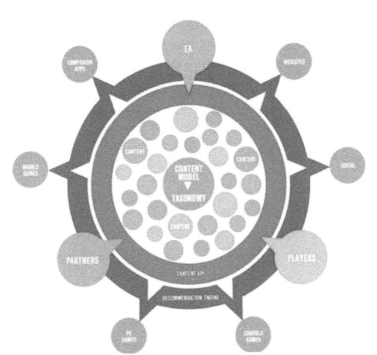

The presenters shared their motivations: "The company had an enormous problem with managing their content across the various divisions and brands: For every title published by EA there used to be multiple content management systems for marketing and support teams, often replicating the content of the other ones via copy and paste. As one can imagine this was highly inefficient, costing the company considerable amounts of time and money while making it increasingly harder to serve content for multiple channels including websites, social networks and in-game."

EA decided to adopt schema.org to manage their content and to serve their content to different devices and platforms. Schema.org provides the foundation of their enterprise ontology (Figure 21.1). According to one of the EA presenters, Aaron Bradley, EA used schema.org to "bootstrap" their enterprise ontology to "extend it locally." Some of the additional properties, such as genres for EA games, are used to deliver more personalization on EA platforms, such as recommendations for other games that are similar.[180]

EA's metadata documentation defines new entities and properties that extend schema.org. These entities and properties support "describing competitive video gaming events ('eSports') with structured data." EA's documentation states: "Wherever possible existing schema.org types and properties have been used. Much new vocabulary was required, however, because schema.org lacks expressive vocabulary surrounding competitions."[181] New entities include GameMode, GamePlatform, as well as new entities that would have wider application such as Region, and Qualification.

EA was inspired by the content management system that the BBC had developed for the football World Cup 2010, which used ontologies to support different services.[182] To implement their ontology, EA chose MarkLogic graph database and PoolParty to managing their enterprise taxonomy. EA plans to extend their ontology further in the future.[183]

---

[175] It is likely that the entity types and properties will be broader and more generic than the original domain model. In many cases the broader vocabulary will work fine, but sometimes an important distinction is required that can't be made with broader terms.

[176] For example, by using the PropertyValueSpecification, https://schema.org/PropertyValueSpecification

[177] https://www.w3.org/TR/annotation-vocab/

[178] "How open standards are developed", http://standards.theodi.org/introduction/how-open-standards-are-developed/

[179] Keynote description, 2017 Semantics conference, https://2017.semantics.cc/aaron-bradley-eamonn-glass

[180] "Schema Markup & the Enterprise: Interview with Aaron Bradley, from Electronic Arts", https://www.youtube.com/watch?v=Ct4Rqy6hlpo

[181] EA, "schema.org Vocabulary Development for Competitive Video Gaming ('eSports')", accessed at https://docs.google.com/document/d/1QMKM-8eZk7Jme6RvEeAV-vLtBWpg1Uly-OuiwmaVAlc/edit#heading=h.2o97i4662v90

[182] "Semantics at Play: Electronic Arts' Linked Data Journey", 2017 Semantics Conference, 12 September 2017 https://www.slideshare.net/aaranged/semantics-at-play-electronic-arts-linked-data-journey

[183] http://www.semiodesk.com/2017/09/22/electronic-arts-multi-channel-content-management/

How to address unique or specialized requirements

A publisher will map the entities and properties that it plans to use to existing vocabularies. It may discover some gaps in coverage.

If a requirements team decides that existing external vocabularies don't cover everything in the domain, they will need to decide how to get that coverage.

If entities or properties are missing in the schema.org vocabulary, and not available in other available vocabularies, online publishers have three options. They can:

1. Propose new properties or entity types **to the core** schema.org vocabulary.
2. Propose a **domain-specific extension** of the schema.org vocabulary.
3. Develop and publish a **new ontology** to cover their domain needs.

In some cases, schema.org may be missing common entities or properties that could be expected to be used widely. This is because the vocabulary is evolving organically, based on suggestions from contributors. If an online publisher finds that they are missing only a few properties or a single entity type that is an obvious subtype of an existing entity, they can propose that these be added to the core schema.org vocabulary. This process is not difficult, though it can take a few months for acceptance and incorporation in a new release of the schema.org vocabulary.

For more domain-specific needs, another possibility is to "extend" schema.org. *Hosted extensions* are part of the schema.org vocabulary but not part of the "core" vocabulary, as they have a domain specific focus, rather than a general purpose focus. They have the schema.org namespace and are subject to the schema.org community review. *External extensions* are built upon the schema.org vocabulary but are separate from it, having their own namespace and review process. For example, the GS1 vocabulary inherits the entities and properties of schema.org, but adds significant numbers of entities and properties of its own that have the prefix gs1:.[184]

The final option is for the publisher to develop its own ontology that is not dependent on an existing external standard. This option is most viable for large-scale publishers (e.g., governments or industry groups) that have specialized domain needs that do not align with existing vocabularies that are designed to address generic use cases. This is a more "go it alone" approach that provides flexibility to address specific needs, but involves more work since it doesn't leverage the collective effort of others. It may be difficult to use generic entities and properties for nation-specific domains, especially in the fields of administrative and regulatory matters.

Developing an ontology: the example of the BBC

The BBC has been a pioneer user of ontologies. They've created and published an extensive collection of ontologies. It seems that for the most part, these are used primarily by the BBC itself, though other parties are free to use them. Because the ontology is public, other parties can find this information described by it easily, whether the information was created by the BBC or another publisher.

The BBC's ontology development is notable for the breadth of information it addresses. Also, the BBC undertook much its work developing ontologies before schema.org was well-developed, so its experience provides another perspective on how ontologies can address specific domains, when the ontology is driven by the business needs of one specific company.

The BBC creates audio and television programming on topics of wide general interest. They also have an extensive web presence providing information about their programming, as well as supplemental information relating to the topics of their broadcasts. They have implemented a number of projects that use open metadata standards (linked data) to deliver content in different ways. The BBC's metadata supports many goals: curating web content for their audience, providing dynamic data-driven content, and allowing multiple perspectives on topics.

The BBC developed a series of ontologies to address domain-specific information they wanted to have available in their metadata. They have been guided by a desire to give an identity on the web to things they would be discussing in their content. They decided to give things URIs on the web to create "business objects." URIs provide a reference, something to point to. It may be easiest to think of each thing as a webpage with a URL, much like Wikipedia, although in practice the URI does not need to have a webpage of content associated with it. In fact, the BBC used Wikipedia to identify topics, and have even created new pages on Wikipedia when a page about a thing didn't already exist.

The BBC's metadata requirements also illustrate their role as an integrator of information. Some of their content was about their own programming. Other content they published discussed topics they aren't the experts on. Rather than recreate information that exists elsewhere, they have accessed that external information and used it in their own content. The BBC decided that when authoritative data existed in sources elsewhere, they would use that information: it was information they didn't want to manage themselves.

Michael C Andrews

The BBC has developed around a dozen ontologies covering internally-focused domains relating to managing content and information, as well as consumer-facing domains relating to topics of interest to BBC audiences:

- Business News Ontology
- Core Concepts Ontology "for representing things such as people, places, events, organisations and themes in the BBC"
- Creative Work Ontology
- Curriculum Ontology
- Food Ontology
- Journalism Ontology
- Politics Ontology
- Programmes Ontology
- Provenance Ontology
- Sport Ontology
- Storyline Ontology
- Wildlife Ontology.

Some BBC ontologies are very specific for entities and properties used in the UK context such as politics and curriculum. Many of the BBC ontologies developed before the full development of schema.org, and few overlap with them.

For ontologies not focused on UK-specific domains, it is interesting to compare the BBC's coverage with schema.org. The BBC food ontology overlaps with schema.org's recipe entity type. It does have slightly different coverage, with more emphasis on recipes in the broader context, "including the foods they are made from and the foods they create as well as the diets, menus, seasons, courses and occasions they may be suitable for." The BBC notes: "Whilst it originates in a specific BBC use case, the Food Ontology should be applicable to a wide range of recipe data publishing across the web."

Another difference is that the BBC vocabulary provides URIs: "While Google, and schema.org, provide a way to represent literal strings in a structured way the Food Ontology provides a richly linked model that more completely describes the recipe and its context."[185]

The BBC is not the only organization to develop its own vocabulary. The Associated Press (AP) is another large publisher that has developed its own vocabulary. The AP Metadata Services offers standardized metadata for content production, management, and delivery. The AP's ontology and taxonomy covers topics in deeper detail than other standards:

- AP Company

- AP Subject
- AP Organization
- AP Person
- AP Geography.

These examples show that no publisher, no matter how large or complex, can dismiss metadata standards because they have insufficient coverage. When required, publishers can develop their own vocabularies. To create an ontology that others can also use, online publishers need to provide:

- A namespace that is stable
- An ontology is published at namespace, for example, PURL
- Documentation on the ontology
- Linking the documentation and the namespace.

While the possibilities are endless, developing one's own vocabulary involves a bigger investment of resources than using existing vocabularies does. It not recommended for most online publishers, especially those new to semantic metadata standards. And if creating one's own entities and properties, publishers are advised to keep it simple. Follow the advice of an experienced ontology builder:

"If you want the data to be used, make it as simple as possible to cover as many use cases as possible but not absolutely every possible scenario. I've wasted too many years working on and with standards that didn't follow this and die on the vine."[186]

For those who decide it is the best option to address their requirements, they need to commit to maintaining the vocabulary so that it is always available, and doesn't become abandoned — a problem that many academic semantic web initiatives have encountered.

---

[184]Richard Wallis, "Evolving Schema.org in Practice Pt2: Working Within the Vocabulary" https://dataliberate.com/2016/03/01/evolving-schema-org-in-practice-pt3-choosing-where-to-extend/

[185] https://www.bbc.co.uk/ontologies/fo

[186] AAC Mapping Validator: How do I handle complexity in knowledge representation?
http://review.americanartcollaborative.org/cookbook/knowledge-representation-vs-api

CHAPTER 22: METADATA USABILITY: MAKING METADATA EASIER TO CREATE

U sability is not another word for "easy." True, making things easy is a big part of usability. But usability also encompasses the ideas of efficiency and usefulness. What seems easy may not ultimately be as efficient or useful as it could be.

> *"It is difficult to get the right values in your taxonomies, especially if your business changes often. Even if you have the right values in your taxonomies, getting authors and editors to use them correctly is a huge challenge."*[187]

-- James Mathewson *IBM*

Getting authors and others to provide metadata is a well-known challenge. Many installed CMSs have missing or inaccurate metadata. It may be tempting to blame authors for missing metadata. But the real fault is often the design of the systems that web teams use. In some cases, metadata specialists have made metadata unnecessarily burdensome to authors. People won't do work that is hard to do when they don't see the benefit of doing it. Metadata has been too hard to create, and too hard to understand. One critic of metadata, Mike Tung, CEO of Diffbot, an AI service, has said:

*"A long line of history (ranging from RDF/microformats/RSS/semantic markup) has shown that requiring human annotation is **never** going to scale in terms of economic incentive and accuracy to all of knowledge."*[188]

Such pessimism can be a self-fulfilling prophesy. People won't use poorly designed tools and flawed systems, and so some technologists assume people are incapable of making use of such tools. In reality, very few vendors have made much of an investment to improve the experience for users and publishers.

A key benefit of metadata is that it can reduce friction when using content. So it is ironic that creating metadata can involve so much friction. It may seem as if metadata makes content easier for audiences, but harder for authors. But creating metadata doesn't have to involve friction. Publishers *can* improve the usability of creating metadata.

The creation of metadata is often described as "tagging." But semantic tagging (adding metadata using standard vocabularies) needs to be distinguished from informal topic tags. The topic tags people see on many websites, and which are used by many CMSs (Figure 22.1), aren't semantic and fall short of the goals of interoperable metadata.

Figure 22.1. In this older version of Sitecore's CMS, the UI for adding tags is not intuitive. Source: Drexel University.

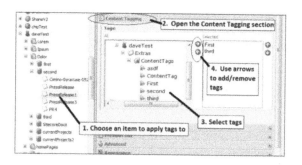

Topic tags are simply labels. The hashtag used in social media another kind of topic tag that is used as a tracking label. A hashtag, such as #ISC2019, is not a robust identifier. We don't know what it refers to. Perhaps more than one thing is using that identifier. Although tags are compact, they are often unambiguous.

Here are some topic tags used by the *Guardian* newspaper:

- Guy Black
- Guy de Maupassant
- Guy Hands
- Guy Lodge on DVDs and downloads
- Guy Pearce
- Guy Ritchie
- Guy Sebastian
- Guyana
- Guyana holidays.

These tags all start with *Guy...* and could refer to music, film, a writer, media, travel, or news. When there is just a label, it can be hard to know. Tags are what most people think of when they think about metadata. But tags are the essence of the metadata quality problems that metadata critics complain about.

Tags show up everywhere: on WordPress websites and in iTunes. We find them in software applications we use to manage our ideas and files. People can relate to the tag metaphor because it somewhat resembles how people label physical objects.[189] In the minds of many authors and web developers, tag labels seem good enough. And they are easy to understand and use. Why bother with more formal metadata?

The problem with self-defined tags is that these tags don't scale. Too many of them, and it's unclear what tags to use. At first, they seem usable. But ultimately, they fail to be usable the more we need to rely on them.

Authors like tags too much. The ubiquity of topic tags is holding back adoption of formal metadata. Tags aren't a viable solution because they lack properties. They aren't semantic.

But publishers should try to leverage what is good about tags. Metadata needs to be user-friendly. Semantic metadata is competing with tags for approval from authors. Metadata needs to be more tag-like in many respects. The best tags will reveal what property they refer to, and will indicate if the value is present, absent, or unknown (Figure 22.2). Metadata should adopt the best qualities of tags — their visual simplicity — without their drawbacks — the lack of useful context.

Figure 22.2. Tag values can be user-friendly and be structured data. Source: Google.

Whether a publisher is building its own UIs for its own tools or evaluating the purchase of tools made by others, it should be familiar with techniques available to make metadata more usable: easier to create, and more reliable.

As a general rule, metadata for static information (information that changes infrequently) will require some author oversight. But metadata for dynamic information that changes frequently should be automated. Automation is most viable when the property needed can be predicted, but the value of the property changes.

The most important rule of metadata usability is to hide the code. Don't expect authors to know any coding or markup. A research team at Innsbruck University notes that raw markup can be intimidating to content contributors: "The generation of schema.org annotations for web content is, especially for people with no background in programming languages or semantic technologies, not trivial. But often these are the people who should actually make use of schema.org annotations: content creators for enterprises or touristic service providers, event promoters or blog editors."

Omeka, an open-source CMS (Figure 22.3) aimed at academic online publishers, does an excellent job providing human-friendly labels and explanations, while indicating the corresponding the machine-readable URI.

Figure 22.3. Omeka UI shows the label for the property, a description of the property, and the Dublin Core vocabulary term. The value is presented as a human-readable label, with a corresponding term from the Getty vocabulary. Source: Omeka.

But hiding code is not enough. Long, confusing, tedious forms are not usable either.

Publishers can improve metadata usability by:

- Improving explanations
- Simplifying entry
- Automating low-level tasks.

Explain important distinctions clearly

Because people entering metadata may not be experts in metadata, they need guidance on making the correct choices (Figure 22.4).

Figure 22.4. Values may be interpreted in different ways. Documentation needs to let users know which to choose. Source: Google Merchant Center.

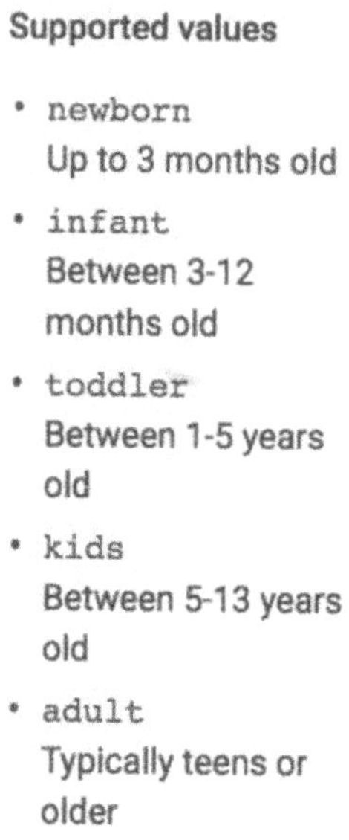

Supported values

- `newborn`
  Up to 3 months old
- `infant`
  Between 3-12
  months old
- `toddler`
  Between 1-5 years
  old
- `kids`
  Between 5-13 years
  old
- `adult`
  Typically teens or
  older

Explain metadata requirements clearly, with simple language and visual indicators. Make clear what's mandatory, suggested, optional (Figure 22.5 and Figure 22.6).

Figure 22.5. IIIF provides a clear picture of what metadata properties are mandatory, recommended, optional, and not applicable. Source: IIIF.

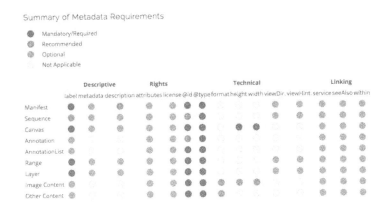

Figure 22.6. Example of distinguishing optional and mandatory properties in documentation. Source: Semantify.it.

In some cases, requirements need to provide detailed guidance. Where possible, they should indicate do's, don'ts, and best practices (Figure 22.7).

Figure 22.7. Google's documentation structures and color-codes advice.

Specify Canonical URLs

Why? The best way to eliminate confusion for indexing when the same content is available under multiple URLs (be it the same or different domains) is to mark one page as the canonical, and all other pages that duplicate that content to refer to it.

Best Practice:

Include the following tag across all pages mirroring a particular piece of content:

```
<link rel="canonical" href="https://www.example.com/your-url/" />
```

If you are supporting Accelerated Mobile Pages be sure to correctly use its counterpart rel="amphtml" instruction as well.

Avoid:

Avoid purposely duplicating content across multiple URLs and not using the rel="canonical" link element.

For example, the rel="canonical" link element can reduce ambiguity for URLs with tracking parameters.

Don't:

Avoid creating conflicting canonical references between your pages.

If users need to consult documentation on how to apply a property, the documentation should provide guidance on whether it is required or optional, how to format the value, and how to use it (Figure 22.8).

Figure 22.8. How to specify a 'sales' price, which may be different from the ordinary price, can be a source of confusion. Source: Google Merchant Center.

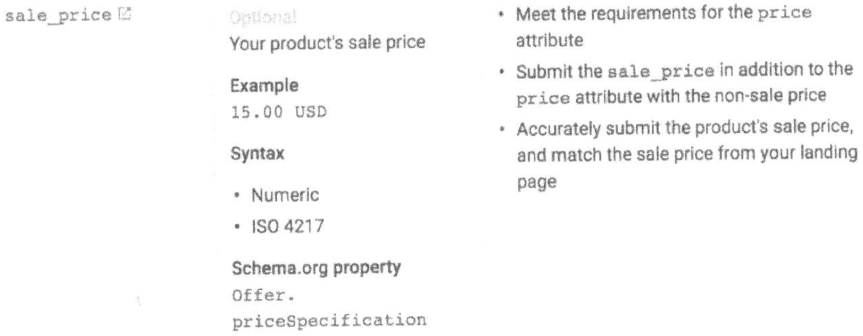

sale_price ☑

Optional
Your product's sale price

Example
15.00 USD

Syntax

• Numeric
• ISO 4217

Schema.org property
Offer.
priceSpecification

• Meet the requirements for the price attribute
• Submit the sale_price in addition to the price attribute with the non-sale price
• Accurately submit the product's sale price, and match the sale price from your landing page

User interfaces for entering metadata need to convey more nuance than a typical online form that has mandatory fields marked with an asterisk, which users often assume is the only information to fill in. The explanation in the UI and online documentation needs to sell the benefits of including the information, not just explain the requirements.

Provide examples, especially for tough judgment calls. For example, a Digital Asset Management system may need to differentiate a photo that depicts a subject from one that shows a subject. By looking at examples, users can see that *depicts* is used when the subject is alone, while *shows* indicates the subject is included within a context (Figure 22.9).

Figure 22.9. Providing examples to show meaning. Source: ImageSnippets

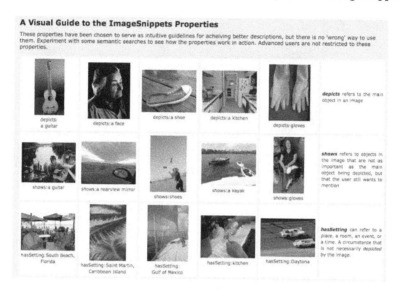

Another area where instructions are needed is to explain the relationships between different kinds of information. Systems should provide advice about what's related (or connected). For example, the UI could note that if you fill out an event, you need to include organizer information.

"Which to use?" advice is also important. Some standards made distinctions that are important but can be hard for users to grasp, even when reading the documentation. Designers of metadata systems should identify user decisions where confusion is possible such as:

- Distinctions between entity types (such as whether to use a general or more specific entity)
- Distinctions between properties (if similar in some way)
- Distinctions between values (such as when indicating a status).

Explaining "Which to use?" is important when property names sound abstract and are consequently prone to confusion. Schema.org has several properties that can cause confusion because they all deal with the topic of the page:

- `mainEntityOfPage`
- `about`
- `mentions`
- `keywords`.

The names of properties may not be self-describing — people can be understandably confused about the correct property to use. UI copy should guide authors on which of these to use, under which circumstances, since the property names alone are not self-evident. UIs can include helper-text or tooltips.

Instructions should also provide guidance on what to do in cases where the user doesn't have expected information. Problems arise when users can't submit metadata because the system's design didn't plan for a scenario, or when users submit bad data because they don't know what to do in a specific situation (Figure 22.10).

Figure 22.10. Provide guidance for common exception cases. Source: Google Merchant Center.

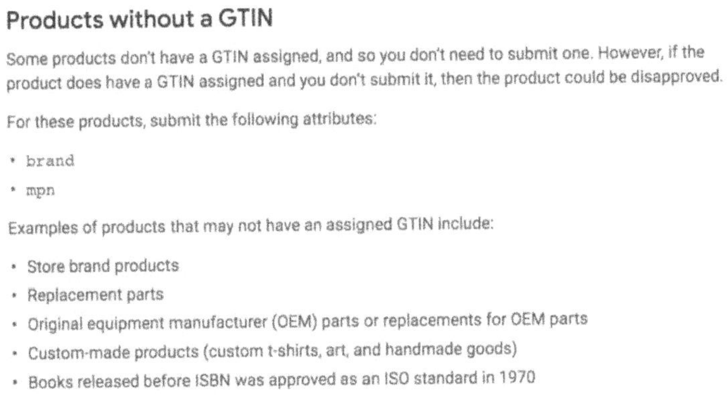

Products without a GTIN

Some products don't have a GTIN assigned, and so you don't need to submit one. However, if the product does have a GTIN assigned and you don't submit it, then the product could be disapproved.

For these products, submit the following attributes:

- brand
- mpn

Examples of products that may not have an assigned GTIN include:

- Store brand products
- Replacement parts
- Original equipment manufacturer (OEM) parts or replacements for OEM parts
- Custom-made products (custom t-shirts, art, and handmade goods)
- Books released before ISBN was approved as an ISO standard in 1970

Systems should not be excessively meticulous. Keep vocabularies broad for areas where information will be sparse. Don't force authors to hunt through detailed properties and values when the distinctions aren't important to audiences or the business.

---

[187] James Mathewson, "What is structured content?" *Biznology blog*, https://biznology.com/2016/09/what-is-structured-content/

[188] Quoted in "The web as a database: The biggest knowledge graph ever", ZDNet, https://www.zdnet.com/article/the-web-as-a-database-the-biggest-knowledge-graph-ever/

[189] The borrowing of physical metaphors such as tags in digital design is called skeuomorphism. Unfortunately, digital environments are inherently different from physical ones, so physical metaphors can be misleading to users.

Simplify entry

When people need to enter metadata manually, it's important that the user interface doesn't get in the way.

> Q: *"What do you think about when I say 'metadata'?"*
> A: *"Ugly, complex interfaces."*[190]

-- Rachel Lovinger *Razorfish*

In some scenarios, the easiest way for authors to add metadata will be by highlighting words that represent entities. This can be done with a tool such as the RDFace plugin for WordPress (Figure 22.11).

Figure 22.11. Example of GUI that allows tagging of entities by the author.
Source: RDFace

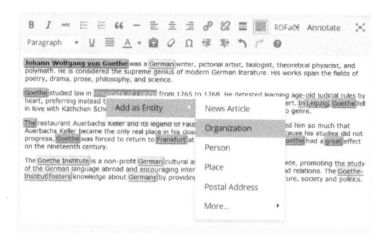

Highlighting is a familiar behavior for most users and it can reduce the amount of text entry.

In cases where authors need to select from a limited number of values, designs can present visual labels, which can be enhanced with color, icons and images to indicate what kind of metadata the label refers to. Authors are comfortable tapping or clicking on visual labels.

---

[190] Rachel Lovinger, "Metadata is a Love Note to the Future", https://www.slideshare.net/rlovinger/metadata-is-a-love-note-to-the-future/8-9\

User interface tips

Minimize forms, and make them less formal. Long forms can feel dispiriting, especially if it isn't clear why the information is being gathered. There is much research on forms usability that metadata can draw from. Some examples of forms usability techniques are progressive revelation, friendly wording, helpful hints, and placeholder text in fields that provide an example of what is needed.

Provide a predefined list of values as options where possible. Don't present everything; only give authors what they need. Make sure the list of values match the likely values required. If reusing enumerated values sourced from elsewhere, remove items that are irrelevant to your use cases, so that users don't need to encounter more values than they would need.[191]

Provide suggested values dynamically using predictive type-ahead (Figure 22.12). Suggested values can match parts of words or synonyms. With suggestions, users don't have to hunt through long drop-down lists.

Figure 22.12. Example of type ahead, with contextual definitions. Source: Omeka.

Another usability problem is the burden of having to choose from a long list of values, especially in taxonomies that have broader and narrower terms. Don't make the user click through a deep tree to find the perfect fit. Consider breaking the task into steps. Users may first choose a broader value, and then be given an option to choose a more specific one. Or they may be presented with a pair of values to choose from, such as "Which is the best description: X? or Y? or None?"

Such questions can be repeated as necessary to identify the most appropriate value.

---

[191]Zeng and Qin, *Metadata* (American Library Association, 2016), p. 197

Automate where possible

Automation of metadata needs to be part of any large scale metadata strategy.

It's important for publishers to understand when and where people need to be involved with classifying metadata. Classification can be done in three ways:

- Manual classification using human judgment only
- Semi-automated, using human-defined rules that are machine-executed
- Fully automated, executed using machine trained classification.

Ideally, human editors will need to be actively involved in some of the total metadata being created. This will generally be for the least routine scenarios.

Some simple scenarios are easy to automate. For example, publishers can reuse metadata values by pre-populating known and recurring patterns. Publishers set up rules to have certain metadata generated automatically. These rules can fill in values based on known relationships between different bits of information.

The next automation level is to let machines make a guess about what key information in or about the content should be included in the metadata. This approach relies on machine learning and other forms of AI. Machines have become good at making certain kinds of guesses, though some of their decisions will need to be checked by humans for accuracy. The use of AI to make suggestions that humans verify is known as automated tagging.

Automated tagging is beneficial in situations where tagging values is hard for humans to do, such as colors and emotions in images. These judgments can be difficult for people to make, but computers with training can detect small distinctions and accurately classify them.

Automated tagging can sometimes find concepts that aren't explicitly expressed in the text. Two or more words used together can suggest that a concept is present.

Automated tagging can also be useful for audio content. It can detect whose voice is speaking at different points of a conversation or audio narrative.

Major tech companies including Google, Amazon, and Microsoft offer affordable services that analyze text or images to classify properties about the content (Figure 22.13). These services can reduce the labor involved with metadata classification.

Figure 22.13. Machine learning image recognition of entity. Source: WolframAlpha

The Wolfram Language can also do the considerably more difficult "artificial intelligence" task of identifying what an image is of.

Identify what an image is of:

For images, Google provides its Cloud Vision API that offers:

- Logo detection
- Landmark detection (for famous landmarks)
- OCR
- Image attributes such as color
- Web detection to find similar images on the web
- Label detection (for broad categories).

Amazon Rekognition is similar service for "Cloud Video Intelligence." These services are improving continually. They can help content staff find which images might relate to topics.

Figure 22.14. Example of entity recognition, finding people, works, organizations, events, places, and concepts in an article. Source: Dandelion

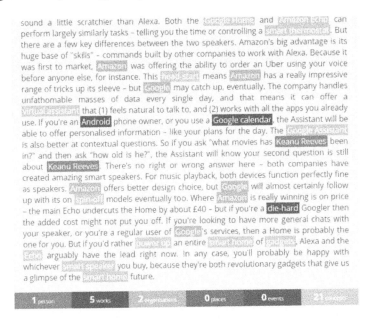

For text content, entity recognition software can be highly effective. (Figure 22.14)

Google provides a Cloud Natural Language API offering:

- Entity recognition, which identifies entities and labels them "by types such as person, organization, location, events, products, and media."
- Content classification, which classifies "documents in predefined 700+ categories."

Amazon Comprehend is a similar service that identifies entities in the text.[192]

While automation can reduce the effort involved with creating metadata, publishers should be careful that automation does not force users to surrender control. Systems should allow overrides to defaults and suggestions. How this is best done will depend on how accurate the defaults and suggestions are most of the time. If automated classifications are right most of the time, but nonetheless wrong with some frequency, then manual overrides should be easy to perform. If automated classifications are rarely wrong, but occasionally need to be corrected, then systems should prompt for a verification to perform the correction. Editors can indicate in what way the classification is wrong, which can help to improve the system's precision when classifying entities.

---

[192] "Amazon Comprehend", https://aws.amazon.com/comprehend/

Don't forget training of editors

While automated tools and good UIs can reduce errors, training authors and editors can help reduce problems as well. Text-based values are often of poor quality when users are confused about how to enter the values correctly.

Publishers should provide simple to understand rules on how to deal with common situations in text entry.

For example, publishers may tell authors to leave a field blank if a value is not available so that authors don't enter values such as *N/A*, *Generic*, *None*, or *Does not exist*. Or publishers may instruct authors never to include dashes or spaces in the fields that involve numbers or codes, or never to use non-text characters such as # in values.

Adhering to a few basic rules for text values can improve the quality of the metadata measurably.

CHAPTER 23:
SOURCING METADATA

Where does metadata come from? Online publishers must get complete and reliable metadata into their content management systems. They need a defined process for sourcing metadata.

Their sourcing process must answer two questions:

1. How will the metadata be added to their content?
2. Who will be responsible for adding it?

Often, if the responsibility for metadata is placed entirely on the author, the process breaks down.

Alternatively, if metadata responsibilities are centralized in a single person or small team, that function may not be able to keep up with the load. Publishers need a balanced approach that makes the best use of available resources.

There are plenty of stories about publishers that create fields for metadata, but later find that these fields are empty, because content creators ignored them. Incomplete metadata can prevent a publisher from realizing their objectives.

Merely creating a field, and expecting someone to fill it in, is not a sound plan. Publishers need to consider the scope of effort involved.

The scope of the effort

All metadata needs to either be created or acquired.

Publishers should aim to reduce the effort required to create metadata, and also aim to get maximum value from the metadata they create.

When publishers decide to include properties, they should ensure they get values for those properties. How to do that can involve a range of approaches.

Metadata is designed for sharing. It can be far more efficient for a publisher to acquire metadata from elsewhere, rather than create it themselves. Publishers have many opportunities to utilize metadata from others, and also to let others utilize metadata they've created. The sharing of metadata with others is in some ways similar to firms sharing code in open source software projects: collaboration reduces the effort for everyone and results in higher quality.

An online publisher's ability to achieve their objectives depends on having good quality metadata. Sourcing strategies will help them get high-quality metadata to fulfill their objectives.

Sourcing strategy is often an overlooked dimension. The challenge of getting complete metadata is widespread, faced by even well-known, sophisticated web publishers. But the challenge is not insurmountable. Publishers have a range of approaches they can use.

By developing a sourcing approach, publishers don't have to rely entirely on writers to create metadata. Authors are no longer saddled with the entire responsibility. Publishers should consider different options. A successful sourcing approach involves using different means to create and acquire metadata.

The means of *creating* metadata include:

- Metadata that staff must enter themselves
- Metadata that machines generate, often with the oversight of staff
- Metadata that auto-populate.

The means of *acquiring* metadata include:

- Metadata that can be acquired from other sources
- Crowd-sourced metadata.

Human-created metadata

Some metadata values will need to be added by humans, who will need to make judgments about what values are most accurate. Who should do this depends on the nature of the content and the availability of resources. Some options include:

- By authors, editors, or webmasters
- By SMEs who might be reviewing content for accuracy
- By contractors following rules and examples.

Human-created metadata is most appropriate for metadata which doesn't already exist, and for which human judgment is required, because machines can't reliably make the correct decisions about what metadata values to include.

Yet because human-created metadata depends on individuals, it can be prone to inconsistency if different individuals apply different criteria. All people involved with making metadata decisions need to follow the same guidelines about what properties to include, and what values to use. For non-technical content, this can be often a simple set of formal guidelines applied during the publishing review process. For information about specialized topics, subject matter experts may need to be involved to ensure the accuracy of values included in the metadata. For example, if the content deals with a biomedical topic, a subject matter expert may need to confirm the precise topics that are indexed by the metadata.

Metadata specialists can learn much from the best practices of economic statisticians, who must all classify data in a consistent way to allow the data to be compared accurately. The United Nations' International Standard Industrial Classification (ISIC) is used by governments around the world (Figure 23.1). It provides detailed explanations about how to classify items so that there is no doubt which classification is correct. It provides a list of entities included in a class, examples of such entities, and pointers to other entities that are not included and should be classified elsewhere.[193]

Figure 23.1. ISIC guidelines for classifying industrial products. Source: United Nations.

2910 Manufacture of motor vehicles

This class includes:

— manufacture of passenger cars
— manufacture of commercial vehicles:
  • vans, lorries, over-the-road tractors for semi-trailers etc.
— manufacture of buses, trolley-buses and coaches
— manufacture of motor vehicle engines
— manufacture of chassis fitted with engines
— manufacture of other motor vehicles:
  • snowmobiles, golf carts, amphibious vehicles
  • fire engines, street sweepers, travelling libraries, armoured cars etc.
  • concrete-mixer lorries
— ATVs, go-carts and similar including race cars

This class also includes:

— factory rebuilding of motor vehicle engines

This class excludes:

— *manufacture of lighting equipment for motor vehicles, see 2740*
— *manufacture of pistons, piston rings and carburetors, see 2811*
— *manufacture of agricultural tractors, see 2821*
— *manufacture of tractors used in construction or mining, see 2824*
— *manufacture of off-road dumping trucks, see 2824*
— *manufacture of bodies for motor vehicles, see 2920*
— *manufacture of electrical parts for motor vehicles, see 2930*
— *manufacture of parts and accessories for motor vehicles, see 2930*
— *manufacture of tanks and other military fighting vehicles, see 3040*
— *maintenance, repair and alteration of motor vehicles, see 4520*

This example shows that even when publishers must create their own metadata manually, they can still reduce the effort required when using existing classification systems that provide detailed guidance.

---

[193] "International Standard Industrial Classification of All Economic Activities (ISIC), Revision 4"

Machine-assisted, human-verified

In some setups, machines review text, images, and video in order to "tag" the reviewed content with metadata. In many areas, such as news articles that use many proper nouns, this can be done with a high degree of accuracy, reducing the effort for staff. But since there may be some ambiguity, a small percentage may need to be confirmed or corrected by humans.

The pattern where machines do much of the spade work, but people course correct, is sometimes referred to as "human-in-the-loop" workflows.

Machine-classified can use different techniques:

- Named entity recognition, which identifies proper nouns in a text
- Topic mapping, which classifies topics based on the co-presence of different word combinations
- Natural language processing, which attempts to understand the structure of sentences, such as what a pronoun refers to.

Machine classification can offer major efficiencies over manual classification. In some cases, it can identify information that might be overlooked by manual processes. Machine classification can sometimes generate errors (such as with homographs — words that have multiple meanings). So humans need to check that machine classification is accurate.

Auto-populated Metadata

While it seems obvious to automate the insertion of metadata into content, these capabilities are sometimes underutilized, because authors and IT staff don't discuss requirements and consider available approaches.

Two approaches to auto-populated metadata are common.

System-generated metadata is useful for administrative and technical metadata. Most content management systems will auto-populate metadata for the author, date published, and some other administrative values.

Template-driven metadata is useful for structural and descriptive metadata. Metadata for many fields can be built into templates. For example, if you host events at a limited number of locations, selecting the name of the location can auto-populate the full details such as the address. This metadata is stored in a database maintained by the publisher that may be separate from the CMS.

It is also possible to auto-populate metadata with external metadata sources. For example, during the publishing workflow, a system could make a call to an API to retrieve and insert metadata coming from another source.

Acquiring other people's metadata

It is always desirable to avoid recreating metadata that already exists and is available. If a publisher's content mentions common factual information, it can be preferable for the publisher to reuse information that other sources have already compiled.

Publishers have the opportunity to use metadata values from other sources, and specialized properties that other sources have developed. Publishers can acquire metadata by downloading files or accessing the metadata through an API.

Externally-sourced metadata can exist in different forms:

- As raw open data that needs to be converted to conform to specific metadata standards (information that's structured but not semantic)
- As an RDF data file, which is already standards-compliant
- As a defined list of values for properties.

Open data (either government- or community-developed) can provide structured information, but such data may not be labeled according to terminology or encoded in the markup used by metadata standards. One of the most common sources of external metadata is the GeoNames geographical database.

Other widely used open data sources include IMDb for film information, the World Bank Linked Data files for comparative data on countries, and MusicBrainz for information about music recordings.

Once open data is downloaded, publishers can process the data to conform to the needs to their internal systems.

Figure 23.2. Metadata about food products is available from the USDA. Source: USDA.

Publishers can also combine metadata from different sources. USDA Branded Food Products Database, which provides information on product names, ingredients, nutrition and portions, is aligned with GS1 standards (Figure 23.2).[194]

In addition to saving time by not recreating this information, publishers benefit from having up-to-date information. Publishers can source current facts through an API call to Google's knowledge graph.

Metadata that is already available in standards-compliant formats is especially useful. The US National Library of Medicine Medical Subject Headings (MeSH) vocabulary is a detailed health property list that's available in RDF (Figure 23.3).

Figure 23.3. The National Library of Medicine's MeSH Vocabulary is widely used to precisely describe health conditions. Source: NIH.

Viruses [B04]
    Arboviruses [B04.080]
    Archaeal Viruses [B04.100] ⊜
        Fuselloviridae [B04.100.224]
        Guttaviridae [B04.100.250]
        Lipothrixviridae [B04.100.450]
        Myoviridae [B04.100.500]
        Rudiviridae [B04.100.700]
        Siphoviridae [B04.100.750]
    Bacteriophages [B04.123] ⊜
        Bacillus Phages [B04.123.100]
        Caudovirales [B04.123.150] ⊜
            Myoviridae [B04.123.150.500] ⊜
                Bacteriophage mu [B04.123.150.500.260]
                Bacteriophage P1 [B04.123.150.500.300]
                Bacteriophage P2 [B04.123.150.500.305]
                Bacteriophage T4 [B04.123.150.500.350]
            Podoviridae [B04.123.150.700] ⊕

Even when publishers can't acquire complete data from external sources, they can often take advantage of enumerated values: a limited set of permitted values associated with a property. Standards organizations may make available enumerated values. These are also called controlled vocabularies. Some are linked to a specific property vocabulary. Enumerated values reduce the effort required to populate values, and improve the accuracy of values.

> *"An enumeration is a list of values suggested by the system to populate certain fields. Enumerations let you standardize the values of these fields, and help with data input or use within queries."*[195]

-- Adobe

Enumerated values are an intermediate step toward getting complete metadata. They offer a range of possible values for a property, though they still require someone or some script to choose which value is the correct one.

Kinds of enumerated values include a list of states or provinces, countries, airports, national parks, and automobile models. These may be available from government sources, given government oversight of these things. In the United States and some other countries, government data is available free of charge.

For example, the International Air Transport Association (IATA) provides a widely-adopted set of standardized two-letter IATA Airline Codes and three-letter City and Airport Codes. These enumerated values provide a complete list of major airlines and airports in the world.

Another good source for enumerated values are IDs from Wikidata. Yle, the Finnish Broadcasting Corporation, is using Wikidata to identify entities in online news and feature articles.[196]

One Drupal developer noted the value of acquiring external linked data to incorporate into one's own content:

"In addition to your own content, there could be various use cases and methods for dynamically displaying data from outside sources and displaying it on your site.

Why would you want to do this? Perhaps another website contains unique data that's unavailable anywhere else. The content is highly relevant to what you publish. Although you don't own or control the resource, displaying this data as supplementary content from this trusted source on your site would enrich your visitor's experience on your site."[193]

---

[194] "USDA Branded Food Products Database Created to Expand the USDA National Nutrient Database" https://www.gs1us.org/details-page/articleid/86/usda-branded-food-products-database-created-to-expand-the-usda-national-nutrient-database

[195]
https://docs.campaign.adobe.com/doc/AC6.1/en/PTF_Administration_Eleme nts_Managing_enumerations.html

[196] See http://wikimedia.fi/2016/04/15/yle-3-wikidata/

[197] "Using sparql and linked open data", https://www.urbaninsight.com/article/using-sparql-and-linked-open-data-for-content-blocks-your-drupal-7-website

Get others to add it

Sometimes others have more expertise or familiarity with certain details relating to the content and are in a better position to add metadata. Such outside parties can sometimes contribute useful metadata. They need access to tools that make the process easy and that reduces errors.

In certain situations, publishers can ask their users to contribute metadata to published content. Most users have little desire to contribute metadata, so it's important to determine that some users are interested in contributing. For content that relates to a well-defined community of interest, especially one that is hobby-related, user-contributed metadata may be viable. For example, non-profit archives have enlisted volunteers to tag photos or recordings about topics that may interest them. If the metadata will make a resource more openly accessible, some people may be willing to contribute to the effort, as the experience of Wikidata shows.

People may be inclined to participate in crowd-sourced activities (Figure 23.4) for a range of motivations: learning/personal achievement, altruism, enjoyment/intellectual curiosity, social motives, or direct compensation.[198] The relevance of the task is important: users are most likely to add metadata during or soon after experiencing content or a physical place or event.

Figure 23.4. Google gets users to crowd-source metadata about locations. Source: Google.

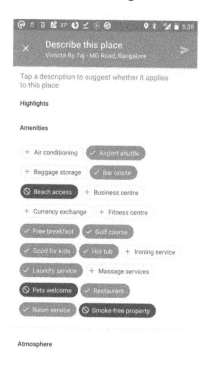

Nonprofits, such as in the cultural sector, use crowd-sourcing to add metadata to their assets. Because of the importance of crowd-sourcing to building metadata, such institutions provide users to tools to assist with metadata annotation. For example, the Europeana consortium has developed the Europeana Annotations API, based on Web Annotation Data Model. With it, users can add comments to images and other media.[199]

Crowd-sourcing depends on behavioral mechanics. When publishers ask users to submit content (photos, reviews) to complete a profile, they need to make the request appealing.

In some cases, publishers can ask for other opinions about already submitted metadata. Publishers can ask users if the information is complete, or if they agree with the information. Some websites elicit user opinions about data quality by providing link asking if the information is correct. Publishers might offer gamified rewards such as badges for contributors based on their participation level. Or they could make a community appeal, asking for help to make the content better for everyone.

Another crowd-sourcing approach is when publishers invite users to add to existing information, so that more details can build over time to complete a profile. Publishers with mobile apps might request users to submit information or content (Figure 23.5).

Figure 23.5. Example of users being prompted to tag photos they upload by

choosing machine-suggested tags. Source: Clarifai.

When users submit information, publishers will want to get it in a format that will work with their metadata. Because the potential volume of such submissions, publishers should try to capture complete and accurate metadata at the time of submission, rather than hoping to add it at a later stage. For example, publishers can ask users to tag the names of people or objects in photos. Publishers can structure ratings and reviews so that users can tap ratings with a minimum of effort.

---

[198] Aikaterini Katmada, Anna Satsiou, Ioannis Kompatsiaris, "Incentive Mechanisms for Crowdsourcing Platforms", https://pdfs.semanticscholar.org/39f6/148d95daf9818d8ba6ede7e619e3f9c035bc.pdf

[199] Europeana, "Annotation Scenarios", https://pro.europeana.eu/resources/apis/annotations#scenarios

CHAPTER 24: METADATA QUALITY

U seful information and knowledge graphs depend on accurate and complete data.

The W3C defines many metadata standards, so it is not surprising they provide a definition of quality:

"Data quality is commonly defined as 'fitness for use' for a specific application or use case."

The quality of metadata is judged by how effectively it does the job it is meant to do. But such a standard provides limited guidance to online publishers deciding how to prioritize metadata decisions. What's ultimately the proper threshold of quality will depend on what the publisher needs to accomplish. In principle there is is no concept of excessive quality, too few errors, or too much accuracy. In practice, it is possible to put too much emphasis on aspects of quality that are not critical to a publisher's current or expected requirements.

Quality and context

Which is worse: bad metadata or no metadata? What's "good enough"? To some extent, the answer will depend on the context.

Metadata quality can be considered from the perspective of coverage, integrity, and utility.

Coverage relates to missing properties or missing values for properties. When no metadata exists, it can't do much. When metadata is uneven, where values aren't uniformly available, this can create problems in some use cases.

> *"Sophisticated search and retrieval capabilities are worthless if the data on which the searches depend is inaccurate."*[200]

-- Richard Bade

Integrity relates to the accuracy of information: how you check and quality-assured information to assure it is accurate.

Utility relates to how the information can be used. It includes how you specify metadata so that it is reliable for machines

The more widely information is used, especially to support automation, the more critical information becomes. A human can understand the meaning of a value that has a typo, but computers will likely interpret that value incorrectly.

> "In order for machine learning, deep learning, etc. to be effective and work the most quickly, the more data that is tagged and defined and labeled correctly the quicker everything goes...labeling and tagging data...It's going to be the job of the future."[201]

-- Mark Cuban *venture capitalist and "Shark Tank" judge*

Metadata quality partly depends on the use cases that rely on the metadata. Quality guidelines and processes make information more valuable. It can save effort, preventing what is known as "defensive" programming. When developing internal requirements and processes, web teams will discuss questions such as:

- What is required, recommended, and optional?[202]

- What's the investment involved to produce the metadata?
- What tasks depend on this?
- What's the cost or effort of fixing poor quality metadata at a later date?
- What's the cost or effort of creating metadata *de novo* at a later date?

Sometimes publishers can't anticipate all future use cases. They need to be future-ready.

---

[200] *Responsible Librarianship: Library Policies for Unreliable Systems* (Library Juice Press 2007), p. 74

[201] http://www.cnbc.com/2017/05/16/mark-cuban-blue-collar-job-of-the-future-is-tagging-data.html

[202] For a standard definition of *must*, *should* and *may* in requirements, see "Key words for use in RFCs to Indicate Requirement Levels", http://www.rfc-editor.org/rfc/rfc2119.txt

Quality best practices

The W3C has developed guidelines, "Data on the Web Best Practices", that provide detailed guidance on different dimensions of metadata quality.[203]

The W3C best practices are motivated by eight benefits, which are useful guideposts for considering the quality of metadata:

- **Comprehension**: that humans understand the structure and the meaning the information described with metadata.
- **Processability**: that machines can automatically process and manipulate the metadata
- **Discoverability**: that machines will be able to automatically discover the information.
- **Reuse**: the chances of metadata reuse by different groups
- **Trust**: the confidence that consumers have in the information
- **Linkability**: connections between metadata resources from different publishers
- **Access**: humans and machines can access up to date information in a variety of forms.
- **Interoperability**: a consensus among data publishers and consumers about what the information means.

The W3C guidelines can be grouped into best practices relating to Completeness, Interoperability, Implementation, and Identifiers.

---

[203] W3C, "Data on the Web Best Practices", https://www.w3.org/TR/dwbp/

Completeness best practices

The W3C advises publishers to think about completeness in terms of different use cases for metadata. They advise:

1. Provide metadata in both **human and machine readable** forms
2. Provide **descriptive metadata** indicating entities and their properties
3. Provide **structural metadata** relating to content types
4. Provide **licensing information** such as copyright
5. Provide **provenance information** when reusing metadata from elsewhere
6. Indicate **quality information** when values are uncertain or estimated.[204]

The issue of how to handle uncertain values is addressed in some metadata schemas. A good example is the GS1 standard, which provides enumerated values for claims about a product. These values are:

- FALSE gs1:NonbinaryLogicCode-FALSE
- NOT_APPLICABLE gs1:NonbinaryLogicCode-NOT_APPLICABLE
- TRUE gs1:NonbinaryLogicCode-TRUE
- UNSPECIFIED gs1:NonbinaryLogicCode-UNSPECIFIED.

Such detail avoids problems that can be associated with not knowing what blank values mean.

---

[204] For a detailed explanation of different metadata such as descriptive, structural, and various administrative metadata, see my book, *Metadata Basics for Web Content*, chapter 5.

Interoperability practices

Since a core benefit of metadata is providing the interoperability of information, online publishers should follow best practices that enhance interoperability. These include:

1. Use machine-readable standardized data formats
2. Use locale-neutral data representations
3. Provide data in multiple formats
4. Reuse vocabularies, preferably standardized ones.

Several guidelines relate to internationalization, a concern of many online publishers. For example, the W3C advises locale-neutrality in metadata: "Data values that are machine-readable and not specific to any particular language or culture are more durable and less open to misinterpretation than values that use one of the many different cultural representations. Things like dates, currencies and numbers may look similar but have different meanings in different locales."

They also recommend that any locale-specific values be identified: "Use locale neutral data structures and values, or, where that is not possible, provide metadata about the locale used by data values." They explain why these practices improve interoperability:

"By using a locale-neutral format, systems avoid the need to establish specific interchange rules that vary according to the language or location of the user. When the data is already in a locale-specific format, making the locale and language explicit by providing locale parameters allows users to determine how readily they can work with the data and may enable automated translation services."

Since information may be expressed in different languages, all text should use the Unicode standard:

"Use Unicode for handling character and string data. Unicode improves multilingual text processing and makes software localization easier."

Interoperability is also enhanced through vocabulary reuse — using a widely used external metadata standard.

Implementation best practices

Choosing the right vocabulary to describe metadata is important to quality. The WC3 refers to this as "formalization." It's possible to be too simple or too complex. The W3 stresses:

"Choose the right formalization level."

Formalization goes to the heart of the coverage issue and involves several competing considerations. On one hand: "Choosing a very simple vocabulary is always attractive but there is a danger: the drive for simplicity might lead the publisher to omit some data that provides important information."

Yet on the other hand: "complex vocabularies require more effort to produce and understand, which could hamper their reuse."

In the end: "a balance has to be struck, remembering that the goal is not simply to share your data, but for others to reuse it."

Always keep reuse in mind when deciding formalization. Make sure that your internal needs don't overwhelm the needs of external users.

"If you are creating a vocabulary of your own, keep the semantic restrictions to the minimum that works for you, again, so as to increase the possibility of reuse by others."

The W3C recommends using common vocabularies wherever possible. "Are simple facts stated simply and retrieved easily?"

Identifiers

Identifiers are vital to reducing the possibilities of ambiguity. They can make the metadata more useful. Identifiers can allow entities, properties, and values to have different labels in different languages.

Where feasible, indicate entities and values with unique IDs to reduce ambiguity for machines. This does not remove the need for human readable labels. The W3C recommends:

1. Use persistent URIs as identifiers of datasets (a collection of statements)
2. Use persistent URIs as identifiers within datasets (specific entities and values.)

URIs are identifiers that look like web URLs. More precisely: "URIs: globally unique identifiers that can be looked up by dereferencing them over the Internet". "URIs are 'dumb strings', that is, they carry no semantics. Their function is purely to identify a resource." Although URIs do not carry semantics, it is possible to make them more human-readable.

Compared with ordinary global unique identifiers (GUIDs), URIs are web accessible and can be linked to metadata elsewhere easily.

URIs are important to how machines can use metadata, and how developers work with metadata. Linked Data depends on URIs.

"When de-referenced (looked up), a single URI may offer the same resource in more than one format. http://example.com/dataset may offer the same data in, say, CSV, JSON, and XML. The server returns the most appropriate format based on content negotiation."

Another best practice is to make URIs persistent. Unlike URLs which can change, URIs are supposed to reliably return the same information over time.[205]

Phil Archer, one of the leading experts on URIs, provides recommendations in his "Study on Persistent URIs." He cites the following URI model as a form to follow:

```
{URI Root}/{Resource path}/{ID}/{String}/{Options}.
```

Archer provides detailed recommendations. URIs:

*   Identify each resource
*   Are permanent and stable
*   Are manageable

- Are unique
- Are clear, concise and short
- Are explicitly linked with each other
- Are user-friendly (i.e. human readable), i.e.
  europa.eu/health/guidelines *not*
  europa.eu/health/1235564798765465498
- Are consistent in format and structure, e.g. europa.eu/health/…
  not europa.eu/healthy/
- Do not contain keywords
- Do not contain file extensions
- Have no 'www' (use a 301 redirection in case it's presumed)
- Are lowercase only
- Do not contain accents or spaces
- Replace special characters !"£$%^&*() with hyphens or underscores.[206]

While URIs to some extent can be human-readable for developers, their primary purpose is to serve as identifiers that are machine readable. For non-technical users, labels can explain what the URI means. Text labels can be managed with metadata standards:

"Best practice is to have an rdfs:label for every entity. If there are multiple possible labels for an entity, a single skos:prefLabel is best practice, with alternate labels as one or more rdfs:label tags. skos:prefLabel is a subclass of rdfs:label, meaning all skos:prefLabel properties are also rdfs:label (s), so it is not required to duplicate data across them."[207]

---

[205] A very good discussion is available by Phil Archer, "Study on Persistent URIs ", http:// philarcher.org/diary/2013/uripersistence/

[206] *Ibid.*

[207] AAC Mapping Validator, "What are best practices for modeling text strings?" http:// review.americanartcollaborative.org/cookbook/How-do-we-handle-textual-descriptions-of-data

Values for 'informative' vocabularies

Text values require special care to ensure that quality is maintained. Some vocabularies such has schema.org follow an "informative rather than normative" approach and often don't impose strict constraints on values. Even some number values are free-text fields. It falls on the publisher to validate their values before validating their markup.

Online publishers need to validate values on entry. Fortunately, many programming frameworks provide validation. For example, Symfony, a PHP framework used to build Drupal, among other products, has scripts that can check the formatting of different kinds of values. It provides different kinds of constraints for basic, string, number, comparison, date, and collection values.[208]

Online publishers should validate different kinds of values, such as

1. Boolean values
2. Text values
3. Numeric values
4. Date values
5. Collections
6. Values that are files
7. Alphanumeric codes.

Although there is no standard list for values to validate, the Symphony library provides a comprehensive set that will be useful to many online publishers.

Basic Constraints Basic constraints assert very basic things about the value of properties.

- NotBlank
- Blank
- NotNull
- IsNull
- IsTrue
- IsFalse
- Type.

String Constraints

- Email
- Length
- Url

- Regex
- IP
- UUID.

Number Constraints

- Range.

Comparison Constraints

- EqualTo
- NotEqualTo
- IdenticalTo
- NotIdenticalTo
- LessThan
- LessThanOrEqual
- GreaterThan
- GreaterThanOrEqual.

Date Constraints

- Date
- DateTime
- Time.

Collection Constraints

- Choice
- Collection
- Count
- UniqueEntity
- Language
- Locale
- Country.

File Constraints

- FIle
- Image.

Financial and other Number Constraints

- Bic
- CardScheme
- Currency
- Luhn
- Iban
- Isbn
- Issn.

These building blocks can provide validation of that text values conform to expected patterns.

---

[208] Documentation on Symphony validation available at https://symfony.com/doc/current/validation.html

Values for 'normative' vocabularies

It is possible for an external metadata schema to declare what properties and values it expects. For example, a location must include a longitude and latitude. The values must be in a certain format.

Such rules provide greater precision. Until recently, semantic metadata didn't have a good, general purpose mechanism to enforce such rules. The Web Ontology Language (OWL) allows some restrictions, but OWL was not considered practical for many publishers.

Recently, the W3C developed the SHACL (Shapes Constraint Language.) SHACL offers built-in constraints:

- Value Type Constraint Components (such as datatype)
- Cardinality Constraint Components (such as min and max count)
- Value Range Constraint Components (such as min and max values)
- String-based Constraint Components (length, pattern, language)
- Property Pair Constraint Components (such as less than, disjoint, equals)
- Logical Constraint Components (such as not, and, or)
- Complex Custom Constraints (for example, combining several constraints, or specifying mandatory values).

The W3C has envisioned how SHACL will be used by authors and others contributing metadata. They note:

"There is a need to have constraints that provide model-driven validation of permissible values in user interfaces. The major requirement here is a declarative model of:

- *Which properties are relevant for a given class/instance?*
- *What is the value type of those properties?*
- *What is the valid cardinality (min/maxCount)?*
- *What is the interval of valid literal values (min/maxValue)?*
- *Any other metadata typically needed to build forms with input widgets."*

Technical details about SHACL are available in documentation:

- "Shapes Constraint Language (SHACL)"[209]
- "SHACL Use Cases and Requirements"[210]

An early adopter of SHACL is SpringerNature, the large scientific publishers.[211] SpringerNature has used SHACL in its SciGraph tool (Figure 24.1). At the time of this writing, it is not yet using constraints, but it plans to do so.

Figure 24.1. SciGraph shapes encoded using SHACL. Source: SpringerNature.

Class: sg:Affiliation

Schema	Field	Property	Datatype
RDF/S	type	rdf:type	sg:Affiliation
	label	rdfs:label	xsd:string
SG	has organization	sg:hasOrganization	sg:Organization
	order	sg:order	xsd:integer
	published city	sg:publishedCity	xsd:string
	published country	sg:publishedCountry	xsd:string
	published division	sg:publishedDivision	xsd:string
	published name	sg:publishedName	xsd:string
	published postcode	sg:publishedPostcode	xsd:string
	Scigraph ID	sg:scigraphid	xsd:string

[209] "Shapes Constraint Language (SHACL)", W3C Recommendation, 20 July 2017, https:// www.w3.org/TR/2017/REC-shacl-20170720/#core-components-shape

[210] "SHACL Use Cases and Requirements", W3C Working Group Note, https://w3c.github.io/datashapes/data-shapes-ucr/

[211] "SciGraph Explorer: Shapes", http://scigraph.springernature.com/explorer/shapes/

Fit Metadata

While best practices are helpful, online publishers can also improve their quality by learning from their mistakes. As the W3C notes repeatedly, reuse is a major goal. Publishers will know their quality is good if others want to use their metadata. If others are hesitating, it may be worth investigating if there are any quality issues making the information difficult to use.

One final tip about metadata quality. Metadata requirements should be written in a consistent way. For an example of how to do it, consult the "W3C Manual of Style".[212]

---

[212] "W3C Manual of Style", https://w3c.github.io/manual-of-style/

CHAPTER 25: IMPLEMENTATION APPROACHES

O nce a publisher has a model for metadata they need for their content, the next step is to decide where and how to begin implementing it. Metadata requirements involve dependencies. The practicalities of implementation are themselves an input into the requirements process. Requirements must be prioritized into tiers, each of which involves a specific scope to implement.

Silos pose the biggest challenge for large organizations, which can have many silos and lots of content. For large organization especially, it's generally best not to try to adopt external standards everywhere all at once.

Even if the organization considers metadata standardization and development a priority, and marshals extensive resources to implement it, a wholesale transformation is likely to fail if attempted all at once. Silos don't get undone all at once. De-siloing will happen through a progression of phases. Different parts of an organization and different domains of content may be in different phases at the same time. The phases are:

1. **Silos** — incompatible and unconnected descriptions
2. **Bridging** — connecting and translating different descriptions, and exchanging information through APIs
3. **Equivalency** — different terminology for properties and values are still used, but are cross-referenced and noted as equivalent
4. **Standardized terminology** — the same standard terminology is used by everyone.

New projects provide an opportunity to introduce standardized terminology. New projects can introduce a new baseline that existing content and systems can reference and build off of.

Introducing external standards to existing systems can entail changes for both content contributors and developers. Both groups are important, yet each will have their own concerns. What is easiest for developers may be more work for content contributors, and vice versa.

Metadata for everyone: inclusive metadata

Standards are one aspect of making metadata valuable to everyone. The other aspect is that the metadata should be *inclusive*. Inclusive means every stakeholder who needs to use the metadata can use it, whether their responsibilities are technical or non-technical. Contributors should be able to use the metadata without needing to understand the technicalities of its representation. No one is left out because the metadata is too limited in scope, and doesn't address their needs. For this reason, SEO metadata is not completely inclusive, because it may not be comprehensive in coverage, and is optimized for search engine crawlers but not for other tasks.[213] Metadata for SEO needs to exist alongside other representations of the metadata (such as administrative metadata) that support other publishing goals.

Terminology is the backbone of inclusive metadata. Terminology can refer to the property vocabulary (the schema or ontology) used to describe types of entities, as well as to the verbal labels for values used to indicate the identity or characteristics described.

When expressed using standardized terminology, entities and properties are no longer defined according to a proprietary data model such as the JSON data models commonly used in APIs. Instead, standardized terminology uses a data schema defined by the W3C or some other international standards group. This approach allows the widest possible use of web content metadata across the enterprise. This approach is inclusive because:

1. All enterprise functions that contribute and access metadata are able to take advantage of it.
2. Standards maximize the exchange of metadata between various enterprise IT systems, as well as IT systems outside of the enterprise.

Standardization is a long-term goal. But in the short-term, forced standardization everywhere could be impractical and disruptive. An inclusive approach can be incremental. The standardization of metadata for different entities and content types does not have to be implemented at the same pace. Some domains have well-developed vocabularies, but coverage for other domains is scant and must rely on more general descriptors. Programming tools and libraries for metadata standards vary in terms of plug-and-play readiness, and performance. Developers generally should not be expected to learn new programming languages to support the idiosyncrasies of a specific metadata implementation. All these considerations will influence how the publisher decides to approach standardization.

When publishers adopt common metadata vocabularies, the schema of the vocabulary will generally be based on an RDF data model. By adopting the vocabulary, the publishers get the data model for free. They don't have to create a unique model to represent their metadata, provided it can be imported into an RDF model. RDFS, the formal model for RDF data, requires some time to learn and understand. In most cases, the majority of a web team shouldn't have to know much about the details of such a model. RDFS is a special vocabulary designed to create other vocabularies. Stakeholders don't need to become experts about RDF data models in order to benefit from using them.

---

[213] Because search engines want to encourage as wide adoption of structured data as possible, they only use a subset of semantic metadata in order to keep requirements simple. There are other features and vocabularies available that can support non-search use cases. While it is generally advisable to follow Google's recommendations, publishers should not conclude that only those recommendations matter. This is especially true as more platforms adopt semantic vocabularies.

Roadmaps

The incremental approach doesn't aim for perfection at the start. It aims instead to make the metadata perfectible — or at least, possible to upgrade and improve so that it will eventually adhere to standards and best practices. Consider a simple three-stage model of how metadata can evolve. Each stage increases the ability of different systems to exchange and discover information, progressing from the basic ability of machines to process routine information, followed by the ability to read or discover specific information automatically, and finally to the ability of machines to understand the meaning of values and their relationships to other values.

Stage 1 (descriptive harmonization - machine-processable, but not fully machine-readable)

The first stage prepares metadata to be compatible with metadata descriptions used by other online publishers. It involves harmonizing existing internal metadata descriptions with how the information is described by widely used external standards. Items are described the same properties that are adopted by commonly used metadata standard.

To prepare to migrate to the schema.org vocabulary, publishers would, for example, change terminology from firstName to givenName. They would make sure terminology is consistent for all data. This step is important for internal uses, and building basic APIs. The metadata might be stored as JSON, without reference to a schema yet. When the information uses consistent entity names, property names, and values, *any* machine can potentially process the information, with a bit of developer oversight. Yet because descriptions don't yet include references about the vocabularies — which defines what information is expected — the information in harmonization stage is not fully machine-readable, where machines can make sense of the information without human oversight. To make full use of the information, developers have to know the structure of the information, and must take extra steps to ensure the information is encoded correctly. While this stage prepares the metadata to comply with external standards, it is not yet fully compliant.

Stage 2 (vocabulary/syntax compliance - machine-readable, but not fully machine-intelligible)

This stage starts to de-isolate the information, by making it discoverable to other parties. Online publishers will publish metadata using properties as described by standard vocabularies — following the recommended syntax and prefix namespacing of these vocabularies. This step is important for visibility in search engines and other platforms that harvest information. By complying with external standards, online publishers let other parties know what kinds of information they can expect to find in their metadata. Metadata that follows conceptual standards (Stage 1), if written in JSON syntax. can be upgraded to JSON-LD by adding context properties indicating the schema ("@context"), and type ("@type") indicating the entity type.

When SEO professionals refer to making information "visible" to search engines, they are typically referring to this stage of readiness. Yet the benefits of reaching this stage can be more extensive than SEO. The metadata becomes interoperable. Different systems use a common, consistent way to define information in metadata, so they can locate and exchange the information.

Stage 3 (deferencable values - machine intelligible)

This stage completes the linking process, so that the data is no longer a silo: it is connected to data elsewhere. Publishers add URI identifiers for entities and values to Stage 2-compliant metadata. This step is needed for linking together different independent items of information. A URI gives a thing a machine-identity. The sameAs property links to another ID on another site and indicates that the data is related to data elsewhere.

Comparatively few online publishers currently provide deferenceable values. But this stage enables machines to understand the meaning of information independently. Instead of requiring a user or a developer specify precisely what they want, the machine can find relationships by itself, and deliver information beyond what was asked for. This stage enables metadata to be as relevant as possible.

Ruben Verborgh, an educator and researcher on the topic of semantic metadata, explains differences in the three stages:

"You can upgrade a JSON document to JSON-LD by providing a relevant JSON-LD context. A context identifies properties and structural elements, but does not create links between resources. Remodeling data to RDF on the fly is tricky. Linked Data transcends your application. Link to external concepts. Reuse external identifiers."[214]

Before converting existing systems and content to standard vocabularies, publishers should make sure both are ready. Can existing systems implement standard vocabularies? Can existing metadata for content be converted easily to standard vocabularies?

Each publisher will need to address its unique circumstances. Migration involves a complex choreography: swapping out the old with the new. It will likely happen in phases. Each publisher will make its own decisions on how to do it. Publishers need to talk to their current and prospective vendors about practical approaches.

Converting existing metadata to a vocabulary standard involves:

1. Mapping relationships between attributes used in existing systems and the properties defined in the vocabulary standard
2. Developing a process to enable migration, such as writing scripts, and doing data cleaning and transformation (known as "ETL").

Establishing a process framework will help teams assess the feasibility of different priorities.

---

[214]   Ruben   Verborgh,   "Web   Fundamentals",
http://rubenverborgh.github.io/WebFundamentals/linked-data-
publishing/#templating-insufficient

Feasibility considerations

Technical feasibility will be a major consideration shaping prioritization and timing. Technical teams need to estimate the level of effort involved.

What changes can be done on a small scale? Understanding the effort involved is an iterative learning process. Estimating effort may initially depend on unknown factors, although these will become better understood as metadata creation becomes regularized and automated.

Some vocabulary standards will be easy to implement because they are widely supported by vendors and outside platforms. Other times adopting external vocabularies may encounter inertial resistance.

In some cases, the publisher will encounter dependencies on other parties that can make implementation more difficult. Some potential sources of friction triggered by dependencies include:

1. Inadequate support for vocabulary standards by vendors and limited compatibility with standards from existing systems, libraries, and platforms that the publisher relies on (CMS products, API providers, front-end frameworks)
2. Consuming platforms utilize proprietary approaches (search, social, API customers).

Technical feasibility will assess what tasks are required to capture, validate and maintain information from different sources. Feasibility will address two distinct decisions:

1. The **degree of compliance** to a standard

    a. selective compliance with most *common* requirements
    b. full compliance with all *mandatory* practices
    c. adopts all recommended *best* practices

2. The **depth of compatibility**

    a. *all* entities and properties follow external vocabularies
    b. *only some* entities and properties follow external vocabularies.

Technical feasibility will also look at the scope of adoption within an enterprise.

- Do all systems have to implement the same vocabulary, or can some systems be not fully compliant, yet interoperate?
- Does everyone have to use the same system?
- Is there one common standard for everyone?

Many projects go haywire when they impose a single solution on everyone, without appreciating the contextual differences within an organization. Publishers should seek to connect the dots in their organization, rather than create a big new dot.

Prioritization approaches

Publishers should prioritize their implementation of vocabulary standards according to the business value standards will deliver. If certain properties and values are needed to support critical business requirements, these should be addressed first.

Business prioritization will also consider the completeness of metadata descriptions. How complete to go? Do entire descriptions have to be standardized, or only parts?

Here's an example of how metadata might be prioritized:

Priority 1: Start with new projects. New projects will likely be a high business priority, and standards may easier to implement compared with legacy content.

Priority 2: Focus on "core" legacy content. This will be content that's important, that has a long shelf life. It is content that is revised often. It won't be going away, so publishers will need to get it described with standards-based metadata.

Once publishers have core content to focus on, they need to determine the *scope* of metadata. They can decide scope by looking at the frequency of entities and properties. The frequency may signify the importance of information and suggest that they should be candidates for properties to include. Publishers will consider business-criticality of information.

Priority 3: Short shelf-life content will often have much topical variation, but has limited long-term use. It will probably be described with a minimal set of generic metadata properties. In the case of broadcast announcements and social media content, publishers will capture the kinds of information most important to initial visibility in relevant distribution channels. In the case of transactional messages, core metadata should support the tracking and manages of any key user actions embedded in the message.

Priority 4: Legacy content that is not revised often may not be a priority if it will be retired in the foreseeable future. However, publishers will want to consider if they are likely to create similar content in the future, and if so, what information they will want to capture in metadata about it.

Getting stakeholder buy-in

Implementation success depends on making the process work for all stakeholders. That means working to make the process simple, and ensuring that incentives for participating are clear. Stakeholders need to be clear on what the benefits of the metadata are.

For stakeholders who are not immediately involved in creating a standards-based metadata system, a certain amount of change management is required.

EBay learned the importance of buy-in when it rolled out its new metadata system, which depended on the entry of a product identifier. Sellers, who sometimes felt burdened by eBay's policies favoring customer rights, didn't see the benefit of new requirements to enter a product ID. The pushback from some sellers led to delays. One industry blog reported:

"EBay have requested sellers enter product identifiers but it seems many sellers simply aren't, or if it's mandatory, they're simply added 'Does Not Apply' as a short-term stop gap."[215]

The confusion seemed to cause bad feelings on both sides. Another blog noted:

"EBay is blaming sellers for its decision to push off next month's deadline to next year, saying it's heard from sellers they aren't ready."[216]

EBay eventually simplified the process further, by allowing sellers to scan barcodes to enter the product ID. Once the system was implemented, sellers could see how their products appeared in the new eBay storefront.

---

[215] https://tamebay.com/2016/06/sellers-are-ignoring-ebays-product-identifier-requirements.html

[216] https://www.ecommercebytes.com/C/blog/blog.pl?/comments/2017/1/1485644234.html/3/40

Cleaning up metadata values

In addition to deciding how to assure new values are accurate, most publishers need to deal with metadata migration. They need a plan for how to assure the quality of values that are migrated from legacy systems or obtained from elsewhere.

A common approach is to prioritize quality by frequency. Most-frequently referenced entities and values may be more important than infrequently occurring ones.

Facebook prioritizes the clean up of metadata according to whether the metadata is in the "head" end of the distribution (high frequency), or the "tail" end (low frequency). Facebook relies on a human review of high-frequency metadata but uses machine learning for low-frequency metadata.

Facebook follows a hybrid process to build the information it uses its entity graph. It:

- Begins with a "vetted source" of data from which to add information
- Fixes the "head" (high-frequency terms) by relying on individuals to review terminology, and by using specialized crowdsourcing to get a more thorough review of important terms
- Fixes the "long tail" (less frequent terms) using machine learning and general crowdsourcing
- Invites user feedback to find incorrect classifications
- Designates individuals to monitor overall quality.[217]

While most online publishers won't face the volume of entities that Facebook does, they too can benefit by using a hybrid approach to reviewing metadata quality.

---

[217] "Under the Hood: The Entities Graph" https://it-it.facebook.com/notes/facebook-engineering/under-the-hood-the-entities-graph/10151490531588920/

CHAPTER 26: THE TECHNOLOGY STACK

Metadata standards allow information to be independent of specific software platforms. Yet what online publishers can do with that information will depend on the tools and applications they choose to manage and make use of the metadata. This chapter will survey, in layman's terms as far as possible, some of the tools involved. What follows is not a technical evaluation of tools, but a survey of the range of tools that are available that could be relevant to online publishers of different sizes and levels of maturity.[218]

Business requirements, not technology, should drive priorities when selecting tools. Technology requirements such as features, protocols, and code-base priorities have the potential to overwhelm business priorities relating to who needs to access information and why.

When first introduced in the early 2000s, the concept of "semantic web" had a rough reception. It was ignored by many content creators and rejected by many developers who felt it asked them to reoriented their practices to accommodate its idiosyncrasies. The early versions of the semantic web failed to get buy-in from two core stakeholder groups: content creators and developers. That suggested the concept was too complex, its value too theoretical and that it wasn't quite ready for mainstream use.

Fortunately, the situation has improved significantly in recent years. Tools are getting friendlier, and use cases for semantic, standards-defined metadata are becoming better known.

But it's important not to jump into implementing a semantic metadata solution too quickly. Teams can become so focused on implementing metadata with such strict compliance to best practices that they can end up jeopardizing projects and goals. A wide range of capabilities and associated complexity are available. Some tools are easy to implement, though they may be somewhat limited in what they offer. Other tools have the potential be transformative, but also represent the bleeding edge of capabilities, and may result in headaches, especially for publishers that lack the technical resources to implement a not-fully mature solution.

Standards-readiness

Standards provide many benefits. Yet information technology is notoriously complex. Legacy systems, diverging trends, and uneven progress in different areas can make choices hard to make.

Before adopting standards, publishers need to ask if their existing setup is ready for the standards, and some cases, if the standards and code libraries that work with standards are mature enough to support specific tasks.

Pragmaticism is important, especially in these early stages of external metadata standards adoption. It is often best to work toward *compatibility* with external standards, rather than try to impose strict *compliance* to a single standard for all information used in every IT system. Not all IT systems can host RDF metadata currently. Custom metadata fields that are used by different IT systems will likely continue to exist alongside metadata properties defined using external vocabularies. Publishers want to make sure that all existing metadata for customer-facing information, in all systems, map to their enterprise's common model for its metadata, which should be based upon external metadata standards wherever possible. They will want to be able to exchange and convert between RDF and non-RDF representations of metadata, to make the data portable. All metadata fields and values relating to content published online should be capable of conversion into RDF, even if the original instance is not in an RDF format. Publishers should aim to create new metadata properties by using standard vocabularies.

The RDF data model can make some tasks much easier, but it may not suit other tasks. Developers may need to work with non-RDF representations of metadata. Not all information stored in various IT systems will follow the conventions of triple statements and URIs for entities, properties, and values. RDF metadata, while increasingly general-purpose when expressed as JSON-LD, was originally designed to be support for specific applications such as SPARQL queries. Developers will likely need to interact with metadata by using existing scripts and queries written in SQL, PHP or Javascript. They may prefer more human-readable values, instead of long cryptic identifiers. For example, if a developer receives values from API as a machine-readable URI, they may need to do lots of work to translate that value into something human-readable.

How metadata is represented is important to different stakeholders. Success with metadata depends on the experience of three kinds of stakeholders:

1. The user experience — how easy and useful the metadata is for audiences
2. The author experience — how easy and useful the metadata is for content creators
3. The developer experience — how easy and useful the metadata is to work with for developers.

The developer experience of RDF, when expressed in JSON-LD syntax, is improving. When structured appropriately, JSON-LD syntax can work with any code designed to work with the JSON. But the most widely used Javascript libraries used by front-end developers aren't oriented to RDF metadata representations.[219] For the time being, relying on RDF metadata exclusively may not be a viable option in many organizations.

"RDF technology is very powerful in setting standards on how to publish, classify or report information. Its strongest feature is the ability to share and publish data in an open way."[220]

-- Vassil Momtchev *Ontotext*

Storing metadata in an RDF data model gives publishers the ability to link together statements stored in different systems. Not all publishers need that capability immediately, even though it offers a big benefit in the long term. If metadata is compatible with well-supported standards, it can be expressed as RDF when that is needed. For example, metadata that uses properties from the Dublin Core standard, which pre-dates the development of RDF, can be expressed in RDF without difficulty. Text values can be converted to URIs. URIs can be converted to human readable values through compaction and expansion, or by using label properties in lieu of URIs, as will be discussed shortly.

RDF allows metadata to connect to different sources. But it will sometimes need to be represented in alternative forms, in order to accommodate the needs of different stakeholders and systems.

---

[218] I will defer from judging which ones are "best" and apologize in advance to any vendor who feels I misrepresent their products. I'm intentionally being inclusive where I identify solutions can work with metadata standards for least some use cases.

[219] Most Javascript libraries focus on non-semantic class attributes.

[220] Vassil Momtchev, GraphDB product owner at Ontotext, http://www.zdnet.com/article/graph-databases-and-rdf-its-a-family-affair/

Technical considerations

Online publishers should evaluate tools supporting metadata creation and management in terms of their:

- Usability
- Deployment practicality
- Implementation-readiness (maturity of solution)
- Future-readiness.

Many online publishers will pursue an incremental approach to the implementation of metadata standards. They will start by working with what they have already, and build upon it.

When considering technology options, it is essential not to let the technology of metadata implementation dictate what metadata is required.

Any selection of technology needs to balance the requirements of three parties:

- Audiences and authors, who need to be able to view a human-readable version of the metadata
- Developers, who need to understand a human-readable version of properties and values while coding, but also need some precision in how these are represented
- Machines, which need machine-readable properties and values that can be interpreted without a human. These will be very precise, but often are hard to read. Some machine-readable representations are even hard for developers to use.

Technical implementation choices can impact the usability of systems. Different actors have different needs when it comes to the "things" versus "strings" debate. Google popularized the slogan: "things, not strings" — to identify entities (things) with URIs. But humans want "strings, not things," because long URIs with alphanumeric identifiers are difficult to read and understand.

Words are human-readable but are difficult for machines to interpret. In metadata, words can be:

- The name of a thing
- A property label
- A text value.

Identifiers (URIs) are machine-readable but can be difficult for humans to decipher. Humans can find these metadata elements difficult to read:

- Subject identifiers
- Property identifiers
- Object value identifiers.

These competing requirements can be reconciled with a little planning:

- Entities and properties get human-readable labels, and values are converted into human-readable formats
- Entities and properties references can be compacted and expanded so that developers can use an easy-to-read short form, while maintaining the reference to the schema used.[221]
- Identifiers are dereferencable, so that machines can know precisely what is being referred to, and determine what other information is related.

This equivalence can be specified using the JSON-LD syntax.[222]

Data architecture is another decision. Technical staff will consider the cost and performance associated with:

1. How metadata is accessed and processed
2. Where metadata is stored.

Decisions about where metadata is stored can influence the ease of creation, maintenance, and use. For example, metadata can be:

- Stored within an asset file, such as some image metadata, or inline within text content
- Injected into content at the time of publication
- Stored in scripts that are separate from the content
- Stored in a metadata repository that is separate from the content.

While a detailed discussion of these topics is beyond the scope of a book focused on strategy, these topics do have a bearing on what capabilities are available, and how easy they are to use.

[221] On expansion and compaction, see https://www.w3.org/TR/json-ld-api/#features

[222] See Karen Coombs "Introducing JSON-LD" https://www.oclc.org/developer/news/2016/introducing-json-ld.en.html

Content management systems and metadata standards

A content management system typically serves as the hub of online publishing operations. A content management system involves a front end that authors use to input content and manage workflows, and a backend database (SQL or NoSQL) to retrieve and store the content.

A CMS will generally act as the repository for the content that has been or will be published. CMSs typically use templates to map the content that is stored with the content that authors create and edit. A CMS will often have some ability to capture and store basic web metadata. However, various CMSs will have different capabilities in this regard. Some CMSs don't capture or store much metadata, and many rely on proprietary fields.[223] WordPress, the most commonly used CMS, has very basic metadata capabilities built in the core product. Drupal, another open source CMS that competes with WordPress, can support for web metadata as RDF and has had these capabilities for many years.

The CMS setup may make different assumptions about the provision of metadata. Possibilities include:

1. Making the author indicate which entity types are addressed in the content
2. Making the site administrator indicate and set up the entity types for authors to use
3. Out-of-the-box entity types are available.

Let's review the capabilities of several widely used CMSs to support external metadata standards

In WordPress, by using a common SEO plugin, an author can indicate the main entity type of a webpage, such as whether the page is a blog post or an event description. It is not difficult for authors but does require extra work, and the metadata that's created is not very expressive.

Drupal offers more robust capabilities. Drupal provides content types out-of-the-box that are often similar in form to the entity types used by semantic metadata standards such as schema.org. In Drupal 8, the site administrator can bake-in the required metadata using the RDF module. The process involves mapping content types to corresponding entity types, and mapping fields appearing in a content type with their corresponding property in a metadata vocabulary such as schema.org. For example, Drupal might describe the entity in the content as "title" while schema.org uses "name", and Drupal's "body" field would correspond to schema.org's "description" property. Once the fields are mapped to the properties, the metadata creation is automatic, so that the author doesn't need to worry about it.

With Drupal's RDF module, it is also possible to build new content types from schema.org entities and properties. There are even UI tools that make the mapping process easier to do.[224] It requires work by the site admin to set up the mapping. Currently, Drupal is standardized on the RDFa syntax, though it is possible to override this default and use JSON-LD instead.[225]

While Drupal can map its fields to metadata standards, that capability is not automatic. It requires manual mapping by the site administrator. "Because of the complexity of the standards and the flexibility of Drupal's entity type and field system, there is no one-size-fits-all solution for Drupal that will automatically map Schema.org properties to every kind of Drupal data".[226]

The most ideal solution is when the CMS provides out-of-the-box metadata properties for common entity types. Sitecore, a popular CMS, has introduced out-of-the-box metadata for content addressing products. It notes: "The schema for Sellable item is based on Schema.org Product Schema. This makes it possible to map the Sellable Item in JSON-LD directly for Google product search markup".[227]

As the discussion of Drupal highlighted, a key task is coordinating an ontology with the content structure, which is represented by page templates (content types). CMSs have fields for author, publication date, and so on which need to be represented by standard metadata vocabularies. Content will also involve free text that discusses entities, which are outside the structure of the page template. Predictable structured content involving lists with fields, or tables, can be mapped to ontologies can so that the author doesn't need to enter metadata manually. This is especially important for dynamic values such as prices that change and are fed from a database.

Sitecore's approach is encouraging, though it so far remains focused on product information. There is a raft of information about content that deserves metadata description, and so far most CMSs do not provide very robust out-of-the-box metadata capabilities. These capabilities can be supplemented, and often should.

Omeka, an open source CMS for scholarly publishing, provides an example of how a CMS can accommodate different metadata vocabularies (Figure 26.1 and Figure 26.2).

Figure 26.1. Omeka, an open source CMS for scholarly publishers, can handle multiple vocabularies. Source: Omeka.

Figure 26.2. Omeka provides an easy-to-use UI to load additional metadata vocabularies. Source: Omeka.

When a CMS missing what is needed, several options are available. The publisher can request these features, or switch to a different CMS that provides better support. But often the easiest and fastest solution is to buy a plug-in to work with the CMS.

[223] "Schema.org - Support In The CMS Landscape", https://typo3.com/blog/schemaorg-support-in-the-cms-landscape/

[224] See "Schema.org configuration tool (RDF UI)", https://www.drupal.org/project/rdfui

[225] Usman Saqlain, "Simple Structured Data implementation in Drupal using the JSON-LD format", March 23, 2017, https://www.caxy.com/blog/simple-structured-data-implementation-drupal-using-json-ld-format

[226] Karen Stevenson, "Create SEO Juice From JSON LD Structured Data in Drupal", https://www.lullabot.com/articles/create-seo-juice-by-adding-json-ld-structured-data-to-drupal-8

[227] On Sitecore, see https://himadritechblog.wordpress.com/2017/10/24/sitecore-commerce-9-is-coming-soon/ Also, "Announcing Sitecore Experience Commerce" https://www.sitecore.com/company/blog/343/announcing-sitecore-experience-commerce-4501

Plug-ins for CMSs

Plug-ins typically provide access to vocabularies and allow authors to highlight content to indicate descriptive metadata.

For entities mentioned within the body of text, some author involvement is generally required. Author annotation is a common way to capture this metadata.

Numerous plug-ins for CMSs are available that add schema.org metadata to content. But most only allow properties relating to the most common entity types such as events or reviews. Publishers should get a plug-in that provides comprehensive coverage of schema.org.

Two popular plug-ins with more extensive coverage are:

- SchemaApp
- WordLift.

Some plug-in products can also work with tag managers that are associated with web analytics packages. A tag manager can inject metadata into content via Javascript. For example, in Tealium's Tag Manager, the process would look like this:[228]

```
u.injectJSONLD([{
  "@context": "http://schema.org",
  "@type": "Organization",
  "url": "https://www.example.com",
  "contactPoint": [{
      "@type": "ContactPoint",
      "telephone": "+1-877-555-1212",
      "contactType": "Lead",
      "contactOption": "TollFree",
      "areaServed": "US"
  }]
}]);
```

SchemaApp, for example, can work with Tealium and Google Tag Manager or via a Javascript API. Using Javascript tags to inject metadata means the metadata is rendered dynamically. But if the publisher uses a plug-in without relying on Javascript injection, the metadata can be stored on the server side, which can deliver faster performance.[229]

[228] See "Tealium SEO (JSON-LD) Tag Setup Guide for Tealium iQ" https://community.tealiumiq.com/t5/Tags/Tealium-SEO-JSON-LD-Tag-Setup-Guide-for-Tealium-iQ/ta-p/9817

[229]See https://www.schemaapp.com/integrations/

Middleware applications

Middleware applications offer a more sophisticated option to a basic plug-in. Middleware apps can enrich the content with more detailed metadata. These applications are separate from the CMS, but are linked to the CMS via an API. Another benefit of middleware applications is that they can support other IT systems such as DAMs.

Some of the better-known middleware applications for metadata are:

- PoolParty
- SmartLogic Semaphore
- Cogito Discover
- TopBraid Composer (Figure 26.3).

Figure 26.3. Example of an ontology editor, a kind of middleware application for managing metadata. Source: TopBraid.

Middleware applications can handle a range of vocabularies and allow custom additions. Some can also analyze text to identify entities and other elements in the text that require metadata tagging. This process is known as extracting triples.

Automatic metadata extraction involves different techniques, which include:

- Named entity recognition

- Natural language processing (NPL)
- Morphological analysis
- Classification
- Concept assignment.[230]

This automation can provide more granular metadata, without creating extra work for authors.

A different kind of middleware application that is useful for metadata management is indexing and search software. Two of the most widely used are:

- Apache Solr
- ElasticSearch.[231]

Although designed to index words in the body of documents, indexing software can also be used to search for concepts by indexing semantic metadata descriptors created by middleware applications such as PoolParty. Indexes are especially useful for faceted searches and aggregations. They can support smarter discovery to help people who don't know what keywords to use, or whether content is available about a topic. Faceted search and autocompletion use metadata to give hints about what content is available. Another benefit of such indexing is that can they can provide additional analytics.

---

[230] These are different techniques for deciding what the text represents. For the buyer of tools, techniques can offer different degrees of accuracy and added value.

[231] http://markbirbeck.com/2016/11/14/schema.org-json-ld-elasticsearch-1/

Metadata databases

When an online publisher has a large volume of metadata, they may want to consider using a database that is designed to store metadata efficiently. Currently, specialized metadata databases are primarily of interest to Fortune 100 firms and large-scale technical publishers. But this approach may become more widely adopted in the future as new pay-as-you-go cloud services become more common.

Database discussions focus on issues such as extensibility, scalability, and query latency. These issues can get quite technical and sometimes spark passionate debate. How publishers store metadata depends on various decisions about speed and completeness. Some solutions work best for small but frequent transactional updates, while others are designed for large batch updates.

Databases that store information follow one of several patterns:

- Data as objects that are accessed by a programming language
- Data as tables in rows and columns, where different tables are linked together
- Data as hierarchical trees, where items are subdivided into smaller units to reveal meaning
- Data as graphs, where different separate statements are linked together.

Large database repositories can store metadata, and sometimes content, from many different applications. These databases include NoSQL ("Not only SQL") and graph databases. NoSQL is a popular approach to "big data" management and analysis of mixed data, such as tables and documents. NoSQL searches the latent structure of the data.

Graph databases focus on the graph data model, which is highly flexible. Graph databases have gradually become mainstream in recent years. Graphs database products generally support RDF standards. From a technical perspective, the value of RDF is that it provides a balance of adaptability over time, and compatibility across different databases:

"RDF ... represents data as collection of <subject, property, object> triples. By providing flexibility for users to represent and evolve data without the need for a prior schema — sometimes called the "schema last" approach — and identifying properties and (references to) subjects uniformly using URIs, RDF has been gaining ground as the standard for global data exchange and interoperability."[232]

Graph databases are sometimes described as "schema last" because they can be changed. That flexibility can help metadata descriptions adapt and evolve over time.

The big benefit of graph databases is their ability to connect and query different sources of information. Unlike relational databases, which are almost always accessed internally within an enterprise, graph databases can be configured to be accessed directly by external parties. Because they can be directly accessed externally, graph databases have a strong rationale for using external metadata standards, unlike internally-accessed relational databases. Graph databases may support the ability to use the semantic query language SPARQL.[233] While traditional "table" databases are excellent for looking up the values of known items, graphs excel in uncovering unknown connections and information. Their value increases the larger the scale of available metadata. With graphs, publishers can look at entities mathematically in terms of distance and neighborhoods, which can yield analytical insights. Such graphs can also be visualized.

Some better-known graph databases are:

- MarkLogic
- Neo4j
- Ontotext GraphDB
- Amazon Neptune (which powers Alexa).

A new type of graph database has emerged called the *property graph database*.[234] Unlike RDF, property graphs are based on proprietary, custom fields. It may not be easy to share or migrate metadata in a property graph database into another application, thereby presenting a silo hazard. The emergence of property graph products has increased awareness of graphs as a database approach yet has diminished awareness of the benefits of following open standards such as RDF.[235]

A recent Mitre Corporation report noted: "The industry's leading products are rapidly changing and are becoming more like each other, in that they are trying to offer both RDF and property graph capabilities".[236] Database vendors are hedging their bets. Even Neo4j, the best-known property graph database vendor, supports RDF.

Publishers interested in using graph databases that support RDF metadata have two options:

1. **Multi-model** databases that can handle RDF, as well a proprietary metadata, which includes Virtuoso, Amazon Neptune, AllegroGraph, Stardog, GraphDB, Blazegraph, and MarkLogic.[237]

2. **RDF dedicated** databases, such as Jena, Algebraix, RDF4J, and RedStore.[238]

Finally, some graph databases position themselves as *knowledge graph* databases. These allow an organization to build complete a knowledge graph of their own. While graph databases tend to evolve organically, knowledge graphs are constructed more purposefully around metadata statements about specific entities.

Several open source products are available specifically to create and store semantic metadata to develop a knowledge graph. These include:

- Open KG
- Metaphacts
- CayleyGraph, the basis of Google's Knowledge Graph.[239]

---

[232] Minh-Duc Pham, Linnea Passing, Orri Erling, Peter Boncz, "Deriving an Emergent Relational Schema from RDF Data", https://homepages.cwi.nl/~duc/papers/emergentschema_www15.pdf http://dx.doi.org/10.1145/2736277.2741121.

[233] Other query languages are Gizmo (Gremlin dialect), MQL and GraphQL.

[234] "A property graph is similar to a graph in that it has edges and nodes, but dissimilar in that the nodes and edges can hold any number of attributes in the form of key-value-pairs." Dorian Voegeli, "A Field Guide ETL from RDF to Property Graph"

[235] Property graph databases may offer features and performance advantages for use cases involving proprietary enterprise data that is entirely internally-facing and not customer-facing. But any advantages are compromised when the information needs to be customer-facing and interoperable with other systems.

[236] Dorian Voegeli, *A Field Guide ETL from RDF to Property Graph* Mitre Corporation, 2018.

[237] See: https://db-engines.com/en/ranking/graph+dbms
[238] See https://db-engines.com/en/ranking/rdf+store

[239] see "Cayley", https://cayley.io/

CHAPTER 27: APIs

APIs are a common tactic to bridge information silos. But not all APIs are equally effective at transcending silos. Some APIs simply expose proprietary silos of information to the rest of the world.

Before examining the limitations of some current APIs, it is necessary to distinguish different kinds of APIs. From the perspective of a content professional, there's a big difference between a transactional or functional API and an informative API. Even though their construction is frequently similar, they serve different purposes. All data is not the same.

In a transactional or functional API, the information is unique to the application and isn't common information. Functional APIs perform an evaluation and deliver a specific result. Functional APIs are typically the sole-source for an answer relating to a specific transaction, answering questions such as "has the payment cleared yet?" An informational API, in contrast, provides published information that could be shared widely, such as "what is the current temperature?" An informational API may be competing with other informational APIs sharing the same information, or similar information.

Transactional APIs commonly answer highly unique questions and rely on custom metadata to provide those answers. The discussion that follows is not intended to critique how transactional APIs are made. Rather, the discussion will focus on informational APIs. This chapter will argue that APIs should embrace external standards for information when the information is multi-user, and supports multiple use cases.

Sharing information with APIs

APIs are a common way to share information within and between organizations. One major advantage of APIs is that they can let different parties choose what specific information they want to incorporate in their own applications.

Two common use cases for using APIs are:

1. To *share* specific information about products, services, or events with other organizations that want to query it.
2. To *get* information from other organizations that is related to content that an organization provides to its customers.

An example of how APIs can be used in content publishing is offered by Edmunds. Edmunds provides information about vehicles for sale. They supply their information to a range of clients, including leasing companies, auto dealers such as Toyota, and marketplaces such as eBay. Those clients, in turn, want to provide information of value to car buyers. Edmunds offers APIs to provide information to their clients on a range of topics. It offers information about used cars, as well as editorial content. It developed a range of different APIs as part of their ecosystem:

- Vehicle API: "true market value, and vehicle incentives offered by auto manufacturers"
- Editorial API: "articles, editor reviews, and road tests"
- Dealer API: "automotive dealerships associated with a given criteria including zipcode"
- Inventory API: "vehicle database via Vehicle Identification Number (VIN)"
- Media API: "photos by tag, by style ID, by vehicle model, and by year."

Edmunds developed APIs to get their content used. They needed to market their APIs can get them adopted by other firms. With APIs, adoption and maintenance are critical issues for long-term success. Although Edmunds offered an impressive array of information, Edmunds recently retired their public API, citing the effort involved.[240]

Why didn't Edmunds' APIs deliver their expected business value? We know Edmunds ultimately decided that the API entailed too much effort. Like many API developers, Edmunds chose to build their APIs around a proprietary metadata model, instead of using external standards. This decision may have made it harder for them to realize their goals. Using external standards can help with API adoption, since developers need to learn fewer details. And external standards can reduce maintenance as well, since information is more easily connected to other systems. API developers can take advantage of a comprehensive set of external metadata standards that exist for information about cars — the autos extension to the schema.org vocabulary.

> *"Use well-known identifiers when describing data."*[241]

-- Gregg Kellogg

To be adopted widely, APIs need to offer information of value and be easy to use. Fortunately, external metadata standards can help deliver those outcomes.

---

[240]See Mark Boyd, "Gauging API Success: Knowing What Metrics to Measure" *ProgrammableWeb,* https://www.programmableweb.com/news/gauging-api-success-knowing-what-metrics-to-measure/analysis/2017/09/27

[241] "Building JSON-LD APIs: Best Practices" https://json-ld.org/spec/latest/json-ld-api-best-practices/

When APIs reflect silos

Most APIs rely on data models that are designed by the API originator. They require other developers to read API documentation to understand what's available in the API, and what attributes and values in the API refer to.

Metadata standards aim to transcend the problems that APIs can spawn:

"Different sites have chosen their own proprietary representations for interacting with their sites, sometimes described using frameworks such as [swagger] which imply a particular URI composition for interacting with their services. This practice leads to **vendor-specific semantic silos***, where the meaning of a particular JSON document makes sense only by programming directly to the API documentation for a given service."*[242]

The value of an API to the consumer of the data depends on:

- The value of the information, such as its uniqueness and applicability
- The ease of implementing, including repurposing information accessed.

For a concrete example of how APIs can deliver different value, let's look at two APIs that cover information about similar domain: food.

The first API, called the "USDA Food Report" comes from the United States Department of Agriculture.[243]

The value of the USDA food report API's information is high. It provides a "list of nutrients and their values in various portions for a specific food."

However, the ease of implementing the USDA food report API is low, as the API doesn't follow metadata standards (Figure 27.1). Users need to know how to decipher the identifier for cheddar cheese (which is NDBno01009) and know that IDs using the letters "cn" refers to commercial name. The USDA using its own data model that provides a "unique key for a food is called its NDB Number (ndbno)."

Figure 27.1. Using the USDA Food Report API depends on knowing a special key called an 'NDB Number'. Source: USDA.

Request Parameters

Parameter	Required	Default	Description
api_key	y	n/a	Must be a data.gov registered API key
ndbno	y	n/a	NDB no
type	n	b (basic)	Report type: [b]asic or [f]ull or [s]tats
format	n	JSON	Report format: xml or json

Format can also be sent in the request header: Content-Type: application/json or Content-Type:application/xml.

To merge the USDA's information with other sources, the developer has to map proprietary keys to standards-based properties.

The second API, called "Open Food Facts", provides a better alternative (Figure 27.2). Like the USDA API, Open Food Facts provides useful information about food. Where it differs is its use of metadata standards. Users of the Open Food Facts API can get an RDF dump of the information, which makes connecting the information to other sources, and using in different contexts, much easier to do. Instead of using proprietary IDs like the USDA, Open Food Facts uses universally-adopted GTIN numbers that appear on the barcodes on food packaging. In fact, their API powers smartphone and other apps that let ordinary users retrieve and add information to the database.

Figure 27.2. Open Food Facts relies on GTIN bar codes and other metadata standards. Source: Open Food Facts.

---

[242] "JSON-LD API Best Practices" (emphasis added), https://json-ld.org/spec/latest/json-ld-api-best-practices/

[243] https://ndb.nal.usda.gov/ndb/doc/apilist/API-FOOD-REPORTV2.md

Avoiding the giant hairball

APIs can be used to exchange metadata between IT systems within an organization, between IT systems belonging to different organizations, and providing metadata to many consumers. The possibilities are numerous, and the potential to create a mess is very real.

Too often APIs try to connect incompatible systems that talk about information in different ways. The API may allow information to be transferred, but it doesn't enable meaning to be shared between systems.

> *"I just have worked on too many projects where the API has been defined by the known use cases, and then more and more functionality gets glued on and the API becomes unsustainable. If we can disassociate the semantic layer from the API layer, we can, when needed, throw out the API layer and replace it without having to do rework against all the wildly disparate data sources."*[244]

-- Developer comment on a forum

When too many APIs try to overcome a lack of standards, they can become a giant hairball. What the information means gets lost in all the code necessary to support how the information is accessed.

An example of the problem of APIs-as-hairballs is illustrated by the Data Transfer Project run by a consortium major tech firms such as Google and Microsoft and others (Figure 27.3). Faced with increasing regulatory pressures to allow customers to move their personal information between service providers, the DTP consortium explored if providing each other with access to their APIs would provide the needed functionality. When they considered the number of different firms that might participate, each with its own proprietary API, they concluded that relying on APIs alone would result in another giant hairball. Common semantics are needed so that multiple, incompatible APIs aren't created.

Figure 27.3. When every publisher has its own proprietary API, it results in a hairball. The Data Transfer Project aims to standardize metadata to avoid this problem. Source: DTP.

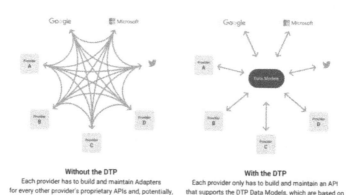

In short, although APIs can bridge silos, when used as a band-aid strategy, APIs can become their own silos that are hard to maintain. Such APIs lack semantics that everyone can understand and use.

---

[244] Developer comment on a forum at http://review.americanartcollaborative.org/cookbook/knowledge-representation-vs-api

Good APIs are built on common semantics

The philosophy of Linked Open Data is to provide URI endpoints that can be accessed. End-users don't necessarily need an API if the information is simple, and you know the URI required to access it. Semantics make that possible.

For more complex queries of semantic metadata, APIs are useful. Metadata standards provide the foundation for semantic APIs. "Use web standards as the foundation of APIs" advises the W3C's "Data on the Web Best Practices."[245]

Developers use APIs to build apps integrating data from more than one source. And they use APIs to disseminate data to different platforms.

Museums provide interesting examples of how APIs can be used. Like retailers, museums need to publish to many different platforms. They have websites, but also apps that visitors might use within the museum. They also have interactive displays in museum exhibits. All these platforms need to be fed from a common pool of content.

Europeana, a European consortium of art and cultural institutions, provides a series of APIs that provide information about paintings and other cultural materials belonging to consortium members.[246]

Each service provides a different set of functions:

- Search API
- Record API (access to data model)
- Entity API
- Annotations API
- SPARQL API (explore connections with other data sources).[247]

For the Europeana consortium, the development of common standards goes together with developing APIs to share information. Their adoption of standards helps make it easier for partners to use the information.

Another way that standards work with APIs is when a standard is available as a service.

International Image Interoperability Framework (IIIF, pronounced "Triple-Eye-Eff") API for images is built upon W3C metadata standards. A major use case is being able to compare images from different sources:

"IIIF gives users a rich set of baseline functionality for viewing, zooming, and assembling the best mix of resources and tools to view, compare, manipulate and work with images on the Web, an experience made portable — shareable, citable, and embeddable."[248]

Like Europeana, IIIF is a product of the cultural heritage sector. IIIF promotes the curation of content by:

- "Combining content from across repositories"
- "Bring[ing] together content from your institutional DAM, library digital collections, and external sources."

IIIF also supports content syndication. By accessing the service, publishers can increase the utilization of their content to support different scenarios. In IIIF's words, publishers can:

- "Publish once, re-use often"
- "Deliver images from your own site for manifold uses; host a single copy and embed in other sites."

IIIF offers a suite of APIs that includes:

- An Image API
- A Presentation API
- A Content Search API
- An Authentication API.

IIIF even promotes open source software that utilizes its APIs. IIIF is designed to accommodate the widest range of use cases possible.

---

[245] Best Practice 24

[246] https://pro.europeana.eu/resources/apis

[247] Sparql, the query language for semantic metadata, is not often used in APIs. Other query languages are preferred. One reason is that open-ended Sparql query results can be uncertain — sometimes yielding a more extensive and exhaustive (and time consuming) result than anticipated. Another reason is that the results retrieved are not formatted in JSON. For these reasons, Sparql is primarily used for human-directed queries.

[248] See "IIIF Frequently Asked Questions (FAQs)" http://iiif.io/community/faq/#what-are-the-current-iiif-specifications

Technical foundations for APIs

API queries are often primitive in the sense that they generally only involve one or two parameters (keys). APIs retrieve values that match the key or keys in the query. They return either a short answer or a detailed record. Sometimes the payload needs to be parsed to get the information actually needed. That is, the receiver needs to run two queries: one conducted according to the limitations of what the API permits it to ask, and a second, internal query to filter out the specific information of interest to the receiver. The receiver doesn't always have the ability to interrogate the API with the exact query they are interested in.

The generic character of APIs, centered around the querying of keys, comes with limitations. Until recently, semantic APIs were difficult to make, so data models used in APIs were simple or fragmented. Most developers prefer working with the simple-to-use JSON syntax, which rarely utilizes schemas. JSON doesn't provide the rich descriptive power of the RDF model that is used widely in standard metadata vocabularies. APIs have primarily focused on getting known data, instead of discovering new information of relevance. As one developer working on APIs for the *Nature* group noted:

"RDF is an extremely flexible and powerful model, however, when it comes to data consumption and access, the average user cares more about simplicity than flexibility. Also, outside linked data circles we all know that the standard tech for APIs is JSON and REST, rather than RDF and SPARQL."[249]

Fortunately, semantic APIs have become much easier with the introduction of the JSON-compatible JSON-LD syntax.[250] The JSON-LD syntax can be used as an alternative to JSON and it offers the benefits of the RDF model.[251]

APIs encompass a range of approaches that go by different names. APIs offer different solutions in terms of how much information is provided, and how the query is formed. Some approaches include:

- Webhooks
- REST
- Hypermedia
- Hydra
- GraphQL
- Nanoservices.

Each approach to APIs has benefits and drawbacks. They vary in terms of how well they support standard metadata vocabularies.

Webhooks

Although not formally an API, Webhooks are a lightweight way to provide some of the functionality that is available in APIs. Microsoft is using Webhooks to work with schema.org-defined "Message Cards".[252]

RESTful APIs

The name REST comes from Representational State Transfer. REST is the most popular approach to APIs, but it can have limitations. Developers need to know in advance the identifiers of resources, which requires a developer to read the documentation. There often aren't semantics in the identifiers.

Developers have started to explore the possibilities of using REST with semantic metadata in the JSON-LD syntax.[253]

Hypermedia APIs

According to the W3C's data best practices, a hypermedia API is "one that responds with links as well as data. Links are what make the Web a web, and data APIs can be more useful and usable by including links in their responses."[254]

The JSON syntax doesn't support hyperlinks — the linking of resources. But the JSON-LD syntax allows resources to be linked.

Hydra

Hydra is an emerging W3C standard. Its goal is to let machines read the documentation. An example of a Hydra API implementation is the New Zealand's Southern Cross Health Society, an insurance company. The lead developer shared his experience using Hydra:[255]

"We are using Schema.org, JSON-LD, and Hydra. Schema.org/Action built a system! We have used the Schema.org/Action and /Event to specify a new generation of customer 'interaction' system."

"API Platform"[256] is a product that can build Hydra APIs. It claims:

"Schema.org improves the interoperability of your applications. Used with hypermedia technologies such as Hydra it's a big step towards the semantic and machine-readable web. It opens the way to generic web API clients able to extract and process data from any website or app using such technologies."

GraphQL

GraphQL has gained notice due to its use by Facebook and Github. The New York Times also uses GraphQL. GraphQL offers the ability to perform complex queries on a single request, generally on proprietary JSON data structures. GraphQL seems to work best on flat records, rather than deep ones that could express more complexity. Some work is underway to use GraphQL for nonproprietary RDF metadata.

HyperGraphQL

HyperGraphQL is an open source extension to GraphQL to bring to it RDF capabilities.[252]

The goal of HyperGraphQL is to provide a GraphQL interface to do SPARQL queries and to get a JSON response. What one gets matches what one states. The viability of this approach will partly depend on the reliability of the SPARQL endpoint.

Nanoservices

Nanoservices are a bit different. BBC has "over 1,000 nanoservices in production. Together, they create a range of dynamic web pages, and also APIs for mobile and TV apps."

"A nanoservice is an independent component that does one job well" notes the BBC. "They are most commonly used to 'template' data. That is, they aggregate, filter, and translate data from one format to another. They may take data from an API and convert it into an HTML component, for example."[258]

---

[249]   Michele   Pasin,   Nature,   https://semantic-web.com/2016/03/30/insights-into-natures-data-publishing-portal/

[250] "JSON-LD 1.0 Processing Algorithms and API", W3C Recommendation, January 2014, https://www.w3.org/TR/json-ld-api/

[251] On mapping JSON API keys to JSON-LD, see "JSON-LD: Building Meaningful Data APIs via Codeship", https://dzone.com/articles/json-ld-building-meaningful-data-apis-via-codeship

[252] See "Post an actionable message card to an Office 365 group", https://docs.microsoft.com/en-us/outlook/actionable-messages/actionable-messages-via-connectors

[253] See "How to Take Your API From RPC to Hypermedia in 7 Steps" https://www.programmableweb.com/news/how-to-take-your-api-rpc-to-hypermedia-7-steps/how-to/2016/09/15?page=4

[254] https://www.w3.org/TR/dwbp/

[255] https://lists.w3.org/Archives/Public/public-schemaorg/2018Feb/0008.html

[256] https://api-platform.com/

[257] See https://medium.com/@sklarman/weaving-linked-data-cloud-with-hypergraphql-d332d768a1fe

[258] see Matthew Clark, "Powering BBC Online with nanoservices" https://medium.com/bbc-design-engineering/powering-bbc-online-with-nanoservices-727840ba015b

Long-term goals for APIs

APIs help shift information from one server to another, but they typically require a lot of human effort to make that happen. There is much overhead associated with APIs. They need to be discovered, which involves marketing them to developers who might be interested in using them. When they are revised, those changes could adversely impact people using the API, so changes need to be communicated to developers.

Longer term, the goal for APIs is to make them "autonomous." When many different APIs all follow a universal metadata description, it becomes possible to perform universal searches, where many APIs are queried at once to retrieve information, instead of each API requiring a separate query.

As one evangelist put it, autonomous APIs rest on four building blocks that make APIs semantic, so machines can find and use them without making developers locate and interpret what is needed:

1. A vocabulary registry
2. Understanding shared at a runtime
3. An API discovery service
4. Programming for the vocabulary, not the data structure.[259]

These features would allow APIs to operate on a completely machine-to-machine basis. That goal may be still far from being realized. But it is worth aiming for.

---

[259] from "Z", "The Future of APIs", *GoodAPI Blog*, https://blog.goodapi.co/future-of-apis-c84a76bc9c85

CHAPTER 28:
GOVERNANCE AND
METADATA MATURITY

.

Online publishers use content strategies to guide what they publish. Publishers that have implemented content strategies sooner or later discover the value of having governance policies and processes to ensure the strategy stays on track. To execute a strategy consistently, publishers need rules and standards. Metadata supports content governance, by introducing standards for terminology, promoting the reuse of information, and enabling better analytics.

But metadata is more than just an adjunct to the governance of content strategy. Metadata itself requires governance. For metadata to transcend silos, the vocabulary used to describe information in content must become, and stay, a common language. Metadata standards must become institutionalized in order to build the momentum necessary to overcome entropy that lets silos persist, and to counter requests for quick and dirty projects that spawn new silos.

Why metadata governance?

When organizations embark on a new transformational project, it is common for initial excitement to be followed to confusion and frustration, as staff start the hard work of translating the objectives into reality. Momentum can flag. Executives may shift focus to other priorities. Some stakeholders may become apathetic, or not want to change.

Metadata strategy is a new concept and needs to draw on the experiences of other kinds of digital initiatives. It can learn from the experience of other new approaches such as design thinking. Design thinking over the past decade has become a popular approach to promote innovation — but it has had mixed success. Some design thinking projects floundered when moving from concept to execution. Innovative approaches such a design thinking involve change management since new practices must replace existing ones. Many experienced design thinking advocates have promoted the value of "stewardship" in design thinking.[260] A novel approach such as design thinking won't be successful if ongoing executive stewardship is lacking.

Metadata strategy also needs executive stewardship. Specifically, stewardship is embodied in a governance structure and framework, which provides a process for overseeing the implementation of the metadata strategy.

Governance should not be thought of as another task to do, adding to an already long list of metadata-related tasks. Governance should be viewed as a process for making sure necessary tasks get done.

> *"It is not just how we name our data, how we define it, where it comes from, where it is going, and the other basic metadata rules that became data governance. It is also the format, the timing, the reason, and how data is going to be shared."*[261]

-- Adrienne Tannenbaum *metadata consultant*

Governance is a structured discussion about what metadata to include. Governance provides a process for high-level, long-term decisions relating to metadata. It makes sure the right metadata is produced. And it makes sure that metadata is not created that doesn't deliver value.

Governance prevents silos from resurfacing. Siloed thinking about metadata can result in more stovepipe systems. New metadata fields are created to address narrow needs, such as tracking or locating items for specific purposes. Fields proliferate across various systems. And everyone is confused about how anything relates to anything else.

Governance promotes strategic thinking about metadata. It considers how metadata can serve all the needs of the publisher, not just the needs of an individual team member or role. When teams work together to develop requirements, they can discuss what metadata is useful for different purposes. They can identify how a single metadata item can be in different contexts. If the metadata describes when an item was last updated, the team might consider how that metadata might be used in different contexts. How might it be used by content creators, by the analytics team, by the UX design team, and by the product manager?

A governance process will make sure all stakeholders meet periodically to review progress, identify problems, and set long-term goals.

---

[260] "Design thinking is intimately linked with the notion of 'stewardship' defined here as the core ability of agents of change to successfully translate ideas into practice to achieve the desired outcomes." UNDP, *Design Thinking for Public Service* *Excellence,* http://www.undp.org/content/dam/uspc/docs/GPCSE_Design%20Thinking.pdf

[261] Adrienne Tannenbaum, "Finding Maturity in Your Metadata Strategy", *Bloomberg,* December 22, 2014, https://www.bloomberg.com/professional/blog/finding-maturity-in-your-metadata-strategy/

Steering governance through a metadata program

Governance guides an ongoing process to build metadata capabilities. The specific artifacts such as requirements, policies, and procedures, are the result of a metadata program that operationalizes governance. Governance defines the direction through collective decisions, while the program implements that direction. Governance focuses on the long-term and the bigger picture, while the metadata program focuses on realizing more specific and near-term tasks. The metadata program is about implementing what's been agreed to in the governance decision-making process.

A metadata program is not a single project that gets delivered. Building metadata capabilities involves change management. Web teams that are implementing a metadata program can draw on a framework developed by William Bridges in his classic book, *Managing Transitions: Making the Most of Change*. The framework provides key components for web teams to consider what they are working to achieve in their daily work. Bridges' framework consists of having a vision and "4 Ps":

1. **Purpose**: explaining why a metadata program is required and what its benefits will be.
2. **Picture**: providing a shared vision of what a metadata program will look and feel like
3. **Plan**: laying out a detailed, step-by-step plan or roadmap toward realizing the vision
4. **Part**: showing people what part they play in the metadata program.

The vision is a short statement about what the metadata program will deliver in the future. It can be in different formats.

A possible format for a Metadata Strategy Vision

"Our metadata program will [*insert how it will impact online information or content*], which will support our business by [*insert key expected business benefit*]."

A good vision will articulate a guiding purpose — why the program exists. It needs to be broad enough to be motivating, but specific enough to feel real.

Metadata must have a clear purpose to be successful over time. Metadata takes time to develop and mature. Its full effectiveness will be apparent only once has sufficient scope to address different kinds of information used in different scenarios. It is easy for metadata-building efforts to falter when parties don't share a common sense of purpose about what they are trying to achieve.

This book has provided numerous ideas for how metadata can improve online information and bolster organizational performance. Each online publisher will have its own unique purpose for a metadata program, which can be either internally or externally driven. For example, the purpose could be internal: to improve sharing of information so that the organization can better assess content performance. Or the purpose could be external: to provide more precise information to customers in order to increase online sales. However, it is written, the purpose will show what is new as a result of the metadata program, and what improvement will be realized — for example, an important benchmark being increased, saved, or made more precise.

The "picture" of the metadata program will provide a concrete image of the practices before and after implementing the program. It will illustrate the change: Prior to the program, operations were this way (chaotic), but after the program operations are a new, better way. It is very helpful to articulate current pain points and keep them vivid, so that motivation is maintained, and one doesn't slip consciously into old habits that can recreate old problems.

The plan will address different dimensions. It will break down goals to define dependencies. Since a metadata program requires change management beyond basic project management, the plan should identify changes that are needed to reach the future state, whether they are administrative (e.g., buy-in, funding, or permissions) or logistical (e.g., creating or migrating metadata or having supporting systems or staff expertise). The plan will indicate key steps and milestones, as well as present a long-term roadmap.

When defining activities, the metadata program needs to indicate roles and responsibilities (such as a RACI matrix)[262] but also define collaboration responsibilities and tasks. It can be easy for roles to become atomized, where individuals focus narrowly on their specific responsibility instead of jointly defining requirements and solutions with individuals in other functions. Collaboration responsibilities will look at how different functions need to jointly own certain requirements and implementation tasks, because they transcend the expertise of any single function. For example, teams members from other editorial and user experience roles will need to jointly define user requirements for metadata.

[262] A RACI matrix lists tasks, and indicates who is Responsible for doing them, Accountable for the result, Consulted about a decision, and Informed about a decision.

How metadata governance complements content governance

Metadata governance both relies on and supports content governance. Metadata governance builds on content governance, having defined processes and procedures in place governing what content is published. Without content governance in place, it is difficult to introduce metadata governance. Web teams need to accept the value of policies and processes.

Effective large-scale content governance depends on effective metadata, especially administrative metadata. Without a metadata strategy, publishers tend to rely on what their existing content systems offer them, instead of asking first what they want from their systems. An existing system may provide only some of the key metadata attributes necessary to coordinate and manage content. That metadata may be in a proprietary format, meaning it can't be used by other systems. The default settings offered by a vendor's products are unlikely to provide the coordination and flexibility required.

Content governance should track important information about content that can be supported with metadata. Online publishers need to know details about the history of the content (when it was created, last revised, reused from elsewhere, or scheduled for removal), where the content came from (author, approvers, licensing rights for photos, or location information for video recordings), and goals for the content (intended audiences, themes, or channels). Those are just some of the metadata attributes content systems can use to manage routine reporting, tracking, and routing tasks, so web teams can focus on tasks of higher value.

Decisions in metadata governance

Governance provides a convening role. Since metadata must serve the needs of the entire organization, it is important that representatives from the whole organization be active in metadata decision making. That doesn't mean that all parties need to participate in all decisions. Part of the process of governance is deciding who needs to be involved in which decisions. Think about the different internal metadata stakeholders: those who create metadata, those who maintain it in code, those who use it to retrieve content, those who use it for analytics purposes.

Governance defines a process to decide metadata requirements, which will evolve as business goals and needs evolve. While some metadata work will be done as a special project, most metadata work will need to be planned and budgeted within other web or digital activities. Metadata strategy needs a program that builds capabilities over time.

Figure 28.1. Metadata governance applies to professional and industry associations such as the Extensible Business Reporting Language (XBRL) consortium as well as to individual companies. This diagram illustrates at a high level the governance process showing guiding inputs and relevant stakeholders for the XBRL financial vocabulary. Source: XBRL.

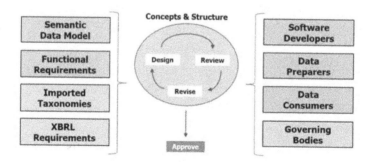

The governance process is necessary to maintain buy-in from different stakeholders (Figure 28.1), who will often have specific interests that can at times be in conflict. Different parties need to understand their responsibilities, as well as feel they are getting value. Some parties will do more work relative to what they get directly, so having a common set of goals is important.

Governance outcomes include securing compliance with common approaches, and accommodating the needs of different parties in a way that the interests of everyone is well served.

A prominent example of how governance works in practice is the work of the United Nations developing their CEFACT code standards to indicate units of measure.[263] The UN developed an "onion skin" model to show how different stakeholders interact. It explains the relationship between universal standards, common standards, and more idiosyncratic ones. The UN's goal with CEFACT is to offer a unified set of codes that cover all the major units of measurement around the world. Their approach to thinking about such a daunting task provides insights into governance issues.

**Figure 28.2. Onion skin model of vocabulary standards for units of measure.
Source: United Nations.**

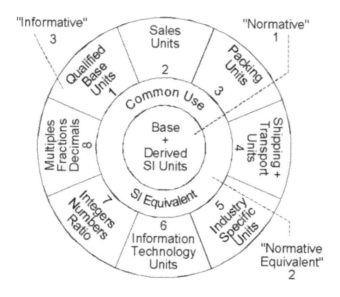

At the core of the onion are global standards that everyone follows (Figure 28.2). These are "normative" values (following an agreed standard) such as SI (metric system) units. The next ring represents commonly used standards that large groups of stakeholders follow, which can be readily converted into the standardized (normative) vocabulary. While not all countries measure weight in ounces, many products such as gold are customarily priced by the ounce. In the outer ring are "informative" values utilized by specific stakeholders for specific purposes, which may require special effort to convert into the standardized vocabulary. The size of clothing, which is described by many different systems, would be an example of an informative value. Many countries and industries use units that are unique and not used by others.

Figure 28.3. The process of standardization and harmonization between the core and peripheral stakeholders. Source: United Nations.

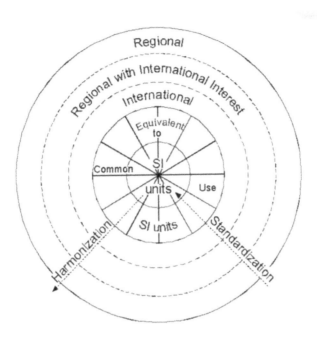

The United Nations considers governance of standards at the global and regional level (Figure 28.3). In the context of large enterprises and organizations, this would be equivalent to imposing standardization across the entire enterprise, or harmonizing the vocabularies and implementations used by different divisions or regional groups. The key governance challenges are deciding: (1) a unified vocabulary for the organization; and (2) where differences will need to exist that must be harmonized.

Let's return to the issue of clothing sizes.[264] Many online clothing retailers sell around the globe. But it can be difficult to impose a single sizing system on consumers that works everywhere. Different clothing size systems exist in Australia, Brazil, China, Germany, the EU, France, Italy, Japan, Mexico, the UK, and the US. Part of metadata governance is harmonizing differences among regional divisions, and ensuring that different expressions of information can be mapped to a common reference value.

The governance process promotes universal (global or industry-wide) standardization where possible and the harmonization of alternative, commonly-used standards where necessary. Governance committees should encourage stakeholders who utilize commonly-used (but non-universal) practices to describe information to adopt universal standard (global or industry-wide) metadata vocabularies where possible. When that's difficult, committees can promote harmonization, so that commonly-used implementations can be converted into universal standard vocabularies. The governance process decides which contextual differences in describing information are important, and how those differences will be managed.

Governance will define a process for developing and requirements, and maintaining them so they continue to meet the needs of an organization.

---

[263] CEFACT is used in the schema.org vocabulary to indicate units of measure.

[264] The example of clothing sizes, while seemingly trivial, expresses the kinds problems that can exist in a multi-division organization, which may have to deal with country- or product-specific ways of measuring loyalty points or describing warranty obligations.

Measuring progress

The governance process provides oversight on how the metadata program is performing.

A metadata program will be responsible for implementing:

- Goals and metrics (the measures of progress)
- Terminology (the properties that are included)
- Taxonomies (the values that are managed as data)
- APIs (the promotion approach).

Governance can address the common problem of redundant metadata. To fight entropy, online publishers also need to guard against the creep of special-request metadata. Organizations can have too much metadata when:

- Too much of their metadata is incompatible because different systems define content in different ways
- Too much metadata is used for a single purpose, instead of serving multiple purposes.

The governance process directs the metadata program to enhance its capabilities over time. Metadata capabilities depend on infrastructure, stored information, and employee knowledge.

Governance oversight can also provide a "health check" of a metadata program. Reviews can check that progress is being achieved, and make sure the implementation of common causes of failure.

Some metadata programs are overly ambitious because they try to do too much, too quickly. They are never delivered, or what gets delivered is not what was intended. Some publishers, especially in the nonprofit cultural sector, pursue completeness without having a sound business case for why completeness is needed.[265]

Other metadata programs are overly cautious. They are timid trials that never develop a critical mass of metadata that can provide value.

Another source of problems is a mismatch of technology complexity to mission-criticality. For example, it is risky to expect novel technology to perform perfectly in a real-time setting. Some technologies were designed to support slower-paced tasks (retrospective, or long-term) and performance is attuned to those needs. For mission-critical features, publishers should stick with proven tech.

[265] Keir Winesmith, Head of Digital at The San Francisco Museum of Modern Art: "Most cultural heritage organizations (like most organizations) are terrible at data. And most of those who are good at collecting it, very rarely use it effectively or strategically." `https://medium.com/@drkeir/against-linked-open-data-502a53b62fb7`

Stages of maturity

The management consultant Neil Churchill developed a five-stage model of how organizations implement programs. This model can apply to metadata programs as well. Programs tend to go through the following stages:

1. **Existence** — an enterprise-wide program for web content metadata is inaugurated, though limited in scope and somewhat exploratory
2. **Survival** — the program carries on, learning from mistakes, but doesn't necessarily have a long-term commitment from executives
3. **Success** — early investments start to show their value
4. **Take-off** — the scope of activities widens, and more staff are participating in the program
5. **Resource maturity** — both funding and processes are well established, and the value of metadata is widely recognized.

Once resource maturity is reached, governance will be nearly automatic. But until then, it will require constant attention.

APPENDIX: OVERCOMING OBJECTIONS TO METADATA STRATEGY

M any online publishers that are interested in developing a metadata strategy will encounter skepticism from within their organization or from their content or technology partners. This skepticism may not challenge the goals of having better connected information. Instead, skeptical voices will question the practicality of pursuing these goals.

A common theme underlying objections to metadata strategy is that the online publishing world isn't yet ready to embrace metadata standards. According to this perspective, because the rest of the world isn't ready, publishers should defer taking action until later. It's never clear when the right time to take action will be — what specific event or criteria will suddenly make the time right to take action.

It's important to separate realistic concerns about the ease of implementing a strategy from vague fears about uncertainty and change. Online publishers may have valid concerns about the readiness of different resources they will need to implement a strategy. These constraints are not reasons to do nothing. Rather, they help inform making realistic decisions and determining a realistic scope.

Metadata advocates should never trivialize concerns others have around implementing changes. Change does involve uncertainties and hard work. But concerns shouldn't solidify into rigid objections used to advocate inaction.

Objection 1: Vocabularies aren't ready

A common objection is that external standards are incomplete or are still immature. They are missing important entities and properties so publishers can assume they aren't useful. Skeptics may conclude they can't adopt external vocabularies because these look different from their current metadata.

Some of these concerns are valid, while some of the concerns reflect a lack of familiarity with how external standards work. It is true that external vocabularies such as schema.org don't cover information about every domain, and even when they do cover a domain, they may provide less depth than is needed. Schema.org is continually evolving and expanding coverage. But it is not intended to be completely comprehensive — it is designed to cover the most commonly used entities and properties. Schema.org is designed to work with more specialized vocabularies, for example, Bioschemas.[266]

Publishers that are focused on common kinds of information aimed at consumers may find that schema.org can meet most of their needs. Some domains have very deep coverage (health, autos) in the schema.org vocabulary, but other domains lack such depth. When publishers have more specialized needs, they can often use intangible entities in schema.org:

- Add specificity to an entity by using `additionalType`
- Create new properties using the `PropertyValueSpecification`
- Indicate complex values using the `StructuredValue`
- Provide structured definitions of introduced terms using the pending `DefinedTerm`.

External vocabularies are designed to be flexible. Their coverage will often appear broader than internal standards. But in many cases, broader terms available in external standards can adequately represent more specific terms in proprietary metadata classifications.

Remember, the goal is to give up proprietary metadata when external standards are available. There's no expectation that publishers will get rid of all their proprietary metadata — especially metadata required for internal use cases. Custom metadata is fine for internal uses, but external uses should aim to rely on external vocabularies.

[266] Bioschemas is a vocabulary for the life sciences that builds on and extends schema.org. See `http://bioschemas.org/`

Objection 2: Tools aren't ready

A second objection is that tools aren't mature enough. Publishers are prudent to consider whether tools will be reliable and offer the features they need. Again, it's important that such caution be based on a thorough understanding of what capabilities are available, and not on sketchy perceptions of these capabilities.

Publishers have more choices now than ever before. That said, the market for semantic metadata tools is still far smaller than the market for relational database systems and other mainstream software applications. The tools haven't had the same level of stress testing. Publishers do sometimes complain that they wish the tools were more mature than they are currently.

At issue is not simply if the tool is ready for the publisher, but whether the publisher is ready for the tool. Publishers need to select the right tool for their specific needs and have the right technical team to support the tool.

Some more-established tools were designed to support academic or scientific research. They can in theory be used for other kinds of publishing but they may not be the best fit. Some of these tools have been around for a decade already. They have improved in their features and performance but may not be geared toward the general needs of web publishers, since that was not their original purpose.

Several small entrepreneurial firms have entered the field in recent years looking the serve the needs of web publishers. They are adding features to make their products more capable and easier to use.

In addition to the startups, some notable large corporations including Amazon have recently introduced semantic metadata tools (e.g., Amazon Neptune).[267] At least one very large CMS vendor is working on adding RDF capabilities to their products.

Given the rapid growth in semantic metadata use and practices in recent years, it's not surprising that tools can lack the level of maturity enjoyed by longer-established IT applications. But the upside is that semantic metadata tools are experiencing continuous innovation. Publishers have options but also need they need to be educated shoppers.

[267] "Amazon Neptune is here: 6 ways customers use the AWS graph database" *TechRepublic*, May 31, 2018, https://www.techrepublic.com/article/amazon-neptune-is-here-6-ways-customers-use-the-aws-graph-database/

Objection 3: Others aren't ready

The third objection concerns the publisher's dependence on others. Publishers worry: "we can't do this on our own; we need the cooperation of others who aren't ready." Others don't yet see the world from the publisher's perspective.

External standards, by their nature, involve agreement and consensus between different parties. And getting different parties to agree involves a dance. Publishers who are unfamiliar with how standards are developed may not understand why consensus is not always instantaneous.

The desire for metadata standards is not contentious. Everyone wants good standards. The debates generally center around how to make standards workable for as many publishers as possible. That means not cluttering up the standards with over-specific features that won't be used much. Standards need to support specific requirements by using a general approach.

Unfortunately, publishers can't sit back and wait for others to arrive at a consensus and expect they will like it. They need to get involved.

Passive free-riding is the tactic of expecting other parties to solve one's own problems. It results in disappointment and in complaints that others made decisions that didn't exactly match one's own situation.

The metadata standards community can benefit from broader participation to address a wider range of needs. Publishers can approach standards communities and share what they are trying to accomplish and how they'd like to use metadata to achieve that.[268] Such participation can sometimes suggest other use case scenarios and increase the reuse potential of the vocabulary.

The best way for publishers to bring along others who need to understand their perspective is to engage peers, share experiences and goals, and suggest solutions that can benefit others as well as themselves.

---

[268] There are community groups or working groups for many external standards such as schema.org and JSON-LD that invite participation, often on GitHub.

The early adopter versus the late adopter

When a publisher spots uncertainties, it may be tempted to hold back and wait until things sort themselves out. Being a late adopter sounds much easier than being an early adopter. But being a late adopter carries hidden risks.

Whether a publisher chooses to be an early adopter of external standards or a late adopter, the publisher can't avoid the work involved with changing the status quo of their operations. While both paths involve effort, the quality of the effort for each is different.

By being an early adopter, publishers focus more effort on choosing tools and standards to use. They get to shape the options that the rest of their sector will get to use. Publishers have the most influence when engaged early. By adopting approaches ahead of their peers, publishers have an opportunity to differentiate themselves. The work they do is strategic, adding value.

Late adopters don't avoid having to do the work involved with change. They reallocate the kind of work needed to lower value tasks. By delaying the transition to external standards, the amount of legacy content that lacks standards-based metadata has grown. Most of the work of late adopters is consumed by cleaning up content and catching up with practices already in use. Instead of creating new value, late adopters are focused on recovering value from out-of-date operations.

Getting ready for more change

Not only do publishers need to change by embracing current external metadata standards, but they need to prepare for new developments in online information. Publishers should not assume that external metadata standards will soon mature and will stop changing. Standards will continue to evolve to address new opportunities. Publishers would be unwise to hope that they can catch up once standards have "settled down."

Online information continues to grow and continues to become more important to different aspects of our lives. New channels keep emerging as well. Online information is becoming interactive.

A prominent example of the changes unfolding is the surging interest in knowledge graphs from major online publishers such as Airbnb, Uber, and many others.[269] While it is still too early to predict precisely how knowledge graphs will influence publishing, it seems reasonable to expect that knowledge graphs will be widely used by online publishers in the near future.

Publishers should expect external standards to expand and be enhanced to support a growing range of use cases.

A metadata strategy should be implemented according to the publisher's capacity to manage the changes to implement. Publishers should debate the right pace of change for their organization. But they should not delay getting started. Publishers can start small, focusing on a primary purpose for their metadata (SEO) and then expanding their focus to address other purposes such as interaction design, analytics, or voice.

---

[269] "Knowledge graphs beyond the hype", ZDNet, September 19, 2018, https://www.zdnet.com/article/knowledge-graphs-beyond-the-hype-getting-knowledge-in-and-out-of-graphs-and-databases/

GLOSSARY

Metadata does involve a certain amount of jargon to refer to major concepts used to structure information. For many people, the most important goal will be to appreciate the intent of the concept, rather than understand its technical details.

The glossary presents short, non-technical definitions of terms used in the book. If you need more detailed or precise explanations of the terms, consult relevant online documentation relating to standards and practices.

API

(Application Programming Interface) A specification that tells developers how they can get information from a publisher that provides an API endpoint.

DBpedia

Wikipedia-as-a-database. It structures key information in Wikipedia as machine-readable metadata. Contains over 4 million entities.

deferenceable

A URI that can be looked up using the HTTP protocol.

entity

A tangible or intangible thing such as a person, place, event, product, or concept, that has specific identifying properties.

enumerations

A defined list of relevant allowed values that are consistent and machine readable. Also known as a controlled vocabulary.

external standards

Metadata standards published and maintained by a collective group that are available to use widely.

graph

A pattern used to model data or information, where discrete statements about facts can be connected together to build larger insights.

interoperability

The ability of different parties to exchange and understand information.

JSON

(JavaScript Object Notation) A simple data model and most common syntax for exchanging data on the web.

JSON-LD

(JavaScript Object Notation for Linked Data) An extension of the JSON syntax that supports linked data. It indicates the schema using a context or vocabulary and supports URIs as identifiers.

knowledge graph

A knowledge base of facts about entities constructed using graph data models.

labeled property graph

A graph database where the publisher can add custom properties.

linked data

Refers to the technologies used to connect information published by different parties.

machine-readable

In this book, refers to the ability of computers to find specific information by relying on standardized metadata descriptions.

machine-intelligible

In this book, refers to the ability to understand the meaning of metadata (without ambiguity), rather than simply find it.

ontology

A formal specification of how to characterize the entities and properties relating to a domain. Largely synonymous with the terms schema and vocabulary.

open data

Data or information that can be republished without prior consent.

open linked data

Used when linked data is also open data.

open source

Software applications that are non-proprietary and are freely available to use and modify.

property vocabularies

Metadata standards used to specify entity types and properties.

RDF

(Resource Description Framework) The data model used for semantic metadata. It structures information as triples: a subject, a predicate and an object.

schema

The formalization of a data model, or more generally, a framework for classifying information. Schema.org is the best known schema for online content.

semantic web

A term used for the overall framework envisioned by World Wide Web inventor Tim Berners-Lee to improve the how machines can understand and reuse information published on the World Wide Web.

SHACL

(Shapes Constraint Language) A new metadata standard used to specify constraints for metadata to ensure greater consistency and quality control.

SKOS

(Simple Knowledge Organization System) A metadata standard used to construct a thesaurus to specify the mapping and labeling of related concepts.

SPARQL

(SPARQL Protocol and RDF Query Language) A query language for semantic metadata.

SSML

(Speech Synthesis Markup Language) A metadata standard used to specify the pronunciation of words.

syntax

The rules governing how to mark up data for machines to parse.

URI

(Uniform Resource Identifier) A string of characters that definitively identifies a resource such as an entity, property, or value. It is machine-intelligible, and is often web-accessible (as when it begins with https:).

value vocabularies

Metadata standards used to specify values (identifiers and enumerated values) in a consistent way that will be understood by machines.

vocabularies

A somewhat less formal term to refer to an ontology.

vocabulary reuse

How widely a vocabulary is used or referenced by other vocabularies.

wikidata

A collaboratively-edited open data knowledge base. Provides machine-readable identifiers for millions of entities and properties and values (information) relating to entities.

ACKNOWLEDGMENTS

A standard disclaimer on Twitter these days is to state that retweets do not imply endorsements. Similarly, acknowledging others need not imply their endorsement of one's views.

While I alone am responsible for the views in this book, my thinking about metadata has been shaped by many people over the years. I want to express appreciation to some of these people and encourage you to follow them on social media.

Rachel Lovinger, with whom I worked together on the Content Strategy Forum community and conference, more than anyone has been responsible for introducing metadata to the content strategy community through talks and workshops at conferences.

Karen McGrane, an advocate for many years of using metadata in online publishing, has inspired me to explore this topic and evangelize its potential.

Joe Pairman, who has a deep understanding of highly complex publishing scenarios, has shared many perspectives with me about the value of metadata in the publishing process.

Aaron Bradley, who runs the semantic search marketing community, has been generous over the years sharing his knowledge about the applications of semantic metadata.

Thad Guidry from the schema.org community has been generous sharing his knowledge and encouraged me to get more involved with the standards community.

Thanks also to members of the information architecture community who have promoted the use of metadata standards, particularly Carrie Hane and Mike Atherton, coauthors of *Designing Connected Content*, and Paul Rissen, who is in the process of writing a book based on his experiences at Springer Nature.

I would not expect all these people to agree with every view I express in this book. I do feel they share with me a common attitude toward metadata: an interest in uncovering its potential, and a pragmatic appreciation that different situations may require different approaches.

I'd also like to acknowledge my wife Kathy for her encouragement while I wrote this book.

ABOUT THE AUTHOR

Michael C Andrews is an American IT consultant with a special interest in content strategy and metadata standards. He is also the author of *Metadata Basics for Web Content*, published by Amazon in 2017.

He started working with online metadata as a technical information specialist at the US Commerce Department in the 1980s, and was among the first wave of people whose full-time job responsibilities focused on using the Internet to access and manage published content. For the past two decades he has worked as a consultant in the fields of user experience and content strategy. He's worked as a senior manager for content strategy with one of the world's largest digital consultancies, and has advised large scale online publishers such the National Institutes of Health, Verizon and the World Bank. He has lived and worked in India, the UK, New Zealand, Italy, as well as the United States.

Andrews has an MSc in human computer interaction from the University of Sussex in England, and a Masters with a specialization in international finance from Columbia University in New York. He also has a certificate in XML and RDF Technologies from the Library Juice Academy. He is a native of Arlington, Virginia.

INDEX